the series on school re

Patricia A. Wasley
Coalition of
Essential Schools

Ann Lieberman
NCREST

SERIES EDITORS

Stirring the Chalkdust:
Tales of Teachers Changing Classroom Practice
PATRICIA A. WASLEY

Incorporating the following books from the
PROFESSIONAL DEVELOPMENT AND PRACTICE SERIES

Stirring the Chalkdust

Tales of Teachers Changing Classroom Practice

Patricia A. Wasley

Coalition of Essential Schools
Brown University

Foreword by Seymour Sarason

Teachers College, Columbia University
New York and London

Published by Teachers College Press, 1234 Amsterdam Avenue, New York, N.Y. 10027

The work described in this volume resulted from a three-year study generously funded by:
    The Coalition of Essential Schools
    The DeWitt Wallace Reader's Digest Fund
    The Exxon Education Fund

Library of Congress Cataloging-in-Publication Data

    Stirring the chalkdust : tales of teachers changing
classroom practice / Patricia A. Wasley ; foreword by Seymour
Sarason.
        p.   cm.—(The series on school reform)
    Includes bibliographical references (p.   ) and index.
    ISBN 0-8077-3421-7 (alk. paper).—ISBN 0-8077-3420-9 (pbk. :
alk. paper)
    1. Teachers–United States—Case studies.   2. Teaching—Case
studies.   I. Title.   II. Series.
LB1775.2.W27   1994
371.1′00973—dc20   94-23350

ISBN: 0-8077-3421-7
ISBN: 0-8077-3420-0 (pbk.)

Printed on acid-free paper
Manufactured in the United States of America

01   00   99   98   97   8   7   6   5   4   3

For the teachers with whom I worked;
they taught me much more than is included here.
For Seymour, Ann and Ted who continue to teach us all.
For Rick for working right alongside.
And for the distance left to go . . .

Contents

Foreword

There is a sizable literature on what teachers think, feel, do, and practice. It is by no means a coherent or focused literature except for its emphasis on teaching as a very demanding, obstacle hurdling, physically exhausting process. Liking children is but one criterion for choosing teaching as a career. If it has been a revealing and instructive literature, it has not made an impact for reasons: The general public still does not comprehend what dedicated teaching entails, and these writings have not been appreciated by the teachers of teachers. Why this is so is not easy to explain, but certainly the explanation must include shortcomings in the educational community. Not the least of these shortcomings is the reluctance seriously and publicly to engage in self-scrutiny and to exercise leadership by accepting responsibility for changing its traditions, practices, and Custer-like stance toward the "outside" world. As a result, it has been that uncomprehending outside world which calls for changes which, however well-intentioned, reveal an ignorance of the culture of schools, the lack of imagination and the rigidity of programs for preparing educators, and, fatefully, how complex the issues are.

The calls for educational change have picked up a lot of steam and stridency in recent years. The seeming intractability of the educational system to change has been noted, criticized, and indicted. It is not surprising, therefore, that there has begun to appear in the literature discussion and description of how teachers experience the pressure (and often the mandate) to change. Dr. Wasley's book is, in my opinion, a remarkable contribution to this literature, and for several reasons. The first is that she presents us with the phenomenology of teachers who willingly undertook to change their thinking and practices. These are not teachers who felt compelled to accommodate to calls for change coming from external pressures and policies that they would rather not have had to confront. These were teachers motivated, albeit in varying degrees, to face up to the need to change. The second reason, already demonstrated in the author's previous writings, is sheer literary skill: a style of writing, a way with words and phrases, a sensitivity to nuance, and a compellingness that together engender in the reader the "it makes sense" reaction, the feeling that you understand another person's encounter with the complexities of personal change. The third reason for my high opinion of this book is that Dr. Wasley always sees and describes these teachers in context. That is to say, she is refreshingly sensitive to the obvious: teachers operate in organized contexts which contain factors for and against change. Motivation to change is one thing but unless the positive factors are stronger than the negative ones, we are asking too much of teachers. Dr. Wasley makes clear that even where motivation is high and the positive factors outweigh the negative ones, personal professional change is rough stuff. Unfortunately, too many people who clamor for change do not have a realistic time perspective about the change process. We are now used to hearing that quick fixes have to be avoided. The fact remains that in practice it is too frequent that the callers for change have unrealistic time perspectives.

This book deserves a wide audience, especially among those who formulate and implement policies for change. If the problems are difficult and thorny, Dr. Wasley's writing (and thinking) skills have the rare virtue of clarifying those problems, of illuminating them in ways that allow us to say "it has the ring of truth."

Seymour B. Sarason
New Haven, Connecticut

Preface

This project began in 1989 when I first joined the Coalition of Essential Schools. I had just finished writing *Teachers Who Lead* (Wasley, 1991a), a book about teachers who hoped to provide leadership for their colleagues by creating livelier classroom experiences. The many teachers I interviewed for that project suggested that they would like to change, but found it difficult to imagine what they should do. All of them, with the smudges of chalkdust on their sleeves or on their behinds that mark veteran teachers, were mired by the long history of schools as we know them and have known them for 100 years.

When I joined the Coalition, I engaged in a series of similar discussions with teachers in Coalition schools who were struggling to change their own practices. They suggested that a series of diverse case studies that were not presented as exemplars (because no one seemed to believe that their work was at that stage yet!), but that showed real teachers grappling with change with their kids and their colleagues would be helpful. At the same time, they were hopeful that I would find courageous teachers, people whose example might spur others on.

My colleagues at the Coalition and I also determined that because the project was to be a long one, 4 years, and because we are a partnership organization, the cases should serve the participants, and others in the organization in some real way while the project was proceeding.

With those guidelines to help focus our work, the selection of teachers took place through a variety of processes and over 2 years, beginning in 1989. We wanted teachers who came from different school cultures and climates. Because the Coalition is a national reform effort, we wanted to work with teachers in various parts of the country. We wanted teachers who taught a variety of disciplines—some who'd reconfigured traditional disciplines and some who had not. We knew that I needed to work with a math teacher because everywhere math teachers were struggling with the consideration of change and the constraints of external exams—local tests, state tests, SATs. We wanted images of teachers who'd been doing this for a while and teachers who were fairly new to change. My colleagues at the Coalition who travel to schools across the country and spend time in classrooms made recommendations. Re: Learning coordinators who direct the state partnerships, and principals and school-based coordinators in Coalition schools gave me suggestions, and, finally, I interviewed interested people over the phone or at regional meetings.

To work with veteran teachers was important. Although a study conducted by Linda Darling-Hammond (1990) informs us that a third of the teaching force will retire by the year 2000, that still leaves fully two-thirds with long careers ahead of them. Furthermore, despite the best efforts of new professional development schools, a majority of teachers will be prepared in traditional teacher education programs for some time to come. We need information about how to help veteran teachers retool if the system is to move in any significant way before everyone retires.

A humanities teacher, an English teacher, a math teacher, a science teacher, and an integrated team of four teachers agreed to participate. Once teachers had been selected, the teachers and I negotiated our working relationship. I went to their schools for a week. A week worked well because it allowed me to see teachers in a variety of contexts, to understand the rhythm of their lives, and it was a little too long for people to retain a polite exterior. We had one lengthy entrance interview and a lengthy exit interview—generally in the evenings. Beyond that, I followed along wherever—classroom work, after-school activities, parent conferences—anything that constituted part of tneir daily work life. I also collected copies of whatever materials they gave to their students or sent home during the week. In addition, we agreed that we would keep in touch for the duration of the study so that I could keep up with what was happening to them.

After the site visit, we agreed I would write the first draft of the case study and that we would work together to negotiate its accuracy. We agreed that if we could not come to agreement about things that needed changing or that had changed, our varying perceptions would be included in the text. We agreed that the principals and other teachers in the school would read the cases for accuracy.

NEGOTIATED RESEARCH

I wanted to find ways to make the research process helpful to those participating. My hope was that the participating teachers would be engaged in reflective practice, that they would get a mirror of their own work. To help me understand if this really happened for them, I wanted a record of what it was like to go through this process. Was it helpful? Invasive? Distracting? The participants agreed to keep track of their feelings about participation and to write about it after the whole process was completed. Should the process return nothing to those who participated, I wanted the opportunity to rethink the strategy.

The casework was done from 1989 to 1991. The weeks spent in the field were both exhilarating and exhausting, both for the participants and for me. I carried a tape recorder and a laptop computer everywhere. The teachers squeezed extra time (generally from their family life) to conduct interviews. I shadowed them relentlessly and asked questions all day long. Principals made time in their schedules, as did other teachers. Students took time from their tasks to explain what they were doing. I went home with mountains of data—school schedules, handouts, handbooks, field notes, interviews.

In the process of the participants' review of each case I came both to value and believe that critical friendship between researchers and the researched strengthens the work of both. Both the teachers and the administrators were very professional in the best sense of the word. They were most interested in the accuracy of the piece, not in their positive portrayal or in that of others. All parties involved agreed that to move forward we needed to look at the difficulties and dilemmas as well as at the gains.

At the same time, they helped me both as an observer in schools and as a writer. They preferred rich classroom detail, feedback that was opposite of what most of my researcher colleagues had recommended. They helped me to eliminate what they considered to be unnecessary detail. They wanted to know as much as possible about what their students were doing. They helped me to sharpen my questions and my note-taking techniques.

The negotiations process raised one central dilemma which we grappled with throughout the project. I feared that we might be creating what could be interpreted as a kind of pronouncement about good teaching, but we all wanted the cases to be provocative for other teachers. To confound matters, the teachers themselves were so invested in the changes that they had made that they found it hard not to be disparaging of their previous teaching practices, and by inference, those of their colleagues. Ironically, all of them claimed that they left no technique, no method behind which might logically lead to such feelings. At the same time, colleagues who read the cases suggested that at times they felt condemned if they weren't doing the things these teachers were doing. They found this condescending, irritating, and not in the least inspirational. We struggled with terms—traditional teaching, conventional teaching, innovative teaching, constructivist teaching. Finally we agreed that it was most useful to think of teaching as a repertoire of techniques, which all teachers continue to develop, and that we would avoid labels that exclude some and invite others.

USING THE CASES

Once the participants and I agreed on the cases, my colleagues at the Coalition and I turned them into working documents to be used in inservice sessions and seminars run by Coalition folk both from our office and from the schools. We used the cases in various educational settings in 1991–92 to see whether they proved useful to practitioners contemplating or in the midst of change themselves. We used them to provoke discussion and to engage people in the analysis of school change. We asked questions: What changes have taken place here? How do you know? What advice would you give to the staff at your school? What philosophy undergirds this teacher's work with kids? What changes in the curriculum? Would that work in your school?

I spent one day using the cases with 25 teachers who believed that change was not necessary; we argued long and hard. Another day, several colleagues and I worked with 50 or 60 teachers who'd been recognized as the best teachers in their districts; they generated a number of ideas beyond the cases with what seemed like brimming enthusiasm. More than once I worked with whole faculties in Essential schools. We used the cases in Socratic Seminars in classes with students at Brown. Several of my colleagues in other universities used them in courses. We used them in a seminar on the management of change. I used them in seminars for school based teams who are not members of the Coalition. We used them with teams of central office and building administrators. I used them in schools that had made more progress than some of the teachers in the cases. One group was particularly helpful: In the summer of 1991, Kathryn and three other teachers—a foreign language teacher, an industrial arts teacher, a math/science teacher—joined me for a 3 day critique of the cases, during which Hurricane Bob joined us. Evacuated from the Coalition offices, we discussed each case very thoroughly while sitting on the floor at a local bed and breakfast built in the 1800s. While the wind howled and the young innkeepers kept the coffee hot, these teachers discussed whether the very important but difficult aspects of change were conveyed in the cases. Their comments helped me to shape chapters 7 and 8.

In all the phases of the development of this book, I benefited from the collaboration of my colleagues in schools and universities, in reform projects, and policy networks across the country. I am constantly reminded that the old adage about "strength in numbers" isn't limited to physical circumstances at all!

REACTIONS TO PARTICIPATION

After the cases were all complete, I asked each of the participants to write about what participation in such a project was like for them. The following excerpts suggest their perspectives.

Kathryn said, "As I think back to having someone study me, I think about a couple of things. It was draining to have someone watch me so closely. But it was very stimulating to have someone to talk to about my practice. I have been observed many times before but to have to process it with someone was unusual."

Judd wrote more extensively:

When I think back to the week we spent together, I see it mostly in varying shades of dark colors. I was not happy or proud of my teaching that week. I think that a lot of those feelings arose from my lack of preparation. In refusing to deliver a dog and pony show, I feel like I went too far the other way. And, it was not a happy time in my life as you know. (During the week I spent with Judd, his divorce was finalized and his son was calling nightly, wanting to drop out of college.) I clearly remember contemplating just walking out of the room at one point. To say that it was emotionally trying is a gross understatement. On the other hand, I would do it again in a heartbeat.

Why? It is a rare and valuable experience to have someone look at what you do in your life. For most people, this never occurs. It opened up windows of self-examination that I never knew existed. The report itself gave me the remarkable opportunity to sit in close proximity to people discussing my work in the most candid way. While some of this was painful initially, most of it was rewarding and supportive. It allowed me to see the strengths and weaknesses of my practice through someone else's eyes. Much different than yearly evaluations, this pushed and probed me to think about what I was doing and not doing on a much deeper and clearer level. It reaffirmed my love of children and my sincere belief that all of them can succeed. It brought me to tears, as you know. How many teachers ever look at their work with such intensity that it makes them cry? Perhaps more of us should have that opportunity.

If there is a problem with this, it is that the experience is filtered through your eyes. While you made a valiant attempt to record what was going on, you are only able to record what you perceive. This became obvious when I read the study. I really believe that we could have spent an extremely long period of time trying to arrive at an agreement about what was going on. I realized that early on and decided to just let it go. I know that the experience was good for me as a person and hopefully as a teacher. It helped me as an educator. It showed me that I could never totally understand all of the intricacies of what it was that I was attempting to do. It also confirmed my belief that teaching has to rank among the most intense ways for an adult to spend time. I wish there were a way to have the kind of interaction the study provided on a more constant basis. I'm not sure what would happen but I firmly believe that it would be good for children.

Jennifer compared participation to going to the dentist!

When I heard you were coming, I felt honored, a little nervous about what you'd find, but interested to see what I'd learn. When you were here, I didn't know how to introduce you to other people without making the rest of the faculty feel like I was tooting my own horn. Then, it was a little like going to the dentist—day after day after day. You kept asking questions about things that hit nerves. By midweek, I felt like we were all going to be exposed as frauds! Then when I got the case, I felt a variety of things. I felt sort of hyper-critical of my own teaching. I'd never seen it so close up before, not even when I'd been video-taped. But I also felt more confident about what we have been trying to do because it still made sense when I read about it.

   You asked me whether participating in the study had done anything for me. Well, it helped me to see my own work and to think about it. When I saw the kids in the case, it reminded me how much I enjoy my students and working with them. On the other hand, I don't think that the study, or my participation as an NRF member or anything else that I've done with the Coalition has made a bit of difference in my school. All of it has made me a better teacher, a more reflective educator, but our school rolls along to the next reform and our district switches direction every time we get a new superintendent. One thing I have learned from working with others is that there are places where the Coalition is working and where change is growing more stable over time. So, I'm hopeful. I'm just waiting, working with a new local foundation so that those of us who are interested can keep going, and so we'll be ready—maybe when the next superintendent or the next principal comes around.

   Mary and Paolo wrote that it was excruciating at first to read about their work in such detail. Eventually they came to see it as an historical document, a record of their professional practices at a particular point in time.
   Elizabeth wrote:

When we take our three boys on road trips in the summer, we play Twenty Questions. Those boys have an endless supply of questions—and that's just what it felt like having you follow me around for a week. After I got over the initial shock that you were going to ask so many questions, I found it to be a positive experience. It validated me as a teacher. Over the years, I've had very few observers. My administrators have been more interested in management than in content. Besides, they have so many people to do that they don't have the time to get into it. I think Ted Sizer uses the phrase, "the compliment of accountability." I was complimented by having to explain what my team and I were doing. I didn't feel threat-

ened but eager to explain what we were doing. I like to analyze what's
going on anyway, and teachers don't get enough time to do that.

At the same time, it was painful. As I talked, I could see what a limited
base of support we had. In part, some of your questions gave me courage
and helped me to be more proactive in writing memos to the administration about what we thought should happen. It's also true that while I benefited personally from participating, the rest of the staff gained nothing.
Not that the case wasn't available to them; it just wasn't talked about.

Their reactions to this project convinced me of two things. First, the
actual conduct of research can and should contribute to the professional
growth of those studied while it contributes to the knowledge base. Second,
involving the participants provides an appropriate check on the researcher's
observational accuracy without compromising his or her ability to write
about difficult circumstances. Documenting changing practices may, in fact,
require more collaborative research methods.

My ambitions were grand, and at this point, as I might have predicted,
I feel a little sheepish, but better informed and much less naive! What I actually gathered reminds me of an old favorite piece of literature, first introduced to me by my own high school English teacher, Chaucer's *Canterbury
Tales,* stories of pilgrims on a journey to gain wisdom and grace. To borrow
strength from Chaucer's form, this book is organized as a frame tale. Thus
the prologue sets the frame. Tales from the individual travelers follow. These
are tales of contemporary pilgrims on a shared journey toward better schooling. These teachers, like their predecessors in old England, set out on a personal quest to find better practices and answers to important questions.
They, like their counterparts, found the road tough going and answers hard
to find. Still, as these teachers were moving along on their journey, they
were willing to pass the time by sharing their dreams, their troubles, their
frustrations, and their insights. Taken together, their stories teach us a great
deal about the magnificent complexity at the heart of changing schools, and
the hopefulness that results from their effort—a fitting epilogue.

Acknowledgments

A 5-year project like this takes the time, energy and goodwill of many more than I can name! This project started over a lunch table with Ted Sizer who believes it important to capture the realities of redesigning teaching from within. He listened carefully before and after each sojourn into Coalition schools, and read all successive drafts of this manuscript. He is relentlessly honest about the complexity of accomplishing what he hopes for students, their teachers, principals, and communities, and believes that honest scrutiny leads to better possibilities. He is also unfailingly encouraging.

Ann Lieberman helped me to conceptualize the project; then she read and talked through successive drafts with me; she is always an excellent and courageous critic. She also provided a critical audience of teachers in her classes at Teachers College and in the staff at the National Center for Restructuring Education, Schools and Teaching.

The staff at the Coalition and in the Education Department at Brown read, critiqued, argued, used the cases, and argued again as each of the cases and the concluding chapters were produced. It has been terrific working with Ed Campbell, Don Ernst, Paula Evans, Susan Fisher, Amy Gerstein, Tom James, Myra Kline, David Kobrin, Lisa Lasky, Sue Lusi, Laura Maxwell, Bob McCarthy, Joe McDonald, Grace McEntee, David Niguidula, Bethany Rodgers, Bev Simpson, Gene Thompson, and Carolyn Wyatt.

All the people—kids, teachers, administrators—with whom I worked in the field were great. These people opened their schools, files, classrooms, and meetings without stipulation because they were good students of their own work and welcomed feedback. The teachers and the principals in the schools represented here read successive drafts of the text and encouraged me to work toward a more sophisticated understanding of the obstacles they faced. In their willingness to acknowledge the complexity of what they do, they never once asked me to change text which cast them in a difficult light.

David Cohen, who read all of the cases just at the point when I believed that the world did not need another book, encouraged me to keep going. Ruth Emery, my high school English teacher, now retired but ever active, harumphed about my faulty grammar, but told me to make the work pop and sing. If there is any snap, any song to be heard, it is at her lively encouragement. Seymour Sarason read each case and then the manuscript; he scrawled notes, phoned regularly, and pushed me to capture the enormity of what we are asking of teachers in this current reform movement. Colleagues in schools and partners at the Education Commission of the States gave me further helpful feedback. I learned a good deal from Sam Billups, Judy Bray, Robert Bullough, Dick Clark, Susan Colburn, Allen Dichter, Faith Dunn, Bruce Frana, Barb Eibel, Marian Finney, Bob Hampel, Marilyn Hohman, Sherry King, Val Klenowski, Nancy Linnon, Jill Matthies, Nancy Mohr, Kathy Mueller, Donna Muncey, Jude Pelchat, and Dave Provan. Brian Ellerbeck, my editor at Teachers College Press, was constant in his willingness to find solutions to the problems that inevitably crop up between life, work, and the completion of a manuscript.

The project was supported in part by the Exxon Educational Foundation and the DeWitt Wallace Reader's Digest Foundation; their interest in understanding change is greatly appreciated. Even with all of that support, I could never have made it through the whole process without the organizational skill and technological prowess of Ginny Pires and Jessica Towbin.

Finally, my husband, Rick Lear, had both the experience and the clarity to see where I hadn't pushed hard enough and where I had misinterpreted or oversimplified. His constant hopes for classrooms where teachers and students dance with ideas, practice thoughtfulness, and complete useful projects are reflected in the stories I tell.

Stirring the Chalkdust

Tales of Teachers Changing Classroom Practice

1
—

Prologue:
Why the Chalkdust Needs Stirring

S everal years ago, when I was working on some of the first case studies included here, a neighbor, Thomas, age 13, was weeding my
flower beds during the late Autumn. Most of the time, I worked in my
office while he pulled weeds, but occasionally, my work done, I joined him.
Thomas was built like a rectangular cement block. His head was shaved
along the sides; a very important rat tail hung half way down his back. He
came to my house on his skateboard and roared home on it at the end of
the day. He was a friendly kid, likable, but he had moments of sadness—
his parents were in the midst of a divorce and his house was up for sale.

One day while we were weeding, Thomas asked me what I'd been
doing up there in my office. I told him I was working on a book. He looked
at me accusingly, "A work book?"

"Nope," I said, "but it is a book about teachers."

"I'm glad it ain't a work book. I HATE work books. All day long we just fill
in the blanks, fill in the blanks, fill in the blanks. It's enough to drive a guy crazy!"

I commiserated with him and then asked him what he did in school
when it seemed interesting to him. "Well, we don't do much that's interesting. Pretty much we do the same old things every day. But I have one good
teacher. Mr. Taglini.

"You know that wall over there in Berlin that's coming down? Well, we
been studying that. Mr. Taglini gets us to bring in newspaper clippings every
day and we watch the news at school and at home. He says we're trying
to piece together the whole story. I been reading, talking it over with my
folks. Mr. West, he lives next door. He fought in the second World War, and

1

so he was telling me about the Russians and the Americans and the British fighting about who should get what, and that's when they built this wall and families were split up and couldn't see each other for years, and a lot of people who didn't want to be in East Berlin tried to escape over the wall and were shot and now it's coming down. There is a lot of celebrating going on over there." Breathless, he concluded, "This is real history! I pretty much figure I'm an expert on the Berlin Wall! You can ask me anything and I bet I know it!"

At that point, Thomas rolled away to a soccer match, leaving me filled with his enthusiasm and flying into the house to capture what he had to say. I sent a silent thanks to the Mr. Taglinis who begin the study of history with contemporary events, who help kids believe in their own expertise on events so distant, but so important to us all.

I embarked on this book for very simple reasons. Far too few children come home from school with the curiosity that Thomas had about what he was studying. Teachers suggest the same—that students seem less interested in school, and worse, that teaching has become both more difficult and more routine. Many are at a loss to know what to do about it or how to do it. I wanted to collect the tales of a few of the Mr. Taglinis in this world— teachers who are working hard to find more engaging ways to reach kids, to make our world and our communities more connected to kids' lives and learning. There is a small but ever growing band of such teachers throughout the country who believe that their professional responsibility is to help kids learn and who have come to believe that in order to do that, despite how much kids have changed, families have changed, and society has changed, they themselves must "stir the chalkdust"; set their own traditional practices and structures under the microscope of their experience; challenge their own thinking about how school might be done. These teachers are pilgrims, newcomers who bring skill and experience to this new century of educational dilemmas, who are working away to create a much broader repertoire of teaching techniques, strategies, and structures to re-energize their own lives and significantly engage their students.

The fact that teachers haven't set clouds of chalkdust aswirl is not surprising. Working in schools—one teacher, one classroom—creates conditions of isolation that work against teachers, preventing many from engaging in thoughtful discourse. There is little time in schools that is not absorbed in dealing with students and their parents, preparing lessons, and grading student work. In addition, schools are hierarchical places. Decisions made elsewhere in the system are part and parcel of the working conditions. (See Cohn & Kottcamp, 1993; Lieberman & Miller, 1984; Lortie, 1975; Sarason, 1971, 1991) For the last 20 years, legislators in every state have made a number of decisions about how schools should be run and central offices have been generating and directing massive staff development programs for teachers. (See Lieberman & Rosenholtz, 1987; Little, 1988; Wise, 1988). Attending inservice courses and implementing legislation took all the give out of already over-full teaching schedules. Traditionally, union negotiations ensured that teachers involved in bargaining made decisions only about bread and butter issues, not about the actual substance of teaching. To make matters worse, students who wanted to train to become teachers went to universities where again they were the recipients of traditional practices. The many thousands of hours of modeling teachers bring to their own class-rooms weights the scale enormously against fresh approaches (Goodlad, 1990; Kerchner & Koppich, 1993; Sarason, Davidson, & Blatt, 1988). My own experience as a classroom teacher confirms for me that the culture of schools is very difficult to change.

Teachers with whom I've worked as a co-teacher, as an administrator, and as a researcher suggest to me over and over and over that despite the fact that their students seem to be less and less engaged in schools, it is very dif-ficult for them to imagine doing the work of teaching differently. The con-versation about it simply doesn't crop up in schools. The discipline centered nature of the day isn't questioned. Whether or not to have multiple periods in the school day isn't raised; the only question is whether to add another period. Teachers haven't had time to think about it. Professional development opportunities, which flourished in the seventies and eighties, provided teach-ers with opportunities to learn new teaching strategies. However, some of the most prominent of these, like the Hunter seminars on more effective teach-ing, did not suggest fresh practices so much as they suggested ways to strengthen whole group, teacher-centered instruction. In addition, although many teachers had ample opportunities to engage in professional develop-ment, they had limited time to prepare to use these strategies or to be coached while trying something new.

All these factors explain why, although many teachers feel increasingly less efficacious, they are at a loss to think of alternatives; it is darned tough to break one's own personal history; it's nearly impossible to change a well-estab-lished system. Many feel very much like Horace Smith, the English teacher who felt himself living a compromise (Sizer, 1985). Although Horace wanted to breathe beauty and vigor and breadth into students' understanding of the world around them and to help them become competent writers, debaters, and consumers, he found himself compromised by the system in which he worked: Too many kids to know them well individually; too many papers to grade to give students much serious help; too short a class period to engage them in provocative discussion; too much material to cover to ensure that many of them understand very thoroughly; too many constraints; too little control.

Many of the teachers with whom I have worked over the years describe their fears about teaching in ways that, in my mind, take the shape of a specter in the following imaginary school:

Two students, with their parents, walked down the hall of their high school to register for the first day of school. The feeling in the school was familiar. For the parents, the school seemed much the same as it had when they attended—new paint; old smells. The students were excited! The school seemed bigger than the one they had previously attended, more adult, sophisticated, but not so different that they felt entirely intimidated. It was a bright, well-lighted place with a good deal of activity around the main office. The time was late summer so, after locating their schedules, students and parents all headed off to the first period classroom just to see what it might be like. They knew no one would be around, but wanted to anticipate what it would be like when school started in a few weeks. The hall was eerily quiet—only the hum of lawn mowers in the distance. On top of each closed door, they looked for the classroom number: 9D, 9C, 9B , 9A. There it was, finally, at the end of the hall. No lights were on. As they walked in, their eyes adjusted, then widened as they stopped cold. The shades were pulled down as if for a movie or film strip; the room was infused with the kind of dust-laden gloom that seeped and poured in through cracks and rips in the shades. A teacher was poised in the front of the room. She stood just in front of the chalkboard on which a number of directions had been written:

> *Homework for today: Read Chapter 12. Answer the questions at the end for review and be prepared to discuss.*
> *End of unit exam: Friday the 17th. Bring $ for field trip on the 29th.*

The board was striped, swiped, smeared in chalkdust, and the writing was thick, layered on top. The chalk tray was full, too. The teacher leaned forward, poised to speak and yet she did not move when the students and their parents came in. Instead, she appeared to be frozen in place—chalk between fingers of the right hand, mouth open as if just about to utter the most interesting tidbit about the material in chapter 12. Her age was inestimable— older, but not old—from an indeterminate time: the thirties? the eighties? the sixties?

She stared out across the 30 empty desks, all neatly pressed into rows. She stared at the bookshelves in which were stacked several large sets of texts, some brighter, some more faded. She stared and she stared and she stared, never moving. She seemed to see nothing at all, or a full house—all the students she'd ever taught. And she was shrouded in chalk dust, dusted in it, webbed over in it. Like Dickens's Miss Havisham, she seemed preserved in the dust of a time gone by, frozen in an action that serves fewer purposes in changing times.

For many of my teaching friends, this specter embodies their fears about their own professional lives. They feel trapped by traditional structures and practices, limited by their own isolation, frustrated by what seems to them an ever growing gap between their students' interests, parents' attitudes towards schooling, and the school's or the state's prescribed courses. Milbrey McLaughlin's (1993) recent research suggests that, in light of these changing aspects of their work-lives, most teachers view their professional responsibilities in one of three ways: (1) They believe they must maintain traditional standards; (2) they must lower expectations for kids; or (3) they must adapt their practices and pedagogy. It was the teachers who believed they must adapt that I was interested in. I wanted to capture these teachers in context to provide some images of teaching done differently. I set out to find some stirrers—teachers who were in the midst of rethinking their teaching practices in hopes that they might re-energize their own lives in the process of engaging their students. I hoped to find classrooms that were lively, where kids were excited, thinking hard, writing, investigating, where they were interested in telling me what they were learning. In my own daydreams, I hoped to collect images of different teaching practices, better teaching practices that would help all of us begin to build a collective imagination to banish the fear of being frozen in a limited range of strategies, in rigid structures—images to raise old chalkdust to fresher, more productive flurries.

THE CASES AND THE COALITION OF ESSENTIAL SCHOOLS

The teachers whose stories I tell all work in Essential Schools, members of the Coalition of Essential Schools. The Coalition is a partnership between Brown University and member schools across the country. The purpose of the partnership is to redesign schools so that adolescents learn to use their minds well. Those that joined agreed that schools would interpret the nine Common Principles, which Ted Sizer (1985) described in *Horace's Compromise*.

The Nine Common Principles

1. *Focus.* The school should focus on helping adolescents learn to use their minds well. Schools should not attempt to be "comprehensive" if such a claim is made at the expense of the school's central intellectual purpose. . . .
2. *Simple goals.* The school's goals should be simple: that each student master a limited number of centrally important skills and areas of knowledge. While these skills and areas will, to varying degrees, reflect the traditional academic disciplines, the program's design should be shaped by the intellectual and imaginative powers and competencies that students need, rather than necessarily by "subjects" as conventionally defined. . . . The aphorism Less Is More should dominate: Curricular decisions should be guided by the aim of thorough student mastery and achievement rather than by an effort merely to "cover content."
3. *Universal goals.* The school's goals should be universal, while the means to these goals will vary as those students themselves vary.

School practice should be tailor-made to meet the needs of every group or class of adolescents.

4. *Personalization.* Teaching and learning should be personalized to the maximum feasible extent. Efforts should be directed toward a goal that no teacher have direct responsibility for more than eighty students. To allow for personalization, decisions about the details of the course of study, the use of students' and teachers' time and the choice of teaching materials and specific pedagogies must be unreservedly placed in the hands of the principal and staff.

5. *Student-as-worker.* The governing practical metaphor of the school should be student-as-worker, rather than the more familiar teacher-as-deliverer-of-instructional-services. Accordingly, a prominent pedagogy will be coaching, to provoke students to learn how to learn, and thus to teach themselves.

6. *Diploma by exhibition.* Students entering secondary school studies are those who are committed to the school's purposes and who can show competence in language, elementary mathematics, and basic civics. Students of traditional high school age who are not yet at appropriate levels of competence to enter secondary school studies will be provided intensive remedial work to assist them quickly to meet these standards. The diploma should be awarded upon a successful final demonstration of mastery for graduation—an "exhibition." This exhibition by the student of his or her grasp of the central skills and knowledge of the school's program should be jointly administered by the faculty and by higher authorities. . . . As the diploma is awarded when earned, the school's program proceeds with no strict age-grading and with no system of "credits earned" by "time spent" in class. The emphasis is shifted to the students' demonstration that they can do important things.

7. *Attitude.* The tone of the school should explicitly and self-consciously stress values of unanxious expectation ("I won't threaten you but I expect much of you"), of trust (until abused) and of decency (the values of fairness, generosity and tolerance). Incentives appropriate to the school's particular students and teachers should be emphasized, and parents should be treated as essential collaborators.

8. *Staff.* The principal and teachers should perceive themselves as generalists first (teachers and scholars in general education) and specialists second (experts in only one particular discipline). Staff should expect multiple obligations (teacher–counselor–manager) and feel a sense of commitment to the entire school.

9. *Budget.* Ultimate administrative and budget targets should include, in addition to total student loads per teacher of eighty or fewer

pupils, substantial time for collective planning by teachers, competitive salaries for staff, and an ultimate per pupil cost not to exceed that at traditional schools by more than 10 percent. To accomplish this, administrative plans will inevitably have to show the phased reduction or elimination of some services now provided to students in many traditional comprehensive secondary schools. (pp. 225–227)

These ideas suggested to Sizer that, put in place in necessary synergistic combination, they would help to construct stronger, more defensible educational experiences for kids and better working conditions for the adults. Sizer selected this strategy—forming a partnership around a set of sound educational ideas that schools were to interpret—because it was more intellectually respectful of people who work and live in schools. To suggest that school faculty should engage in their own diagnosis about what needed to change to improve learning for students was almost heresy in the prescriptive 1970s and 1980s when almost everyone who did not work in schools mandated for those who did what it was they needed to do to improve. Most agree that the long-term effects of those mandates were limited. The Coalition also acknowledged at the outset that just as no two students are alike, no two schools are alike; therefore, schools would interpret these principles in the context of their local culture and community.

In 1989, those involved in the Coalition were finding the task of translating the nine Common Principles into action quite difficult. Whereas the principles seemed full of common sense and sound educational thinking, their implementation required radical change for everyone—teachers, principals, parents, and students. Faced with such an unfamiliar task, the teachers, not surprisingly, responded in various ways. Some said, "Translate these ideas? Sure. I already do most of them." Mission accomplished with no changes necessary.

Others suggested they needed more direction. "You want me to change? From what to what? Show me what it looks like. Give me a model."

Still others said, "We're trying, but what does all this mean? Taken seriously, it looks like we'll have to challenge everything that currently exists—certification requirements, graduation requirements, schedules, departments. Do we really have the authority, the knowledge, the expertise to make decisions like this?"

These tales are about teachers who are in the thick of interpreting the principles into action. The individual stories help us to understand better how the principles translate in different settings and contexts, and how variously people interpret these ideas. Collectively, they delineate many of the tensions and challenges between established structures and changing practices.

THE TALES

Five case studies follow. They are of pilgrims in progress and should not be considered exemplars or models that the Coalition recommends. Unromantic, they show the real difficulty people experience in attempting change. What the Coalition did hope was that this work would provide multiple examples of teachers struggling with the ideas in their own contexts; in reading and discussing them, all of us might build our own diagnostic capacity for rethinking schools in our own contexts.

Chapter 2, Kathryn's Tale, is the story of a teacher who was about to quit, defeated by the system, but who decided to take one last swing at teaching in a new, smaller, alternative high school. It is about how the structure of daily life in schools—the schedule, the courses, meetings—influence the nature of teachers' and kids' work together. It is about an exhausted, worn-down teacher who becomes alive in a new, more educationally sane environment, and, with her students, flourishes.

Chapter 3 is about Judd, a seasoned science teacher. Because his team started in a hurry to take advantage of new funding, his story is difficult. Despite their good intentions and high hopes, in their second year the team struggled to work together, to work with the rest of the faculty, and to survive in a politically volatile system. This case is more discouraging than the rest, but it is important because difficulty, complications, and confusion are generally more abundant in school reform than clarity, ease, and simplicity. We need to learn more about negotiating tough circumstances and about redirecting good intentions gone awry.

In chapter 4, we meet Jennifer Rochambeau who is a math teacher. Jennifer teaches in a large, suburban comprehensive high school; part of the faculty is experimenting with becoming an Essential school. As part of that effort, Jennifer and her colleagues in the math department are in the midst of rethinking what mathematics instruction might look like. In addition, she and her colleagues are on interdisciplinary teams and hope to blend with, and eventually influence, the rest of the high school. Jennifer allows us to glimpse what is possible when teachers within a department begin to see themselves as knowledgeable and capable of important curricular decisions made to enhance student learning.

In the Team's Tale, chapter 5, we meet Mary, Paolo, Enrico, and Michael, four teachers who work together in a school that makes decisions by consensus. This team has just convinced the rest of their colleagues in the school to let their team keep their high school students for the whole day, much like elementary schools do. They've asked to try this for a semester to see if it serves students' needs better. We join them for the first week of the new semester and the new program and then return at the end of the semester to see what changes they made. (There was follow up in each of the cases, but this case also includes a section entitled *Eighteen Weeks Later* because we felt it important for readers to share the mid-stream changes these teachers made as they developed a new curriculum.) We see all the bumps, glitches, and miracles that occur the first time teachers try something new. It is a powerful reminder of the uncertainty that accompanies new beginnings. It also suggests what happens when teachers take the nine Common Principles seriously over time. We watch their staff, settled into a schedule that might seem radical in many schools, elect to adopt another less familiar schedule as they continue to work to help their students succeed.

Chapter 6 is about Elizabeth, an English teacher in a large regional high school, who, with three of her colleagues, carried one group of students through their 4 years of high school and was just beginning again with her second group. They and their students demonstrate the benefits of knowing kids well. Their new students help us to see how difficult change is for students as well as for adults. At the same time, Elizabeth and company demonstrate again how critical stability and commitment are to change.

The cases all have similar elements, although they are not all arranged alike. Each includes an introduction and a section entitled "A Changed Job," about the teachers' descriptions of their previous teaching roles and their new roles. All the cases contain a section that describes teachers' work in classrooms and in meetings. As Kathryn notes, "When I decided to change my teaching, I didn't realize that I would be in meetings for the rest of my life!" The section, "Stepping Back," reveals their reflections on what changed, what supported and what challenged them, and concludes with the essential learnings I gleaned from each case. Because I want to convey that the road to better schools is one that takes a career to travel, a concluding section, "Since Then . . . ", tells what each of the teachers is up to now, and includes brief reflection from them about what they've learned about reforming schools. Undoubtedly by the time this book is in print, they will all be illuminating some further point along the road to better schools.

Chapter 7 reviews the common places where the teachers all stopped on their journey. They stopped at compelling and difficult places, but places where they might gather strategies, techniques, or understandings, all of which helped to build better schools for their students. Chapter 8, the Epilogue, marks our progress, offers an opportunity to think about what has been learned, and notes the paths left as yet uncharted. Appendix A is a simple chart that outlines the supports, challenges, and essential learnings teachers encountered, and allows readers to compare the cases at a glance.

The teachers who worked with these cases over the last several years asked that I extend a few words of their wisdom to those about to read the cases. They suggest that two guidelines are important: (1) Put aside the notion that one can learn only from teachers who teach in the same kind of school, the same aged kids, the same discipline, and who work with kids from the same economic background. Techniques, strategies, structures, personal reflections, and big ideas can and do transcend all of these personal identifiers. Schools, teachers, and kids are much more the same all over this country than they are different. (2) The phrase, "we already do that," should be banned from one's thoughts prior to reading about these teachers. Such a ban allows a fresh reading of someone else's circumstance, which may generate a solution to an old problem, highlight a slightly different approach, or help others to see new possibilities. Thus, our hope is that the journey these teachers took will shed some light for others as they wend their own way down the road toward lively schools.

2

Kathryn's Tale: A Humanities Teacher Talks About Change

"*F*or me, the hardest part about changing the way I teach was learning to trust kids and their own voices," said Kathryn Montegue, a high school humanities teacher. After having taught in large, conventional, urban high schools for 18 years, she moved to a smaller, innovative 7 through 12 high school called Westgate. Because had she moved to a school that held different expectations for staff and students, she found herself teaching quite differently. In the fall of 1989, I followed Kathryn for a week to see how her teaching had changed in a changed structure and what the effects were for students. The following case study shows us what a staff like Kathryn's can do when they determine that school structures and adult practices should focus on student learning.

A CHANGED JOB

"For me, trusting students and their voices meant a clear pedagogical shift," reflected Kathryn. She learned to believe more fully in her students' intellectual capacities and to respect their personal integrity as she watched them become more engaged in their own learning. Kathryn was in the process of exploring what had happened to her as a good conventional[1] teacher, and to her pedagogy, her curriculum, and her relationships to students and colleagues as she and her fellow team members worked to incorporate the nine Common Principles of the Coalition of Essential Schools into their classrooms. Surrounded by her students on the subway back to school, she grabbed time to reflect.

We were headed back to Westgate High School, a small, inner-city, 7–12 school, after a field trip to a downtown law firm. This particular trip was one

11

of the activities in the integrated curriculum that Kathryn and her fellow team members had developed as part of the year-long humanities course for 9th- and 10th-grade students centering on the essential question, "What is justice?" She had contacted this law firm in hopes that they might establish an enduring partnership. She hoped that these students would be able to work well with the attorneys who had agreed to participate so that by the time the students were seniors, those who would like to become lawyers might be able to do internships at the firm. More immediately, the firm had promised to help with the mock trials.

If learning to trust students' voices was her greatest challenge, Kathryn had certainly come a long way. Her students had just demonstrated the clarity and the authority of their voices in an exchange with eight seasoned attorneys on complex legal issues and procedures in the American judicial system. Kathryn had said almost nothing during the entire two-and-a-half-hour visit.

Kathryn's 15 students ranged in age from 13 to 16; they were racially mixed and displayed typical teenage hormonal hysteria—some were 4'6" while others loomed 6'2". The only specific instructions to the students prior to their meeting with the attorneys had been given outside the tall building that housed the law firm. Kathryn stopped, pierced the kids with her most direct gray-green gaze, and announced, "No gum and no hats. Got it?" The kids shuffled; hats came off. Some swallowed their gum; a few chewed surreptitiously.

Once inside the elegant offices, two attorneys met the students to take them on a tour of the various departments within the firm. They visited the huge word-processing department where they experimented with a Lexus database that could access records of any court case on any subject from the Supreme Court register or from the state law register. Because there had been a recent case of rape in their neighborhood, the kids entered "statutory rape" into the computer. A list of all the statutory rape cases appeared on the screen by case number and date. They walked through the library, which was organized around a series of moveable stacks. They toured the accounting department and the copy center. Each of the departments was large and full of people working busily.

The students were then ushered into an imposing boardroom with a long mahogany table, leather chairs, a bar, and a big window overlooking the city. A buffet lunch was set up at one end of the room. Kathryn, who had not said a word since our arrival in the offices, grinned. Her face was radiant with excitement. She whispered to me that the kids were learning all kinds of things: They were seeing a variety of possible careers; they were experiencing the city at work; they were seeing the kinds of technological support systems that have become crucial to our society. She couldn't talk fast enough in her excitement.

While the kids wolfed the lunch, she worked. She talked with one attorney about their plans to do mock trials in which the firm had agreed to participate. The attorney asked about the kids. Kathryn noted that they came mostly from impoverished families, many of which were very troubled. Still, she bristled a bit when the attorney made a big fuss about the kids' abilities in the face of these difficulties. Kathryn believed in these kids in a way that was not soft—that did not excuse them because of their circumstances, but that demonstrated her certainty that they were as capable of anything they put their minds to as people who came from more privileged circumstances.

After lunch, the senior attorney suggested that they might start with a discussion on legal proceedings. One of the students opened by asking how poor people could get legal representation. Kathy, one of the guides on the earlier tour, explained that their firm, like most others, did *pro bono* work. She gave the kids a definition. The students pushed. How much *pro bono* work did they do? Who decided what cases they would take? How did someone contact them in order to gain access to the attorneys in this firm? Finally Tyrone, who had asked the original question, said, "Well, I got myself a lawyer!" and everyone had a good laugh.

The senior attorney asked the students what they knew about legal proceedings. The kids described the two kinds of law—civil and criminal—and explained court procedures. They described the players, too. A woman attorney asked why the prosecution went first in the courtroom. The kids explained by describing opening comments and what should be included in them and how the prosecution set the stage. The attorneys elaborated. One noted that a tremendous amount of work goes into the preparation of the trial. A student asked, "Why do trials take so long?" Another asked, "What is a hung jury, and what is a mistrial, and what is the difference?" The senior attorney straightened his tie, cleared his throat, and observed that the kids were asking excellent questions, and hard ones at that. One of his colleagues fielded the questions about trials. "Who determines whether a case is subject to state jurisdiction or federal jurisdiction?" another student asked. The lawyers looked at each other and laughed; one attorney remarked that these kids wasted no time getting to the heart of the matter. Then he went on to explain, indicating that this was a troublesome issue, but noting that the prosecution usually made the determination based on the government's best interests.

During the discussion, the students did not raise their hands but spoke out in turn, as the attorneys did, giving way when they overlapped. The whole group was respectful and attentive. The attorneys asked the kids to speak up and to identify themselves as they spoke, which they did. When several students appeared to dominate the discussion, the senior attorney asked to hear from those who had not yet spoken, and the more verbal students held back. Mark, a ninth grader who wanted to be an attorney, asked what proportion of their time was spent in preparation for a case compared to the time spent in the courtroom. The attorneys gave a variety of examples, citing different types of cases. The lawyers asked the kids about plea-bargaining. One student explained, "It's designed to relieve the courts because they are so over-booked." Another added, "People can negotiate the plea outside of the courtroom so that they move towards getting what both parties want."

The students asked more questions. "In drug cases, who determines whether it will be a federal or state case?" "Does losing a case have anything to do with an attorney's salary?" Everyone laughed again. The lawyers asked the kids if they knew what contingency fees were. A student answered, "If you win, you gets the money; if you loses, you don't get nothing." More laughter; the kid grinned.

After an hour and 15 minutes, Kathryn reminded the group that their time was running out and that she would like them to conclude the conversation with some discussion of closing comments. One of the girls noted that it was in the closing statements that people asked for what they wanted as an outcome of the trial. One of the boys said it was a terrific time to ask for all kinds of money and to reflect on the American way of life, apple pie—that kind of stuff. The entire group laughed again, and the senior attorney said with good humor that there was not much more they could add.

The students stood up, thanking the attorneys for the lunch and for the conversation. The attorneys told the kids that they looked forward to seeing them in court for their mock trials and congratulated them on their excellent preparation. As they filed out of the room, the kids chatted with individual attorneys, pursuing questions of interest, or explaining the cases they were working on.

As the students left, the attorneys were visibly surprised and delighted by the visit. They commented that this must be an exceptional group of kids. Kathryn replied that these were ordinary kids, but that all kids can be exceptional given a learning environment into which they can sink their teeth. She made arrangements to call one of the attorneys to finalize plans for the mock trials. The attorney said that she would like to come out to their classroom to help the kids with their preparation. "Anytime," Kathryn replied. "We could use you!"

The kids were jubilant on the way home. They knew they had done a good job. Kathryn, visibly pleased with them, relaxed her business-like demeanor. Her face softened, and as the subway carried us uptown, she moved back in time to describe her teaching experience before she came to Westgate.

REFLECTIONS ON A CONVENTIONAL CLASSROOM

Kathryn taught for 18 years in a large comprehensive junior high school in the heart of one of the largest cities in the United States. She was an English teacher, and like the other 120 teachers in her building, she taught five 45 minute classes a day. She had 175 students a day, an average of 35 students in each class. During the time allotted, she attempted to impart to her students an appreciation of the great works of literature—American and European—a task for which she had been prepared in countless literature classes, both undergraduate and graduate. In addition, she hoped to teach them to write clearly, to read critically, and to express themselves well. Kathryn loved her students and got a great deal of pleasure from working with them.

The organization of the school was much like other comprehensive schools across the country. The school day was controlled by bells signaling the beginning and the end of each class. Each teacher taught in his or her own classroom. For the most part, Kathryn worked alone without much contact with her peers. Except for passing in the halls, bolting sandwiches during their 30-minute lunch break, or attending infrequent staff meetings, she seldom saw her colleagues and rarely talked with them. "I was always conscious of the bell. Do I have 10 minutes of motivation? Do I have enough time to go over the homework? I was always racing, watching, and looking; the kids started shuffling their books before the end of class and I could tell they were not focused on what I was talking about. I was focused on the management of it all." Despite the time constraints, she carefully planned her lessons in advance and had the plans ready in case the administrators wished to see them, as they occasionally did.

Kathryn believed that she was a good teacher. She worked well with students. She invested a good deal of energy in preparing and conducting her lessons. She had been given every indication by her administrators that she was good. Although the administrators seemed distant to Kathryn, "I knew I was doing a good job because I always got an S (satisfactory) on my review, and because I was left alone a lot of the time—the administration didn't bother me." Her attendance records were up to date, and she managed all of the requisite custodial tasks well. Furthermore, the administrators frequently let her know when special programs were available—a show of their confidence in her. As a result, she participated over the years in several special programs. "I was happy when new programs came into the school. Nobody else wanted them; nobody else cared about them. I think they thought, 'Ah, that crazy lady down the hall, she's doing that Shakespeare program again.'"

These programs constituted the bulk of Kathryn's professional development—they influenced the way she taught far more than the university courses she took to maintain her credentials. Kathryn was involved in a program to bring Shakespeare to life, in a law program, in a program to break down stereotypes in both sex and race. She was involved with a poets-in-residence program and with a program to determine the effects of stress on students' lives. All of these programs brought lay people into her classroom and enabled her to take her students out of the classroom and into other workplaces. Each added both to the course content and to her pedagogical skills. She actively pursued these kinds of improvement opportunities over the years.

Life behind Kathryn's classroom door demonstrated good conventional teaching practices. Her classroom was arranged so that she sat in the front of the room. "There were wonderful bulletin boards," she recalled. On the walls were posters with lofty quotes from great American philosophers, which she got from other teachers who left or from school trade stores. The students' desks were arranged in rows. "Sometimes the desks were arranged singly in rows, sometimes in twos—depending on the year. I had a series of textbooks, usually not enough. Grammar books, literature books, series. I followed the textbook through the year, so the lesson would consist of whatever page we were up to at that point. I put some examples on the board, I discussed several points, then I would see if the kids could do it on their own. Then they got an assignment. I lectured a good deal. They wrote. Sometimes they'd ask a question. Active student participation was minimal because I believed that the sign of a good class was a quiet class. Once in a while, we would do group reading that would involve reading a piece of literature together. Sometimes, some years, I'd have workbooks, and groups of kids would work on a particular task.

"Students worked independently. I corrected their drafts; then they would recopy them and hand them back in. I believed that my professional responsibility was to cover the material, to prepare the kids for state exams, to make sure they had practiced for their reading test—and my students did well." She called parents when something was wrong.

Kathryn had two children of her own during the course of those 18 years and felt that she had orchestrated her life so that she could both work and parent successfully. "It was very convenient for me in terms of my family. If I needed to go home, I could."

Although the working conditions remained fairly constant over time, Kathryn described other changes that eventually caused her to feel dissatisfied. When she had first gone to that school, it had been a very exciting place. "I was a politically active person. Decentralization was just starting and it was very exciting. We (the teachers in her department) formed a curriculum support group and developed a nice camaraderie. They were a tremendous source of support; we were there for each other."

Unfortunately, that faded. "Everything changes. The administration changed several times, and I was becoming increasingly dissatisfied with my job. Enrollment declined to 600 kids and 50 staff. Everything was a battle. People were reined-in in their jobs. To get a bus pass, you had to smile at the right time; to get paper, you had to know the supply guy; and I did— I'd worked there long enough; I'd paid my dues. But the focus was on discipline, keeping the kids in line. It is the bureaucracy that strangles you. People were not interested in teaching; they were interested in holding outside jobs, not making waves, getting out at three. You couldn't get close to the time clock at 3 o'clock, the line was so long. The administration did not force collaboration. It became divisive. Then it became blacks versus whites—and that was the worst."

In her 15th year, the superintendent heard of Kathryn's dissatisfaction. He asked her to start a mini-school. She and two other teachers were offered the opportunity to set up the kind of school they thought would produce better learning. "It was very exciting to me. I could order my own materials; we were told we could hire who we wanted; we could really work together. We could celebrate kids' birthdays, take kids to the theater! We had one floor within a regular school building. I can't tell you the ideas we had. We spent the whole summer just planning, calling, writing, and setting things up in the classes—it was very exciting. The problem was that the superintendent just wanted someone to start a mini-school, and he really had no intention of giving support. He was an interesting guy; I'm glad he gave us the opportunity, but he didn't help us. So we couldn't survive. The rest of the school was very hostile to us, and that changed it. We found out we couldn't hire who we wanted. People were transferred in who couldn't be put anywhere else. These people had no idea what it was we were trying to accomplish, and they didn't want any part of it." It was at this point that Kathryn decided that she needed a change.

Like many other practicing teachers in the United States today, Kathryn felt a diminishing sense of satisfaction in her work. She recognized that the goals she had once believed possible—helping students to appreciate great literature, to write well, to express themselves clearly—seemed unrealistic and unattainable in the midst of her large comprehensive school. And, like countless others, she began entertaining notions of a career change. She had spent hours trying to determine what she could do besides teach when a friend outside the school system suggested that she apply for a job in another of the city's schools—one that had developed a reputation for innovation. Kathryn didn't know much about the school, but she applied on the strength of her friend's enthusiasm and was hired.

AN INNOVATIVE SCHOOL ENVIRONMENT

When Kathryn arrived at Westgate, she learned that it was a member of the Coalition of Essential Schools and that it had been working to incorporate the Coalition's nine Common Principles for 2 years. The school seemed to provide just the kind of environment Kathryn was looking for, so rather than leave education, she moved her files of good lesson plans across the city to her new classroom.

When I met her, Kathryn was in her 3rd year at Westgate, her 21st as a public school teacher. Westgate was an alternative school located in a moderately poor neighborhood, a school of choice in a large urban school district. The student population was 40% black, 40% Hispanic, and 20% other. As an Essential school, Westgate focused on helping young people learn to use their minds well, stressing that students should be the workers.[2] It emphasized personalization and the mastery of a limited number of centrally important skills and areas of knowledge. It promoted high expectations, trust, a sense of personal decency, and a respect for diversity.

The school was divided into "houses"[3] of about 75 students each. Each house had an interdisciplinary faculty that worked exclusively with the students in that house. Each staff member also took responsibility for the social and emotional welfare of about 15 student advisees. Students in grades 7 through 10 studied a common core curriculum, with three classes per day—humanities, mathematics/science, and an advisory period. Each student also participated in a community service project. Additional subjects—languages, music, physical education, and library skills—were offered before and after school. An intramural physical education program, in addition to library, music, and gym, among other educational options, was offered at lunch time. A typical student schedule looked something like this:

8:00–9:00	Spanish/Library
9:00–11:00	Humanities
11:00–1:00	Math/Science
1:00–2:00	Lunch/Recreational Activities
2:00–3:00	Advisory
3:00–5:00	Daily Extended Options

Students were grouped in two-grade blocks—7th and 8th, 9th and 10th, 11th and 12th. Kathryn, as a humanities teacher, worked with three teachers on a team that took responsibility for the 9th/10th humanities curriculum. Kathryn had two 2-hour humanities classes and an advisory period each day. Each Tuesday morning, while the students were working at various projects in the community, she and her colleagues planned and refined the curriculum. Kathryn's typical daily schedule looked like this:

8:00–9:00	Meetings and Planning
9:00–11:00	Humanities (first group)
11:00–1:00	Humanities (second group)
1:00–2:00	Lunch
2:00–3:00	Advisory
3:00–3:30	Meetings and Planning

More often than not, the teachers worked together through the lunch hour. On Friday mornings at 8:00, the advisory team met to plan activities and to discuss students' progress and support. The whole school faculty joined together in weekly meetings to participate in shared decision making about the governance of the school. In addition, teachers conducted two hour-long conferences with the parents of each of their students during the course of the year.

Resources were allocated in some uncommon ways in this school. Each of the teams—the teaching teams and the house teams—was given a budget with which they could plan during the course of the year. Kathryn noted that the teachers had moved away from dependency on textbooks. "Sometimes we use pieces of the texts. We use novels. We use all kinds of materials. We write stuff. I have brought in stuff from the Legal Outreach program I did at my old school." In addition, the teachers were each given $250 for supplies and, rather than spending the money independently, Kathryn's team had collaboratively planned what they needed and who would order what.

Leadership for Change

Furthermore, the school was organized to reduce the bureaucratic impediments teachers normally face and to develop broad based leadership. There was a copy machine on each floor. Teachers were not required to document how many copies they made or when. A telephone was available for use across the hall from Kathryn's classroom. A teacher–coordinator was on full-time release from the classroom to provide support to the 7th/8th-grade team and to the 9th/10th-grade team.

As the coordinator, Mary Wells filled a variety of roles: "I make sure that each teacher in the group has the materials, knows what they're doing, why they are doing it, that they get support when they need it. I run team meetings, do proposals and agendas ahead of time so that people can think about it." Mary functioned as the liaison between the two humanities teams in the house to ensure consistency for students as they moved from 7th through 10th grade.

Mary's other major responsibility was to help teachers who had just come on board. Although most of those who joined the staff at Westgate were experienced teachers, few of them had had the opportunity to function as "generalists."[4] At Westgate, the humanities teachers taught writing, language arts, history, civics, geography, and expression. Michael Thompson was new to the team that year and had never taught English before. Mary read all of Michael's first round of student papers. The two of them worked together on his comments to the kids. Mary noted that the teachers worked together all the time, not just once or twice a year during an evaluation, that they had established an on-going process of building a better support system for teachers. Mary had provided similar support for Kathryn, but in a different way. Kathryn was an experienced English teacher but was unused to such intense collaboration, and was inexperienced at giving students more choice within the curriculum. Mary watched her teach and encouraged Kathryn to let go of many of the decisions she liked to make and to let kids participate more.

Finally, the administrators at Westgate worked as partners with the teachers in the educational endeavor. "I see the administrators as a source of help," commented Kathryn. "Their concerns are very much focused on how teachers and kids grow. And they are always accessible to me." Kathryn described her principal, Rebecca Hoffman, as "a very stimulating person. She keeps me going. She keeps asking questions. Her own perspective is light-years ahead of where I am, so she makes me think about things. Most of the time, she's really interested in deepening our thought, which is very valuable—for the kids, for us. She has a wonderful way of putting things." Rebecca had been a kindergarten teacher. When she went into administration, she started several elementary schools, so Westgate, her first high school, was significantly influenced by elementary philosophy.

Rebecca was fearless about confronting difficult issues, and so kept the staff probing their basic assumptions and their daily practices. During a faculty meeting Rebecca pointed out that everyone became extremely tense around grading periods. The comments on the reports sounded very much like the standard, rather empty phrases she used to write on report cards when she was teaching. As she reviewed the reports, she felt that teachers seemed to revert to old behaviors during times of high stress. As a result of Rebecca's insight, the faculty grew to understand that they must push themselves to be more communicative in the reports home—that they must push forward instead of reverting back.

The principal's office, a converted classroom, was across the hall from Kathryn's room, right in the midst of a number of classrooms. The administrators did not evaluate teachers. Rather, they rearranged the schedule so that teachers had time to work together to examine curriculum, pedagogy, and assessment.

Kathryn's Role

Kathryn perceived her role as focused on facilitating the best possible learning circumstance for each student: "My professional responsibility is to really examine what's happening for each kid." That meant knowing her students very well and assuming a variety of responsibilities in order to ensure that each student could learn. Therefore, her schedule was organized so that she dealt with only about 45 students each day. She walked kids through all kinds of problem-solving situations to ensure that they would be able to focus and to concentrate.

She was also responsible for 15 advisees—students with whom she became very close. It was her job to know these students well and to become a trusted adult for them, to help them learn to cope with the daily complexity of both school and adolescence. Kathryn saw them frequently and was very aware of their particular concerns, problems, and strengths.

During my visit, she took one of her advisees out shopping on a Saturday to replace the student's coat, which had been stolen. She knew most of her students' parents and was in frequent contact with them.

Kathryn's role in the school was complex. As a humanities teacher, she was expected to be a generalist with responsibility for writing, language arts, history, civics, geography, and expression. The curriculum for the year was organized to consider the question: What is justice? Kathryn and her colleagues built curricular units that included activities in all of the disciplines mentioned—not as discrete activities in geography, history, etc., but as activities embedded in the larger question so that students could see the interconnections.

Kathryn also supervised student teachers, organized field trips, and was the house team leader for her unit—half of the 9th/10th-grade team. She taught writing on computers and helped students to develop keyboarding skills. She was responsible for attending humanities team meetings, whole faculty meetings, and house meetings. Recently, she had been asked to travel to different schools across the country to conduct staff development activities for other teachers interested in changing their working circumstances.

Kathryn, now in her mid-forties, had been married to her attorney husband for 22 years. Their daughters were teenagers. She spoke frequently of her family with great affection and occasionally mentioned the conflict she experienced between caring for her home family and caring for her school family. She noted that changing roles for women posed challenges that could be weathered but that were challenges nonetheless.

A DAY IN KATHRYN'S CLASSROOM

Standing in her classroom—she almost never sat down—Kathryn was a small woman with the voice control of an actress, quiet and personal at times, conversational at others, commanding when necessary. Her large gray-green eyes dominated her face. She opened them very wide when she meant serious business, piercing students with them. She had robust mannerisms, quick and staccato speech patterns: "Focus, focus, focus! Jimmy, you left your hat on. There are ladies in here. Come on, now. No time to waste. Let's focus!"

Despite her small stature, her quick and decisive movements gave her a commanding presence. She was confident without being arrogant. She laughed easily and, in softer moments, communicated a strong sense of caring. She frequently linked arms with students and fellow staff members, as if to draw them deeper into personal conversation.

Kathryn's room was in a 90-year-old building and was painted a deep eggshell blue. The color—selected for its ability to blot out decades of scarring—was harsh and cold. There was a bank of closets along one side of the room, one of which was locked. Across the room was a row of windows. The shades were pulled down over two of the windows, at half mast over two others. The windows were covered on the outside in thick wire mesh. Several large housing projects loomed beyond the windows. Vibrations from commuter trains rumbling past periodically shook the room.

Along the top of the board were five questions the Westgate faculty and staff had collaboratively devised to help their students develop good habits of mind during their years in the school:

> How do we know what we know?
> What's the evidence?
> How else might it be viewed, seen, considered?
> What's the viewpoint?
> What difference does it make?

On another wall was their essential question[5] for the year: What is justice? This question provided the guiding focus behind everything they studied in their humanities block during the year.

Kathryn had arranged the room to accommodate several kinds of flexible groupings. "The main part of the room is a circle of desks for whole-group instruction. I've tried to make three different work areas in the room: the round table in the back can accommodate four students, the rectangular table in the back is another, and the three chairs by my desk are another. But I need room for a fourth group." Kathryn threw up her hands as she wondered why she worried about the arrangements she'd made. "The kids move the desks where they want anyway!" She longed for a larger room and desks on wheels.

Off to a Flying Start

By the time I arrived in Kathryn's room at 8:15 on a winter morning, the day after our visit to the law office, she was already in the midst of her third meeting of the day. The first had been with her humanities team members; they had added an extra meeting to the day because they wanted to devote their regular planning session entirely to a discussion of mini-Exhibitions.[6] The special meeting had been called to discuss a growing concern that their two-hour-block periods with their students were being eroded by interruptions and special activities. In order to present a clear case to the staff, the group wanted to document how much time they had lost in recent weeks .

Kathryn's second meeting had been with her house advisory team. This cross-disciplinary group—one math/science teacher, two humanities teachers, an art teacher, and the resource room teacher—took responsibility for approximately 80 students. Their purpose was to pay particular attention to the emotional, physical, and intellectual well-being of their advisory students while they were in school. The first item of discussion was how they were going to raise money for their big annual trip. Each advisor took his or her students somewhere during the school year—usually to a university, so the students could begin to think about what they might like to do and where they might want to go to college. Last year, Kathryn had taken her students to her alma mater in Massachusetts. This year she wanted to take them to Philadelphia.

Next, the teachers talked about arranging a trip to the local planetarium to see a new exhibit on "The Seven Wonders of the Universe." Outings were encouraged, and because several were already scheduled, they had to plan this particular trip several weeks down the road.

Kathryn's third meeting of the morning was with Micki Sherman, her student teacher. Micki was in her last quarter of work before graduating with a degree in education but was struggling over whether to go ahead with a career in teaching. Her experience at Westgate had been very different from the usual student-teaching preparation, and she was not sure that she wanted to teach in a regular comprehensive high school. Kathryn and Micki went over the student papers Micki had graded and reviewed the lesson Micki had taught the day before. The two appeared to have a good rapport—easy and supportive. Kathryn was encouraging, while offering constructive criticism.

As they finished, a student came in looking forlorn. He was tall, yet looked very young. Kathryn immediately turned her attention to him. "Hi, Charles. What's up?" They sat down at two desks. The student started to cry. Kathryn put her arms around him while encouraging him to talk. He sobbed out that his grandfather, with whom he lived, had had a heart attack. He had been taken by ambulance to the hospital the night before, and Charles had no idea how he was. Mary Wells, the humanities coordinator, came in and joined them, while Micki ran off to find Charles's advisory teacher. The room was quiet and calm, full of caring for the student. Once found, the advisor helped Charles arrange a visit to the hospital and secured an excused absence for him.

The Daily Advisory Session (Part One)

As Charles was leaving, two teachers rushed into Kathryn's room, distraught because the second copy of the film, *To Kill a Mockingbird,* was missing. Kathryn checked their schedules and then pointed out that they could show the film to their students together. At this point, students began streaming in for a half-hour morning advisory. To accommodate one of the teachers, the usual hour-long advisory had been divided into two half-hour sessions at the beginning and the end of the day on that day. The purpose of the advisory period was to allow teachers to catch up with a small group of students, to check on their progress, to make sure that they were progressing in school. Several students met with Kathryn who sat at a student desk in the large circle. They called Kathryn by her first name, as they did all the teachers and administrators.

During the few minutes before class, the activity in the room intensified. The librarian popped in to tell Kathryn that he missed her—that he never saw her anymore. The art teacher stuck his head in to remind her of the schedule change. Kathryn asked a student whether he'd enjoyed doing his homework last night. He looked sheepish. Her eyes opened very wide, and she gave him the look. "I charge a lot for notebook rental space here, Frankie. One more time and you will be in heavy debt. Ask George. He knows." As he came up to pick up his notebook, she said, "Come on, Frankie, let's get with it. You can't get smarter when you leave your books here. They belong with you."

Kathryn addressed her advisory students, all of whom were in her humanities blocks. Kathryn liked to use advisory time to help her students learn the organizational skills they need to be successful. "Okay, you people. We have no time to waste. Focus, please! Please get your writing folders out and write what you intend to do today. We have a busy week, a busy schedule—no time to waste. Please focus and write silently for 10 minutes." She was very brisk. On the blackboard was a schedule of the students' activities for the day:

1. Art/writing
2. Exhibition question #4
3 Bail discussion
4. Read short story on the Civil War

Kathryn moved purposefully around the room from student to student. She stopped beside two kids. "Gentlemen, if this conversation is not dedicated to what you are writing, I don't want to hear it. Focus. Focus."

After 10 minutes, Kathryn asked the students to put their writing away. "Does anyone have any questions about what you will be doing this week?" She asked whether they had games this week. Several of the kids told her what was going on in their athletic programs. She asked two boys if they were nervous about a playoff game. One looked nonchalant; the other grinned and nodded. She wished them luck.

The discussion turned to *To Kill a Mockingbird*. She asked how many students had finished reading it. Most raised their hands. One student turned to his neighbor and moaned, "How did you finish already? It's too long . . . too long." One of the kids observed that when Atticus went to Tom's house to tell his wife that Tom had been killed, she knew even before Atticus said anything. One of the girls snapped at him, "Well, Atticus took off his hat, that's how she knew. She just knew. People don't always have to say things. I know. I've had it happen to me." Discussion was lively, and the half-hour passed quickly.

Kathryn closed the discussion by reminding the kids that they needed to watch their time as they all had a major portion of their mini-Exhibition for the trimester due on Friday. She told them she was available to them if they were having difficulty. Some of the kids packed up and moved out; others left their books but drifted out into the hallway to see their friends. She caught Adam on his way out. "Adam, your math book has been here for days." He responded, "I gots . . ."

"I gots? I gots?" Kathryn's eyes were very big. He grinned and took his book.

She grabbed Tommy, a learning-disabled student who spent part of his time in the resource room and part of his time mainstreamed into regular classes. "Tommy, on time for Spanish tomorrow, huh? It's important that you get there on time." He nodded on his way out.

Teachers' Time to Plan

Because it was Tuesday, the humanities team of five teachers was scheduled to meet while their students were out doing community service work. In this school, the teachers generated their own 2 year, rotating curriculum. Everyone taught the same thing at the same time, so there had to be consensus on what was to be taught when. Each interdisciplinary team had two-and-a-half hours a week to work together to plan curriculum, develop instructional strategies, and build mini-Exhibitions to assess student performance. These meetings provided a rich source of professional growth and generally extended through the lunch hour. The group straggled into Mary's room. They pulled the desks into a small circle and moved quickly into frequently difficult substantive discussions. They were debriefed about the field trip to the law firm. They shared articles on racism to enhance the study of *To Kill a Mockingbird*. They adjusted their instructional schedules to accommodate the PSATs.

The bulk of their discussion, however, involved the revision of the mini-Exhibitions they were creating to gauge student progress on the essential question for the year, What is justice? They had generated the mini-Exhibitions earlier—a series of 10 to 15 exercises from which students would choose in order to demonstrate their growing understanding. The teachers discussed the specific wording of particular questions. They debated whether kids should be given more opportunity to create other approaches to the mini-Exhibitions and whether they should be limited in access to resources. They juggled the order of the questions, wondering whether they should build in complexity, à la Benjamin

Bloom,[7] or whether the questions should be of equal value and complexity. They discussed the number of questions and how different kinds of students respond to different quantities. They argued over the efficacy of creating both advanced questions and standard questions, and whether doing so would intentionally reduce the expectations for some of their students.

During the discussion of the mini-Exhibitions, the teachers ranged back and forth among the activities they were planning to do in class, the readings they had prepared, and the evaluative exercises. They checked to determine whether they were actually teaching what students needed in order to complete the mini-Exhibitions. One question asked students to determine whether jails administer justice. This led the teachers into a discussion of whether they would go ahead with a proposed visit to a prison. Kathryn spoke passionately against the trip. She had gone to a nearby correctional institution with a group of teachers; they had been shown clean rooms and inmates watching color TV, eating three regular meals a day, and playing basketball. Kathryn's fear was that many of the students might miss the major point—that the inmates were confined, restricted—because the living conditions were so much better than those of many of the kids. The teachers talked about whether the kids should be allowed to suggest unreal punishments (punishments not currently admissible under our legal system) or whether they should deal only within the realm of the legally possible.

Much time was spent on what topics students should be allowed to examine. Each of the teachers in turn suggested and defended particular topics. Two teachers felt strongly that kids should deal with murder cases. Others thought they should be allowed to choose. Kathryn, after listening carefully, suggested that they broaden the questions so that students might deal with crimes of discrimination, involving rape, race, gender, and class. Another tense debate: Should students be taken to see another film that featured white people's struggle for black South African freedom? One of the teachers, himself a black South African, felt very strongly that students should see the film. An African-American teacher believed it misrepresented the political situation and over-idealized the role of whites and diminished the role of blacks. The majority of the staff wanted to see the film. Mary, who facilitated the meeting, turned the group repeatedly to their task. All members seemed to listen to each other. Because this issue was not resolved, it was tabled for smaller meetings before or after school.

Work continued through the lunch period. Several of the teachers pulled out lunches from home; others skipped lunch. The teachers analyzed where individual kids were and what might best be done to help them. No student was disparaged or devalued in any way. The group broke amicably; everyone reminded everyone else of what they had promised to do before next week's meeting.

The Humanities Block

At 11:00, Kathryn's second group of students arrived for their 2-hour humanities block. She greeted them as they came in, reminding some individuals of things they needed to do, asking others how things were going at home. On the right-hand side of the board, Kathryn had listed all the assignments that were due and when.

> Assignment 18: Final drafts I, II, and III and all pre-drafts.
> Assignment 18: Drafts due Friday.

Assignment 18 was a mini-Exhibition—several pieces of work to demonstrate students' understanding of *To Kill a Mockingbird.* The students had choices in three categories. In the first section they were to explore the development of viewpoint by rewriting part of the text from another character's vantage point, or they could create a scene that had to have happened but that wasn't described in the book. The second section asked the kids to engage in literary analysis—a comparison of characters or the use of the naive narrator. The third assignment asked them to deal with the social issues presented in the book. One choice was to explore Harper Lee's representation of blacks; another was to compare and contrast Lee's portrayal of blacks with Paul Lawrence Dunbar's poem "We Wear a Mask."

Kathryn began the class by asking for homework from the previous night. "I got it from some people but not from others. I can see evidence that you worked on drafts, but I haven't seen the results. There will be detention on Friday at lunch time for those people who do not hand in all three sections. If you were absent, call somebody. I would like as much typed as possible. I'd like everybody to work on the computer, even my computer-shy people. Are there any questions? There will be no time in class on Friday to work on the assignments, so bring them finalized, ready to go. For the next hour, I'd like you to take out your writing files. This will be a silent writing period for 1 hour. I am available to anyone who needs a conference. Who needs to work on computers?" Several students raised their hands. Kathryn took a huge ring of keys out of her purse and unlocked a small closet on one side of her room. The students rolled out four computers and one printer and quickly hooked them all up to portable outlet strips.

Some students went to work on their mini-Exhibitions; others continued to work on stories or essays they'd been doing. Kathryn glanced at several students sitting together in the back of the room. "Michael, focus, focus." She walked over to three other students. "Come on. I want you to spread out. Three of you together is no good." Her tone was very brisk again, and she stayed right with them, prodding them until they scattered in different directions.

Three visitors walked in with Mary Wells. They were accompanied by a student who was working for the school's Community Education Center as part of his community service requirement. His job was to show visitors around the school. No one in the classroom paid any attention to them; visitors were commonplace.

Kathryn leaned over one of the girls who was working on her conclusion to one part of the mini-Exhibition. She said that she was working on it because Kathryn wanted her to. Kathryn said, "I wanted you to? I wanted you to? What about you?" The girl grinned and then described where she'd been having difficulty.

The school's assistant principal walked in and pulled Kathryn aside for a minute. Kathryn had attended several meetings about problems of home–school communication. The assistant principal reported that they had made some progress but that it would be helpful if Kathryn could come back to the school that evening for another meeting to hear parents' concerns. Kathryn said she would be there.

During the interruptions, the room was quiet and students continued to work. Those on the computers helped each other occasionally without disturbing the rest of the class. Kathryn moved immediately toward any students who looked as if they might disturb others. She was stopped by a student who asked, "What do you want me to put in here?"

"I can't answer that; you have to make that decision."

"No, but you put some editing notes here. Read 'em. I don't know what you mean."

Kathryn grinned and sat down to see what she'd suggested. She worked with this student for about 5 minutes. She looked up once and said, "If you are not working in a comfortable place, move to where you will be." Another student asked to go to the bathroom. Kathryn had a list going in her head. "After William."

Two students sitting across the room from each other carried on a complete conversation without words. As discreetly as possible, they gestured back and forth. Kathryn missed this.

Tyrone was working on run-ons: "It's like two sentences where you got no period," he explained to me. "You gotta put in a period. I'm always looking for 'em." He waited for Kathryn to get to him. He was a ninth-grade student and smaller by a long shot than everyone else in the room. He wanted her to read one of his mini-Exhibitions. In this section, he had decided to adopt the persona of one of the characters in *Mockingbird* and to rewrite a scene from that character's perspective. He'd chosen Boo Radley, the troubled adult in the story.

"Did I use the words right?"

Kathryn clarified, "You mean the vocabulary?"

"Yeah."

She sat beside him and asked him to read his piece to her while she looked on. He read, "'They are always talking about somebody. People have malevolent minds.' Is that right?"

"Hmmm . . . 'malevolent.' Yeah."

Tyrone looked pleased and resumed his reading. "'. . . malevolent minds. Some people can pass for good but not most.'"

Kathryn stopped him after several more sentences. "Okay, this word is used correctly but this one is not." She helped him search for a better word. They then discussed how he could indicate who was speaking. Kathryn said, "Well, you have two choices here. You can either write a monologue where only one character is present and speaking. Or you can put quotation marks around only that part which is spoken language."

Tyrone nodded, "Yeah, I see." They moved back into the text. Tyrone resumed reading. "'I see a few kids. Let me move from the window. I don't even know when was the last time I was outside walking around. My amble way is a shame.'"

They worked through the use of the word *amble*. First they identified its part of speech as he used it. Then she had him identify its more common use as a verb. She encouraged him for using new words.

Tyrone read again, "'Gee, I'm so slow but I wonder what Atticus's kids are doing. I wonder what Atticus's kids are going to do next. I wish I wasn't in such a bewilderment.' Is that right?"

This time they worked through the meaning of the word *bewilder*. Kathryn asked, "What is another word that means bewildered?"

"'Sly,' maybe?"

"Tell me more."

"Like, you don't know what they're going to do next?"

"How is Boo feeling at this particular moment?"

"Sad. He doesn't know what they're going to do next. He's like . . ."

"Well, what are you when you don't know what you're going to do next?"

"Wait. When you don't know what you're going to do next, you're confused."

"Yeah, there you go. 'Bewildered' means confused."

They discussed how he would change *bewilderment*. She asked him to think about two more things—first, adding periods where he read the breaks in the text he'd written. She had him read it again and again to her so that he could hear where he put the breaks in.

Her other suggestion was about the introduction. "Suppose Rebecca and I hadn't read this book, and we walked in and picked up your paper and started to read it. How would we know what was going on?"

"Yeah, so I have to have an introduction, right?"

"Just identify what your paper is about so that, you know, someone who hasn't read the book can enjoy what this character is doing." She squeezed his shoulder affectionately and congratulated him for his hard work. The conference took approximately 8 minutes, during which time the class continued to work. Kathryn circulated for another 5 or 10 minutes, then said, "Please wrap up what you are doing in the next 5 minutes. Those of you working on computers, don't forget to save your work and print out a draft. Tomorrow you can give me your drafts so that I can do some editing in order to make this deadline. It is very important that you finish the *Mockingbird* mini-Exhibition by Friday. We need to move on."

The room broke into activity. Two girls argued about racism. One said, "I don't think things are much different today." The other disagreed: "I never experience racism today." Her friend roared at her, "That's because you live with blacks! What do you expect? And there ain't any racism here in this school. But what about the other schools? What about South Africa? What are you thinking of, girl?" Kathryn told the class to take a 5 minute break but to be back promptly because they had another important discussion coming up. The students dispersed, many arguing on their way out.

When the students returned, Kathryn hustled them into their four work groups. Kathryn handed out two actual court cases in which the judge had to determine bail. Each group got one case. Each group selected a prosecuting attorney, a defending attorney, the accused, and the judge. The kids argued about who would take what part.

"You can't be the judge; you've already been a criminal. No criminals ever get to be judges!"

"I want to be the prosecuting attorney here so I can knock old Mike into jail for life!"

"Okay, okay, let's get serious. Who's going to do what?"

Once they had settled on their roles, they reviewed their cases and the circumstances that would influence the judge's decision to post bail or not. The student judge needed to determine whether or not bail might be paid and, if so, how much. Kathryn reminded them that they must be able to explain their decisions and the processes they used to arrive at the decision. Each of the groups went to work, given 20 minutes to deliberate.

One group argued at length about the constitutionality of bail.

PROSECUTOR: I don't think any bail should be posted. This criminal is a repeat offender. He's just going to go out and commit another robbery.
DEFENSE: What difference does it make whether the judge posts bail or not? This man is a poor man—otherwise he wouldn't be robbing nothing! Where's he gonna get the money for bail? Bail serves the rich and

defeats the poor. It's just another example of how the legal system hurts poor people. Is that constitutional?

CRIMINAL: I don't think so. I'm never going to raise any bail money. I got starving kids at home!

JUDGE: Bail is set so that criminals can come and go before they're proven guilty—it's "innocent until proven guilty"—so that's constitutional. Get off it. Starving kids! More like you got starving friends.

DEFENSE: Yeah, but how can a poor person take advantage of that? And what does it look like for him? He has to hang out in the jail instead of being able to go to his job and everything.

PROSECUTOR: That's what you get for stealing. He didn't worry about other people's rights.

In each of the groups, students were leaning forward, arguing their points. Occasionally a burst of laughter or a loud groan emerged. The room was noisy but charged with activity. Kathryn walked from group to group, sitting down for a few minutes, listening in, contributing to the conversations by asking students to clarify, then moving on.

After 20 minutes, Kathryn asked each of the judges to announce his or her decision and to justify it. Mike went first. He determined that the criminal must post $15,000 bail. He set it that high because he didn't want the criminal on the streets and knew that the criminal couldn't raise that kind of money. Kathryn asked them to find the handout she had given them on bail. She asked them to locate the three factors a judge must consider in the posting of bail and then to analyze Mike's decision in light of those factors. The students began to argue about whether the bail was too low or too high. Emotions escalated, as did involvement. Kathryn did not participate other than to keep track of the speaking order. "Billy, then Martha, then Jason." The discussion lasted for 20 minutes. One student stood up and walked around the room, pacing back and forth but engaged in the debate.

The assistant principal came in again, this time to check with Kathryn about an early dismissal: would it be all right for the kids to attend a meeting about school jackets? The student discussion continued despite Kathryn's diverted attention.

Kathryn asked that each student function as the judge in deciding on the second case. The rationale for their decision needed to be determined before they left for the day. The room quieted quickly as they set to writing for the remaining 5 minutes. When their time was up, Kathryn asked them to put their names on their papers and to tell her what they would be doing that evening and the next day in class. Several of the students reviewed their work agendas—some reading, some serious work on their mini-Exhibitions.

The Daily Advisory Session (Part Two)

The room emptied except for those students who were in Kathryn's advisory. Gradually her full complement of 15 assembled for the second half of that day's advisory. Her businesslike demeanor dropped again; she became relaxed, more like the students. Both she and the kids were excited; it was a student's birthday. He had been sent on some fictional errand so they could set up chips, cookies, and sodas for a celebration.

The kids arranged things at whirlwind speed, then strained at the waiting. Two students hung out the doorway to announce his arrival. They all shouted and hollered and sang "Happy Birthday" to him as he appeared. He looked surprised, noted the goodies, appeared pleased, and said, "Thank you." He sat down with his friends, grinning from ear to ear, and the kids fell on the food. Mary walked in to say that her group's trip to the law firm had also been exceptional. Noting the party, she sat down with Kathryn, and they immediately resumed the discussion from the early morning meeting of the humanities team about whether instructional time was being eaten away. The kids merrily drank sodas, ate chips, and belched.

Food devoured, the students gathered on one side of the room and sang popular songs. They sat on the desks, close to each other, all wrapped up, arms and legs swinging. Three of the boys moved into rap songs. As Mary left, Kathryn told me it had been difficult to get this group to bond. She wanted them to develop a strong relationship with each other—to become special friends and a support group within the school. She reviewed her attempts to draw them together at the beginning of the year. She had tried discussions, but only a few would get involved. It didn't happen when they worked in their journals. It didn't happen when they read together. Finally she took them to the park one Friday afternoon, and they began to have fun. "It's the fun I want for them. I want them to have fun so that they can begin to share experiences." It took several months of team building activities and a variety of approaches to get them to form a group. Kathryn had been vigilant, watching them and looking for another activity, a new technique to try.

She also understood that it was during advisory that she learned the most about her students. For instance, a year ago one of the boys had performed a whole rap song. Kathryn let him know that she felt cheated because his school work was so poor. If he could memorize all those words just by listening, then he certainly had the ability to do the work and to learn. She had told him that he should be able to work harder. "This year," she noted, "he is doing much better. Just fine." She moved in to sing with the kids, then reassumed her brisk persona.

She explained the PSAT test, which was coming up soon. The kids groaned and asked how they could get out of it. She told them that they couldn't—that they needed to practice on these kinds of tests because they would have to take the SAT for college admission. The practice exams would help them to do better on the SAT. She gave them a letter to take home to their parents, snapped her fingers, clapped her hands, and marshaled people into quick cleanup before they left.

The kids scooped up crumbs, shot baskets with plastic pop containers, and rearranged their desks. Soon the room tumbled with coats, books, jibes, and teasing as the students prepared to leave 10 minutes early to go to the special meeting about school jackets. Kathryn went with them after stopping one of the students to remind him, "NO excuses. Do you hear me? Get that homework done!"

After the announcements about the jackets, the kids streamed out of the auditorium. Kathryn and her colleagues traded insults and guffawed about the day's events. There were no derogatory comments about students. They seemed spent from the demands of their schedules. Several of them gathered on the way up the stairs to discuss the imminent evening meeting with the parents. After attempting to sort out the issues, they agreed to meet a few minutes early to get clear.

Back in her room, Kathryn worked with two students who had questions about their mini-Exhibitions. She then conferred with Micki about the day and about their plans for the next day's activities. Despite a continuous flow of students and colleagues in and out of her room, she put on her coat at 5:00 to head home to make chicken soup for her daughter who was home sick; she would be returning 2 hours later to attend the parent meeting. As she walked out of the school, she linked arms with another teacher–friend while they shared the disappointments and triumphs of the day.

STEPPING BACK

Kathryn's role as a facilitative teacher appeared to be significantly different from her earlier description of herself as a good "conventional" teacher. Activities in her classroom were unlike most of those I have observed in secondary schools. At no time did I observe a lesson that involved the whole group using a standard textbook nor was the room always quiet nor were the desks in rows. Kathryn was often silent and nearly invisible in the classroom. She handed out no fill-in-the-blank worksheets; she gave no multiple-choice tests.[8]

At the same time, most of her students seemed to be engaged in serious work, and most of the time, the quality of their responses appeared to be thoughtful and complex because they were dealing with complicated issues. There was evidence of authorized opinion—they had done some research in order to solidify their ideas. More importantly, I did not see any evidence of the deadly torpor that affects so many students in the classrooms in which I have taught or observed around the country. Their ability to ask and to discuss important questions on legal practices on the visit to the law firm was impressive. Their ability to engage in serious discussions about emotionally loaded issues like justice and equality without taking the classroom apart also was noticeable. They were clearly struggling independently to master certain skills that they recognized as important. In addition, the relationship between Kathryn and the students was warm and caring but did not avoid the personal confrontation of tough issues like student motivation or personal problems. It was not a soft place—but it was a safe place.

What accounts for these differences? Kathryn is an intelligent and capable teacher but would be the first to claim that she is no more so than thousands of other teachers who labor in other classrooms across the country. The school was not enriched—there was no fancy technology, little new equipment. Indeed, by most standards, the school was run-down and in need of additional resources. Although students chose to attend this school, many came from the surrounding neighborhood. They seemed much like other heterogeneous groups of kids in large cities across the country.

Admittedly, Kathryn had demonstrated a predisposition to change over the years. She had participated in a number of programs: Legal Outreach, Shakespearean theater, sexual and racial stereotypes, poets-in-residence, and a project that researched stress in kids' lives. She had chosen to participate in these programs because they had provided more real-world experiences for her students and had offered her a means by which to grow professionally. Although she had maintained traditional teaching methods, she had taken advantage of these programs even though this had meant frequently rearranging her regular curriculum.

At the same time, when teaching in the larger high schools, it had never occurred to her that she might want to disregard the major portion of her planned course of study or the methods she had used for so many years. Although she had used different teaching methods when experimenting with new programs—group activities, role-playing, inquiry sessions—she had not incorporated these methods into her familiar repertoire of lessons. In this sense, Kathryn's experience had been similar to that of most other teachers; recent research conducted on the effectiveness of staff development efforts has shown that programs developed by outsiders seldom change teachers' instructional repertoires in any significant or lasting way.[9]

In order to investigate what had caused or enabled Kathryn to discard her more familiar teaching methods when she came to Westgate, I asked her to reflect on those conditions and circumstances that had supported her and to dig around in the challenges she had encountered. The case concludes with what might be characterized as the essential learnings about changing practices.

Support

There were a number of conditions at Westgate that enabled Kathryn to experiment with less conventional teaching methods. Westgate provided a rich collaborative learning environment for teachers. "It was a great experience coming here. It was wonderful. I couldn't believe the people; they were so interesting. Every meeting I was in, there were so many ideas being tossed around: Why don't we try this? Why don't we do it this way? Here's how we'll do it—we'll take a group of kids out to a museum, y'know . . . That's what it was like!"

The structure of the school had an enormous influence on Kathryn's teaching. She walked into a school where the daily schedule looked little like most high schools. She had only two classes and 2 hours with each. The length of each class propelled Kathryn to use different teaching methods. She had fewer students. She had 4 hours of regular planning time each week during which she was expected to meet with her colleagues. She spent 1 hour a day with 15 students whom she got to know very well. With them, her job was simply to get to know them well and to help them in any way she could to do well in school. In combination, these conditions made it nearly impossible for her *not* to change.

The school had been set up to foster collaboration among the adults in the school. Kathryn attended weekly faculty meetings to discuss the general concerns of the school and to share ideas. The norms of the school expected that teachers would participate in discussions and in decision making. She talked about the fact that the faculty read things together, many provided by their principal who was a voracious and wide reader. She had to do some catch-up reading—the series of books from A Study of High Schools: *Horace's Compromise* by Theodore Sizer (1985); *The Shopping Mall High School,* by Powell et al., (1985) and *The Last Little Citadel* by Robert Hampel (1986)—and what she read made sense to her. She believed she had found a place that shared and articulated her particular educational philosophy. The faculty continued to read and to discuss articles about education, about teaching and learning. Over time, they continued to shape their shared philosophy so that the school had a clearer sense of purpose.

The humanities team meetings and the house meetings provided two more regular opportunities for collaboration. She noted that because they had regular time to work together, if something wasn't quite right they'd just keep at it until it got better. This was distinctly different from her previous schools where time to work together had been so limited that they had had little time to engage in meaningful discourse or to resolve conflict. The humanities team used its time to continue refining and rearranging its 2-year rotational curriculum. All teachers were expected to function as knowledgeable generalists. Kathryn came from a system in which she had spent each class period just on English. She was full of questions at first. How was she to teach the fine arts, all that she would normally cover in English and Social Studies, and computers, too? How important was her depth of expertise in subjects that she had not taught before? How could she be sure that her students would be successful in college courses that were completely discipline centered?

Mary Wells described the power of the team's collaboration. "Getting people together in groups to share ideas is a liberation, and it unleashes people's possibilities, excitement, intellectual growth, in a way that they never experienced before as professionals. . . . It's the process of transformation that keeps the groups alive and makes people risk and connect in ways they never have before. If teachers use their minds instead of staying behind teacher-directed activities and working in isolation, the flip becomes true. They become student-directed and more open to thinking, learning, challenging, and questioning." Kathryn found what Mary said to be true. She and her colleagues generated essential questions like "What is justice?" and over time, she came to understand that the kids read literature, wrote, discussed ideas, and engaged in creative projects. She learned gradually that if activities were structured so that students had choices in the work they undertook, they developed expertise. In addition to the expertise she had as both an experienced teacher of adolescents and as a teacher of English, she needed the ability to guide them and to help them organize their own work. Although each student was writing about a different topic, each of them was learning to develop an idea, a point of view, gather research from multiple sources, refine ideas, put them on the computer, refine them again, and share them with others. At the same time, they might be following a court case, reading the newspaper, or learning about how the court system works. She cautiously gained confidence that she and her colleagues were designing activities that enabled students to gain both factual knowledge and depth of understanding. She lectured less and spent less time preparing her own notes and more time preparing activities that allowed the kids to interact with the central ideas or concepts—like the bail activity. Kathryn added that her team members were glad to have her guide them in incorporating some of the stuff she'd done before, so she felt empowered to write and to recreate the curriculum.

Mary Wells was important in fostering Kathryn's gradual growth from a teacher-centered classroom to a student-centered classroom philosophy. Mary facilitated the collaborative team meetings so that their time was well used. She ensured that they stayed on task and made sure that they had an agenda organized for the following week by the time they left. She was also skilled at facilitating conflict, encouraging people to say what they felt and believed, and then helping the group search for acceptable compromises or suggesting time to think. In addition, she watched people teach and coached them along. In Kathryn's case, Mary prodded her to relinquish her central status in the classroom, encouraging her to give the kids more choices, to trust the kids as reasonable and responsible learners. Mary encouraged Kathryn to feel more comfortable as a generalist. Kathryn described one time, "I remember in the first year I was here we were going to a trial, and we had the kids reading in a small book Mary wrote for the kids. She had written it on two levels— intermediate and advanced. And she suggested that we tell the kids there were two levels of the booklet and that they could choose whichever they liked. 'Wait a minute,' I thought; 'I know who can read at what level.' Mary said, 'Try it, and if you think a kid makes an inappropriate choice . . . '"

"'What about the kid who can do the harder one, but takes the easier one?' I grew up in a culture that always suggested that kids would take the easy way out."

"Mary said, 'It's all right. You can talk about it with the student, but it may be the right thing for him at that moment, or you may want to suggest that he should read the harder one.' Mary trusted the students, but I didn't. It was ridiculous to me. But I tried it because she said to, and it was wonderful. For the most part, they picked the books that I would have given them."

She told another anecdote about the anxiety she felt on their first outing. In her old school, she had counted the kids every couple of blocks, so on the way back from this outing, she was furiously trying to count the kids when Mary said to her, "Kathryn, it's okay. They're all here." Kathryn learned that in this school, trust between teachers and students was an integral part of the learning process. She, as a teacher, shifted from worrying about controlling the kids to believing that they were honest and legitimately able to participate in the decision making about their own education. Mary really helped her in this regard, but provided very different support for other teachers as they needed it.

Another circumstance that provided Kathryn with support in the change process was being allowed to start slowly. She talked about teaching new things in combination with things she had brought with her, so that she was on familiar ground at least some of the time. "We did geography, which I wasn't very knowledgeable about, but I knew the law material and was comfortable with the curriculum." The staff was sensitive to a newcomer's needs.

Kathryn's advisory team also met once a week before school. Each of them had an advisory group, and because each of them taught all of them, they often discussed students, not swapping stories about what a pain Jamie could be, but working to figure out how to provide each student with enough support to be successful. Early on, this group bolstered Kathryn's confidence as a member of that team by crediting her ideas. "A kid was going to be kicked out of Spanish the first week I was there, and she was in my group. I just couldn't understand why it was happening. And someone said to me, 'Well, what do you think should happen?' I said, 'First of all,

I think we should speak to her family.' And someone else said, 'Well, go ahead; do it.' And I did, and things all turned around and I made it happen! I just went on my instinct, but I got support for the work I was doing individually with kids. I realized I didn't have to wait to find out how things were done around here. I could just do it."

The fact that change was encouraged at all levels made a difference for her. She went several times to Rebecca, the principal, with an idea and each time was encouraged to try her ideas out. Rebecca tended to the norms of the school. Because she had started the school afresh, she was able to eliminate the discussion about whether they should change or not, the discussion that holds so many high schools back. Although she was restricted by district and union seniority hiring policies, she helped the staff to devise a process to acquaint potential candidates with the norms of the school, so that they were more likely to get teachers who wanted to be in the school. Rebecca changed her own role in that she did not evaluate teachers. This enabled her to function as a provocateur, to keep their direction clearly in focus and ask difficult questions when they veered from their shared ideas. Kathryn's example about her comments at grading time were characteristic. Rebecca also raised money to pay teachers for time to work beyond the regular school day, and she argued vehemently with the district and the state to protect the school's right to make its own decisions.

Kathryn stated clearly, though, that the greatest single factor that had supported her in her process of change was watching the benefits for her students. "What really made me change was seeing how very powerfully new approaches moved the kids. I saw those kids really handling the material, digging in, very confident. It embarrasses me now, but I didn't always believe that students could handle sophisticated work, that they could do research, conduct sensitive discussions, and work their own writing over several times, mostly because I didn't ever see them do it. Since I've been here, I have watched students become champions of provocative issues. I've watched them read, ask for more information, and read some more. Then I've watched them struggle to write what they feel, what they believe, instead of the teacher-pleaser kind of stuff I used to get. And these kids belong to the same population of kids I worked with before, the same." Her voice trailed off as if she were disappearing into her old classroom, looking for past students she might be better able to help now.

Challenges

Kathryn was far from a Pollyanna who glossed over the difficulty of change. She talked about her own fears after she had been hired and as she struggled to change. "I felt scared to death. I mean, I was tense the summer before I went to work. I went to a meeting with one of the house groups; we had to decide what we were going to do that first week of school right down to the minute. It was so scary to organize every minute. The parameters were bigger. It's quite a responsibility to decide what you're going to teach, to decide what the kids should learn. You're grappling with the real nitty-gritty: What do we want kids to get out of school? What's important here? How do we do that? At the pit of my stomach was the fear that I wasn't smart enough, that I didn't know enough to make these decisions for kids. I had not had the opportunity before, and because these decisions had always been made for me, somehow I doubted my own abilities.

"Another thing was that I was good at standing up in front of a class. And I was used to that. Just give me a textbook and I'll do great. So I was scared. Was I good enough? Would I be able to make this change? I was really afraid that I wouldn't have control, and I wouldn't be on top. I was afraid that I couldn't do it in a way that would really help the kids. This was for other people who really knew about learning styles, really knew a lot more than me. I also worried about whether I was *really* teaching if I wasn't standing up in front of the class."

Mary Wells confirmed that Kathryn had really struggled with the control issue and that she had vacillated between her old conventional teaching style and the coaching stance. Kathryn still felt uncomfortable and embarrassed remembering severe moments of panic, moments when she had been afraid that things were out of control and when she had felt that she would be judged harshly because of the noise and the disorderliness of the students' learning.

"I remember the first day when I met the kids and they called me by my first name. It blew my mind—the whole thing—the whole school calling each other by first names. That first day, I took the kids upstairs and they were noisy and my old training came out: 'All right, now that's enough noise on the stairs.' I used my sternest teacher-voice and barked out directions. It was the part of me that believed that a quiet school is a good school, and that I would look as if I couldn't handle the kids if they weren't in rows and silent. When we came to the room, I had assigned seats for everybody. The kids told me later, when everybody relaxed, 'Kathryn, you were really something—you yelled at us on the way up to the classroom. All we were doing was talking.' I went through a number of tense moments like that. Those memories embarrass me now; I don't like to talk about them because I think, 'What did my colleagues think while I was barking at the kids like that?'"

Collaborating with others posed a number of problems. "One difficulty was that I was working with people with all different experiences. That's hard." Frequently they had different ideas about things. They argued a good deal about standards and grading and how they might best measure kids' success. They argued about the value of field trips, for instance. She recalled a period early on when they split right in half. Half of the group did not want to go outside the school and half did. She felt passionately about the fact that students learn better when they get first-hand experience, and she felt angry with her dissenting colleagues. Because they had agreed to teach the same things, they couldn't just close their own classroom doors or open them and go out according to their own preferences. They argued for weeks, which left them all tense, exhausted, and divided. Finally, they reached a compromise: they agreed to experiment. They would try a couple of field trips and then reassess their value.

She observed that the adults didn't really know how to work together; they were unsure how to resolve conflict, and they didn't know how to share the work load. They had to practice being collaborative. Furthermore, each of the members of the various teams had different strengths and weaknesses, and they had to work at juggling that. And they had to learn to confront controversial issues.

It was also difficult for them to turn work off. Kathryn frequently talked on the telephone at night to her colleagues about their projects and plans, and they talked earnestly at every possible moment during the school day.

In addition, participation in the governance of the school, in the nurturing of kids, and in the determination of the curriculum, all took time that was in scarce supply. Unfortunately, their school day did not grow, nor did the numbers of days in the week. She felt constant pressure to find more time to do all of the things that needed to be done. She sighed while she explained that even though she had fewer students, as a generalist concerned with their total well-being, she needed to spend more time with each of them. And, though she gained a half a day a week to work on the humanities curriculum with her colleagues, the issues they were debating—like what it is that students really need to know—were complex and required careful consideration as well as the time to air diverse views and opinions. Shortage of time was a constant frustration.

Changed relationships with students posed additional challenges. She had never had to worry about getting students to bond into a cohesive working group before and found that she had to cast around for ways to make this happen. She gathered activities that helped her to do this from inservice courses, from her colleagues, from books. She had to work more frequently with parents, which was initially unappealing. Now that she was in the thick of it, she believed that she needed to forge even stronger bonds with the home, as well as with outside community support agencies, in order to help the kids. She called the parents of her advisees regularly.

An unsettling and difficult insight she gained once she had embarked upon the road to change was that she would never be done honing her skills as a teacher. She realized that she would never "arrive," that she would never know everything she needed to know in order to be good at what she does. "I don't think I know enough. I have to learn right along with the kids, and that's been a very difficult transition, to feel comfortable with that. I worked in a system for years believing that I had to know it all, that I should be the definitive voice of knowledge.

"Another major challenge is that you're never off duty; you just can't sit down and say, 'Open your workbook to page 40 and do it.'" Kathryn noted that frequently there were no breaks for her, and that she was often unaware of how fast she was moving. By the end of the week, she was simply exhausted. "Teaching this way requires an enormous amount of energy."

On a more personal note, Kathryn mentioned on several occasions that her new job brought challenges and difficulties at home. It impinged on her family life, and she frequently felt conflicted about that. There were more meetings, more phone calls to be made from home in the evening, and a good deal more time spent at school. In addition, she was frequently invited to travel around the country to speak to other groups about the kinds of changes she was attempting with her colleagues. Although she loved the travel, it added new complexities.

Despite these difficulties, Kathryn believed that she was on the right track. The benefits of changing clearly outweighed for her whatever distress she'd gone through in the process.

Essential Learnings

Kathryn and I, over time, looked back at her experiences to distill what we characterized as the "essential learnings," the understandings we gained about the conditions that made these changes possible for her. They fall into four categories: structural changes, system changes, role changes, and changes in beliefs.

Structural Changes

Kathryn was able to go into a school that had all sorts of structural changes in place: an integrated curriculum and multi-aged grouping. She talked about the benefits of watching students grow over time. "Last year, Miguel wouldn't speak. He actually sat in class like one shy little kid who never is allowed with the rest of the kids. But through the year, he gained confidence. I worked with him, quietly, on the side. All of a sudden, halfway through, his hand was up during the class discussions. He would read a little bit. It was halting and it was difficult, but he did take the chance and today, at the law firm, you know, he talked! That's a teacher's dream, to see a kid grow like that." In addition, planning time for teachers was built in, plus a greatly simplified schedule, a governance council that required the participation of the entire staff, and advisory periods. Although all of these structures had been in place when she arrived, each year they shifted and changed a little as a result of the constant fine-tuning of the staff. The fact that they were in place, and that they were subject to constant refining, facilitated Kathryn's transformation.

A System of Support

Although Kathryn was an experienced teacher, the shifts she made in her teaching were not at all insignificant. She had been able to make major changes in the 3 years she'd been at the school because there was an entire system of support in place to enable her to do so. The small staff at West-gate shared a philosophy that was represented in the structural changes they made. Rebecca fenced for them at the district and state level, helped them to hold their focus, and encouraged them to clarify whatever it was that they needed to work on next. She fostered experimentation. Kathryn's team members helped her to clarify her own thinking and also provided her with both strategies and confidence in herself and their collective effort. Mary's teacher leadership position provided Kathryn with individualized support, which enabled her to adapt to the school in a productive way. She also encouraged Kathryn, recognized her strengths, and made sure others shared the advantages of those. Kathryn increased relations with parents through conferences and phone calls. This enabled her to provide better support for the students. Participating with students in the advisory sessions enabled her to learn slowly, and over time, to embrace her students as part-ners and collaborators. Participating in the Coalition provided her with prin-ciples against which to measure and analyze her work. The network of schools enabled her to gain more strategies from colleagues in other schools and made it possible for her to share her own expertise. The cul-tural norms of the school were consistent in structures, leadership, and strategies with the intentions of the school—to help students learn to use their minds well.

Role Changes

Kathryn, as advisor to a small group of students, was charged with ensur-ing their success and was encouraged to do that by providing students with whatever they needed to go forward. She was not allowed by her col-leagues to resist this role because she did not have specialized training. She was told to use her own best instincts and to borrow strategies from her colleagues to care for the students. Somehow, this seemed easier for her in a system that really provided that for her. She was a curriculum generator and fine-tuner. She and her colleagues worked hard to use more contem-porary materials in order to link students' work to their lives. She taught a variety of subjects within the humanities discipline. She built performance assessments and worked with the entire staff to move the whole school towards performance assessment. She constantly added to her pedagogical repertoire as she worked to interpret what students did as real intellectual workers in the classroom. In doing so, she became a far greater diagnostician of their individual learning needs. She asked herself different questions: Was she giving kids enough responsibility? Was the lesson structured enough to be helpful to them, open enough to provide them with some personal choice?

Changes in Beliefs

Finally, as a result of all of these other circumstances, Kathryn's beliefs about how learning takes place shifted over time. She began to see the necessity of student engagement to deep understanding. She gradually saw that she could construct lessons that didn't involve giving them information, but required that she guide them as they constructed it. Mary described it this way, "Another tremendous leap in beliefs is from deliverer-of-instruction who kicks kids out of class if they are disruptive to the teacher-as-problem-solver with individual kids. Being a partner in the responsibility for the success of each kid is radically different from "Take it; it's here if you want it." Kathryn also came to believe that teaching is a profession one never masters, that it, like learning itself, was far more dynamic and rich than she had previously believed—enough to keep her going for years to come.

—

When we had finished examining what it was she'd changed from and to, I asked Kathryn whether, after 3 years, she felt that she was back into settled practice, whether she could relax a little, put her feet up, pull out a trusty lesson plan.

> For 18 years, I almost knew the pages of the text by heart. I don't know the pages now. There's a lot I don't know—about material, about subject matter that I'm teaching or working with, about how kids learn. I don't feel settled because there's so much more to do. I did a lot more group work the second year than the first. This year, I'm doing more individualization. I'm going to work on that part of it. I have to do it—for kids like Tommy (the learning-disabled student). I know he learns better that way.

She smiled and said that once she got better at individualizing, she'd move on to something else, constantly building her repertoire of coaching techniques.

"You know, I take new things with me to each class and I explore new ground, and it's okay with them. Their voices get stronger every day. I learn how to trust their great capabilities, and we learn together."

SINCE THEN . . .

Currently, Kathryn is in her first year at another new school. Since I had observed her, she had been promoted to team leader for the 9th/10th grade humanities team at Westgate, had spent another year coordinating the team and teaching full time, moved to a brand new high school with several other colleagues from Westgate, and now was starting a third new school. They were interested in building, with some differences, the same kind of school—a school in which both students and teachers flourish. "The new principal and I are working very closely together to build what we hope will be a warm, supportive, and academically demanding environment for another group of inner-city kids. I hope we empower the students to take greater control of their education and their lives. We're working closely with families so that we can foster intellectual and social goals for the kids. It's a small school. We've learned that small schools, where people know each other well, are essential to providing meaningful educational experiences." Kathryn, flushed with enthusiasm, noted that her experience at Westgate had prepared her to take on this new challenge.

We paused for a minute to talk about what she had learned while at Westgate.

I learned that teaching is ever changing, not static, stimulating, intense, exciting, and most of all, fun. I also learned that it is critical for teachers to accept greater responsibility for the overall running of the school. Every decision a school makes affects teachers and kids! In the time I was there, Westgate got larger. New staff was added. That's tough. It's hard to bring new people on board. As the staff grew, governance issues took more time. Sometimes power struggles among staff interfered with our focus on pedagogical work. An uncomfortable feeling can settle on the entire staff. It's hard to remember to focus on what's fair for kids, not just what the adults feel comfortable with. When our expectation for students is that we will have very different, much more personal relationships, adults have to reshape their relationships as well. Sometimes issues of 'political correctness' sidetrack us from the real issues of teaching and learning. It gets tough when we confuse ownership of the curriculum and decision making with the process of compromise and collaboration. Communication must be clear and it gets tough when people don't always say what they mean. Sometimes I feel that we are confused about governance issues—a staff run school, democratic participation, those issues. Other times, I think we are confused by an informal atmosphere and the corresponding maintenance of academic and social standards. Almost all of it is tough!

But all that struggle among adults has been worthwhile. I think about my students there and here at this new school. The projects, the directions, the academic presentations, the ways they feel more in control of their lives and their futures, their work, the choices they make. Most of them have more going on in their lives because of their participation in this type of schooling. All of this contributes to their power, their ability to make a difference in the world.

3

Judd's Tale: A Science Teacher Joins Re:Learning

D riving to school at 6:45 AM in the fall of 1990, Judd Marshall, a secondary school science teacher, explained what the last 2 years had been like for him. "After 20 years of teaching, school seems a lot more serious. It's more devoted to children. More frantic. More consuming. It's a lot more tiring. It's a lot more fun. It's a lot more painful sometimes. A lot more exciting sometimes . . ." As we pulled into the parking lot of Dillingham High School, the sun was just half way over the horizon, deep tropical fuchsia. Its strength influenced the rest of the sky—orange, red, pink, purple. As we moved toward the school, Judd reminded me to look for sun spots, which are hard to detect with the naked eye. He told me that he had seen them twice when there was just this kind of sky.

Dillingham was a large high school facility in a mideastern city of 60,000 people. Built to accommodate 1200 students, it housed 660, a result of declining enrollments. Forty-four percent of the students were black; Hispanics and whites made up the rest. There were 47 faculty members. The basement housed an ESL program for adults during the day and a high school equivalency program in the evenings.

The school's long history reflected the changing demographics of this and many other urban American schools. While Judd signed in at the front desk, a counselor who had been at the school for 30 years considered the shifts they had experienced:

> We used to be the premier academic school in our state. Very rigorous.
> Prestigious. We've had lots of famous people go through this school—
> well-known politicians, a Nobel prize winner. Then when the blacks moved

in and the whites fled to the suburbs, the school changed. The poor kids came to us without basic skills. They didn't like school, and the teachers had a hard time making the shift. For a while in the seventies, it was a dangerous place. Lots of fighting, maybe some drug-dealing. We had policemen here. The school is better now, much safer, but we still have the highest dropout rate in the state. Fifty-five percent of our students drop out before they finish high school. That's above the national average. Now teachers work their tails off just to keep the kids in school, never mind basic skills. And I don't think the community thinks much of this school.

He suggested that for a number of years faculty and staff had struggled under the community perception that the school was the "black" school, a place where kids couldn't—didn't—do much; a place where academic standards were very low.

While the counselor described the history of the school to me, Judd chatted with the swimming coach, predicting this year's potential. That settled, mailbox checked, we went up to the third floor, which housed the Telemark program—a new program for some of the school's 9th- and 10th-grade students. This program was one of the first projects to emerge out of the Re: Learning, a new state initiative that combined the forces of the State Department of Education, the Coalition of Essential Schools, and the Education Commission of the States. Its purpose was to build systemic support for schools as they implemented the Coalition's nine Common Principles. The Telemark team, of which Judd was a member, was then in its second year. Telemark had two interdisciplinary teams of teachers working with 150 ninth- and tenth-grade students but the rest of the larger high school continued its business as usual. I had come to spend a week with Judd to see how he and his colleagues had started their efforts, and how this new approach was affecting his teaching and his relationships with kids and with adults. By all accounts, the changes the Telemark team was attempting were causing great struggles.

Judd had long been recognized as a nonconformist. He relished his reputation as an old subverter, a faithful sixties hippie. He looked the part, a cross between Willy Nelson and Kenny Rogers. Born and raised in the city where he was teaching, he knew people everywhere—from the local donut shop and restaurants to the sidewalk cops and desk clerks at an elegant old hotel. He was a friendly man, energetic and passionate. His second divorce had recently been finalized, and his son was calling frequently from his first term in college to say he wanted to come home. Judd chuckled; he told him to stay put till the end of the year, then they could reassess. But he noted that he himself struggled to stay interested in school. He loved to give speeches, which he attributed to his Irish heritage, and waxed eloquent on any number of topics from the absurdity of school schedules to his dream of nonstructured, nongraded schools. He frequently flared up in anger when talking about administrators and their inept, inconsistent decision making, and he blamed them for many of the problems at Dillingham. He was also angry about the lack of interest from the larger faculty about the Telemark project and felt that his involvement in the project cost him old friendships. Judd was astonished to find himself constantly thinking about work and the need for change, completely absorbed in a way he hadn't been in the last 15 years as a teacher. In the midst of his renewed commitment to education, he made no secret of the fact that he would like to find an alternative to classroom teaching, to do more of the consulting work that had grown as a result of his involvement in Re:Learning.

A CHANGED JOB

The Telemark team had its own faculty room, converted from a large classroom. A coffee pot, a microwave, old couches, a coffee table covered in current magazines, four old oak teacher desks heaped with papers and books, and a round table with a number of chairs made the place look comfortably cluttered, homey. Other team members were already gathered—some worked at desks, others clustered at the table. Students wandered in and out to say good morning. Teachers asked the kids to run errands. Constant movement and side conversations formed a backdrop to the more central action, which occurred at the round table in the center of the room. Only Telemark team teachers came here; the rest of the faculty seldom visited the third floor and never spent time in this room.

Judd opened his briefcase and ruffled through a pile of papers. Fran Mellon, the 9th-grade civics teacher, was in the midst of recounting an upsetting incident. Her students had told her that one of their team members, Jack Fisher, was trying to sabotage their program by explaining to the kids that heterogeneous grouping was detrimental to them. Apparently, he had asked his 9th-grade English class to line up, and then had prompted them to identify the smartest kids in the class. He had requested those kids to step out of the group and had explained to them that in homogeneously grouped classes these kids would be working with others as smart as they are and that they wouldn't be held back by those less bright. Fran had already had a call from a parent who was coming in after school to discuss the validity of Jack's assertions. She wanted help from the rest of the team: What should she say?

The group was a little stunned. Judd spewed a string of unprintables and then said, "How is it that Andy supports this program one hundred percent but assigns Jack to our team, when he knew that Jack didn't want to work with us?" Andrew Zanchich was the principal. Maria D'Agosta, the 10th-grade-team English teacher, suggested that everyone who could should attend the meeting. She wondered where the articles were that describe the detrimental effects of homogeneous grouping. She reminded them that the professors from the local university were also coming in and that they had a meeting at 3:30 with them.

Tom Michaels, the 10th-grade history teacher, came in fuming, waving Andy's latest directive, "All teachers must submit their photocopying to one of the secretaries. Teachers and students will not be allowed to use the photocopy machines because they are breaking far too often." All of the teachers exploded over this new procedure, irritated at being punished for the misdeeds of a few. They might not get the things they needed by the time they needed them. They predicted multiple screw-ups.

Judd handed out an article, "Pushing School Reform to a New Edge: The Seven Ironies of School Empowerment" (Glickman, 1990). Fran said, "Why is this man giving me this stuff at this hour in the morning?"

Leslie Tersch, one of the 9th-grade science teachers, asked, "Am I in here?" Judd said she was. She asked, "Well, tell me what page I'm on so I can get right to it."

Judd shook his head. "You are as bad as the kids."

"I'll read it; I'll read it!"

Tom changed the subject by asking whether anyone had any good resources on the Middle Ages. He was doing a unit on monasteries. Maria whipped out a photo album she had brought to share with their students. (She and Tom shared the 10th-grade students, taught in the same room, and did some planning together.) Her cousin was a monk and she had visited him. She showed how monks are buried.

Dorothy Simms, the 10th-grade math teacher, asked about the visitors who would be observing their program during the day. Maria, who coordinated their schedule, noted when the visitors would observe classes and when they would be in meetings. Everyone was invited to a dinner, which Dillingham High was to host for the visitors that evening. Mid-sentence, the bell rang.

The vice principal's voice boomed down the hall. "All of you people should be in your classes by the time the bell has rung. Move . . . now!" The forcefulness of his command conjured up the image of boot camp, a drill sergeant. . . . The teachers and students scrambled.

History of the Telemark Team and Judd Marshall's Involvement

In 1989, Dillingham High was one of the first schools selected to participate in Re:Learning. Andrew Zanchich described how they got involved:

> When I came here, the school was a real war zone. A lot of fights. Not a whole lot being taught. The schedule was really screwed up. For a couple of years we had some workshops, some team-building meetings. Then we

went through regional accreditation. They said we needed to improve our expectations for our students, that we needed to increase our involvement with our kids. So we were looking for some vehicle to help us improve instruction. Re:Learning sounded like a good thing to me. Re:Learning schools were supposed to get $30,000, the chance to travel, and the chance to work with people from all over the place. The district is so busy with other problems that they are not able to attend to the needs of high schools. So when I got a call to consider our involvement, I went to a few symposia, read *Horace's Compromise, The Shopping Mall High School, The Last Little Citadel,* and got very excited. In the summer of 1988, I gave every faculty member a copy of *Horace* as they checked out in June for their summer reading.

Judd had taken his copy to the beach.

I never read stuff like that. I read stuff about science, but not stuff about schools in general. My 16-year-old son ran out of reading material. He is a voracious reader—so he read it in a day. He flipped it into my lap and told me that it was pretty good. When I read it, I was furious. I thought this guy Sizer must have done his research in my school, and I didn't know about it!

During that next year, Andy held conversations for the faculty to consider joining Re:Learning. By the next summer, Dorothy and Judd had volunteered to go to a summer institute sponsored by the Coalition. Sitting on the steps at Brown, Dorothy had said that they should call their Re:Learning program, whatever it might be, "Telemark," a symbol to suggest that they could learn a new turn to get themselves out of a defeated educational system. She accurately predicted that Andy would want to start something before the next school year began. Andy called several teachers together on July 9th, before school started in 1989. They decided to begin by giving five teachers a group of 70 ninth-grade students, and a block of time during which they could work out a schedule. The team included math, science, history, English, and computer teachers. The hope was that they would be able to integrate instruction and curriculum and to personalize learning for more students. In order to get an English teacher, Maria D'Agosta from special education was recruited with promises of support.
    Judd described why he had felt compelled to participate:

I used to be a pretty standard kind of a teacher. I lectured a lot and then gave the kids work to do. We had worksheets and some other assignments. My labs were demonstrations rather than real participatory labs. I played Trivial Pursuit at lunch time with a crowd of guys. We would make very meticulous notes of the way the board was at the end of each lunch period, and we would pick it up the next day. On Friday afternoons that same group would go over to the Inn to hoist a few pitchers of beer. When I was off duty, I was off duty. I coached a lot of things—track, swimming, theater—and enjoyed doing those things with kids.

Around about my 17th year, I began to feel pretty burned out; I was ready to leave teaching. Test scores were going down. Absenteeism was going up. Dropouts were going up. The reputation of this school was rotten. Frustration level of the teachers was going up. The ability to have any effect on anything seemed to be going down. My sense of isolation was going up. And there was not much coming back in. Everything was going out and nothing was coming back. So, when I went to the summer institute in Providence, it came as quite a shock to me that I got interested. Even though I really wanted to spend a year planning the program, I did not want Andy to organize this without me. I felt that I had something to contribute, that I might be able to help establish the program in the school. Now I think I was pretty hasty in that decision—hindsight is always so much better than foresight.

New Structures; New Relationships

The first year, the team worked closely together. Dorothy taught math; Judd, science; Maria, English; and the team hired Tom Michaels, a first-year teacher, to do social studies. The major challenge the team faced was the students. Accustomed to low expectations of their abilities and to many dismal experiences in school, the students found it hard to adjust to new approaches. They had a difficult time moving as a group and did not like having double-blocked periods, mostly because they felt that they were missing valuable social time. The teachers claimed that although they attempted to engage the students in more rigorous work, the children were resistant. In the midst of their struggles with the students, which took most of their energy, the teachers used their common planning time to meet with parents and to build small bridges between and among their disciplines. They also spent considerable time trying to communicate with the larger faculty about the program, but felt that the other teachers were simply apathetic, did not want to know, and would rather complain about Telemark than try to understand it.

Because they were one of the first Re:Learning schools in the state, the group was under constant scrutiny. A number of outsiders visited. They received one of eight awards given to educators by a well-known local community organization; the award came with a small grant. With that grant and part of the money that came with membership in Re:Learning, the Telemark team members traveled to Re:Learning symposia around the country. Although Andy made these trips available to the entire faculty, only teachers on the team chose to go. Despite the offer to participate, many of the faculty resented these privileges—trips, smaller class loads, and an additional planning period per day for the Telemark team members. At the end of that first year, the computer teacher left, and Andy wanted to expand the program to the 10th grade. When volunteers were requested, the larger school faculty seemed at once more apathetic and more resentful of the program than they had been the previous fall. Only one volunteer came forward.

Despite low enthusiasm from the rest of the faculty, Andy, two vice principals, Maria, and Alice Fremont, the home economics teacher, went to the summer Trek, a Re:Learning seminar designed to help faculty manage the process of school change. They joined staff from two other states in an attempt to build a broader base of support for their efforts. The Dillingham team concentrated on how they might expand the effort at their school. But by the time school started, additional budget cuts had affected their planning. No acceptable contract was negotiated and several teaching positions were lost. Andy took on additional administrative duties because one of his vice principals was reassigned. A new superintendent arrived and announced his dissatisfaction with the dropout rates and the low standards at Dillingham. In addition, he implied that because enrollment had dropped in the three city high schools, he would be working with the board of education either to consolidate the three schools to two or to develop a choice program by the 1991–92 school year. If the schools were consolidated, the Telemark team might be scrapped. If it became the magnet program, the rest of the faculty would be forced to join in or to transfer to one of the other schools. Morale was not good.

Against this back drop of uncertainty and resentment, Tom, Maria, and Dorothy moved up to the 10th grade with their kids. In order to fill a new 9th-grade team, four new faculty were recruited. Fran, the only veteran in the school to volunteer, taught history. Leslie Tesch, a teacher with 3 years' experience in private schools, was hired to replace a retiree. Andy assigned Jack Fisher when no other English teacher volunteered because Jack had been involved in team teaching in the past. Jack made it very clear that he was a loner and that he did not want to participate. He told the team members that he would try to undermine their efforts and did not show up for the first full day of school, which was a planning day. Despite pleas from the team to Andy to find an alternative solution, Jack remained assigned to the team. Andy had hoped that when pushed, Jack would retire. Frank Taro, the band teacher, agreed to team-teach biology for 10th graders with Judd so that Judd could also serve on the 9th-grade team, which included a new teacher unfamiliar with the school. A permanent sub was hired to teach math because no replacement could be found. Judd agreed to teach both 9th- and 10th-grade students and to carry the stagecraft class, while teaching 9th-grade science. A new computer teacher agreed to help, but 2 months into the school year, she disappeared. No one seemed to know what had happened to her—just that she probably would not be back soon. No substitute for her work with the students was found. In the 3rd month of the 2nd year, the team was having difficulty finding time to plan together and to maintain a good relationship with the larger faculty, and was worrying about their abilities to solve internal team problems—given that they had four new members and no shared values or experiences.

A DAY IN JUDD'S CLASSROOM

As Judd gathered up his stuff and hustled off to class, the day seemed to whoosh forward, like a wave of human exchange, roaring into the halls and classrooms, carrying students, visitors, and adults onward at a significant clip, occasionally knocking over chairs and garbage cans caught in the great movement. Judd understood that no single person could control the direction once set in motion—influence, maybe, but not control.

Judd's schedule varied from day to day, but on this day it was as follows:

1st period	9th-grade science/stagecraft
2nd period	double block 9th-grade science
3rd period	double block 9th-grade science
4th period	planning
5th period	double block 10th-grade biology
6th period	double block 10th-grade biology
	double block 9th-grade science
7th period	double block 9th-grade science/planning

The team designed their own schedules and worked around students' elective schedules and their own staffing problems. Judd had the most complicated schedule of all. He team taught all of the science classes in order to make sure that they had enough staff to cover all of the double-blocked periods.

His classroom was a huge, traditional lab—black counters with gas jets, microscopes set around on the counters. The room was divided into two. On each side, long lab tables were set up to form squares. Each square seated 20 students around the outside. In the middle was a catch-all table piled with science books and scraps of paper. The walls were bare except for a few haphazard pieces of big paper showing student-groups' work. Around the back counters more books were scattered, generally in bad repair. Except for the precision of the squares, the room had an abandoned feeling.

First period was a difficult one. Judd taught both 9th-grade science and stagecraft simultaneously. He explained that he shared responsibility for this class with Maria, a non-science teacher, and that when she took the science, he and the stagecraft students worked in the auditorium, building sets. However, because she had never taught science, she needed time to prepare units, so for stretches of time, he had both groups. When this was the case, the science students sat in a square of desks on one side of the room and the stagecraft students sat in a square on the other side of the room.

A voice on the intercom called everyone to do the Pledge. The students were slow to respond; Judd barked at the kids to attend. Announcements followed; students visited rather than listened. Introductory routines finished, the stagecraft students settled in to reading the newspaper, magazines, or novels, or doing homework—whatever they wanted—for the remainder of the period. Judd gave the 9th-grade science students a photocopy of the front page of the *New York Times*. They were to find 25 words they didn't know and make a list. In addition, he gave them a newspaper article about a newly discovered fault line in the midwest. The students went to work. Individual students came up to Mr. Marshall's desk so that he could answer questions. He, too, read the paper every day first period. He justified this activity by explaining that the kids see few adults reading, attempting to stay informed. In a recent article he had written for a local education newsletter, he described how teachers must be flexible, not rigidly locked into traditional disciplinary practices.

> A lively teacher who is a guide, touchstone, and model for an inquisitive student must be open to the millions of possible pathways that inquiry might take. I know that if I were more scientist than teacher, I would still be in the labs and hopefully in the running for the Nobel Prize in microbiology. But I'm not. I'm more teacher than anything else. Even if I don't know about a particular subject, I can coach and cajole a group of kids to a higher level of understanding about that subject than they currently possess. And I'll probably soak up a little knowledge about it myself on the way. (Local Newsletter, 1991)

His philosophy played out in a serendipitous approach to curriculum and instruction. He called one of the stagecraft girls over to him and got her squarely centered in his line of vision, face to face. "Yo, Marie, where you been?"

"I didn't come to school for a while."

"I know that, but how come?" She shrugged, not rude, just lethargic.

"Listen to me. You're so close. You could be done at the end of this year. But you gotta come. What about the night school? You think you'd like that better? You're eligible, you know. You don't like coming days, go nights. Just say the word, I'll help you. If you stick with days, you gotta come every day, okay?" She said okay, but her sister had a baby and she had to help. She squeezed his arm and slowly moved back to her seat.

Gina, a large 9th-grade student, shared her list with me. "Postpone, sanctions, sacrifices, hostile, influential, prolonged, destabilized, component, molecular, expectancy . . ." Gina said, "Mr. Marshall says that if we can read the front page of the *New York Times,* we can read anything. We do this every week." I asked her how she liked it. She said it was okay. I asked her whether she learned the words she looked up. She grinned and said that sometimes one stuck. Gina recently spent 60 days in juvenile detention for stabbing her brother. Everyone agreed that she seemed to be doing fine.

Tom came in to borrow a knife so he could fix the librarian's glasses. As half the period passed, Judd asked the 9th-grade students to summarize the article on the newly discovered fault. They discussed it for a few minutes, everyone wrote a summary, and he asked them to hand in their work as they left.

Another group of 9th-graders came in. Fran entered, worried about a new testing program. Judd told her not to worry; their program would come out fine. She wandered back across the hall. Judd gathered the kids up around the blackboard, told them to bring something to write with. They had been working in groups, and each group had agreed to pursue a project on recycling. They had not yet decided what they would do specifically and so, must gather some information. Judd reviewed potential resources they might wish to use and wrote these on the board. They began with the phone book and moved on to the library. The kids paid close attention, contributed, wrote down whatever he did without any prompting. The lesson was slow-moving but thorough. Several students from across the hall poked their heads in. A student aide wandered in and sat down. Because he had no work to do, he put his head down and dozed off. Maria came in to do some science planning. She sat at the table in the middle. As the period neared its end, Judd said, "You know why I like doing this? Because you all know a lot of stuff. You don't all know all of it, but each of you knows something, and between you, you know a lot." He gave them a 5 minute break and told them to meet him in the library.

During the 2nd period, the students looked through various resources for materials on recycling. Some found articles in the *Reader's Guide*, while others attempted to locate things on microfiche. Judd worked with Leslie, who had come in to talk about their plans for a field trip to a recycling center for all of the 9th-grade science students. The district required paperwork that takes nearly 6 weeks to clear. Judd was disgusted at the barriers the district places in teachers' ways, clearly suggesting that they ignore the rules. Leslie was not tenured, didn't belong to the local teachers' union, and wanted to follow procedures.

An announcement came over the intercom. "Tim Pagliaci has been suspended. He should not be allowed into any classes." It was the vice principal's booming voice. Judd called a student over who had been rude to another student. This particular boy had a problem dealing patiently with a mainstreamed student in his group. "Joey, you gotta get a grip here. To treat him that way is awful, just awful." Joey explained that the mainstreamed student was slow and had to be reminded to do his part frequently. Judd said, "So what are you in such a hurry for? You've got time to help him. He needs your help, okay?" Joey listened and nodded. Maria came in to remind Judd that their meeting with the visitors from the two other schools would be held on the third floor. She wanted him to be sure to be there.

The bell rang and the students scattered. Judd went back up to the third floor and into the meeting. Teams of nine people from Midvale High School in another Re:Learning state and four from St. Clair High in a mid-eastern state had gathered with five people from Dillingham. The three teams had worked together at a summer institute, the Trek, sponsored by Re:Learning. There participants had explored methods and tools they could use with their faculties back home to support their efforts to rethink common practices. During the school year following the institute, each team had hosted one visit of their "critical friends"—those teams they were paired with during the summer—and made one visit to each of their schools. The hope was that each team would gain some objective feedback about their own progress from the visitors, and that they would gather additional insights into their own work as they saw how others were approaching change. The meetings generally lasted two days; this was the first day, and the faculty from Dillingham, the host team, explained their progress since they were all together last.

Andy began by noting that their district was experiencing a good deal of upheaval. They had a new superintendent, an inability to pass any kind of referendum, and an administrative policy on non-retention that meant that some of the students who came to Dillingham hadn't passed a single class in the last 4 years. The superintendent was determined to bring down drop-out rates and was, at the same time, considering a redistricting measure that might close Dillingham.

Judd described that in light of all this uncertainty the Telemark staff had had difficulty accomplishing their major goal which was to expand their team to the 10th grade. The new team members had not had any inservice so knew little of the Coalition. One of them did not believe in teaming, and so was not supportive at all. Because their collaborative planning time came at the end of the day, the teams weren't using it very well. To top it all off, they frequently heard criticism from the larger faculty who rejected the opportunity to participate when it was offered to them, but complained about the perks Telemark staff received. All in all, the report on their progress suggested problems.

The Midvale team talked briefly about the fact that they were in the midst of planning a whole 9th grade program for the next year. Teachers in the building applied to be part of newly forming teams and had significant release time to build an integrated curriculum. The other school teams were quiet—daunted by and envious of the thoroughness of their approach. Asked for feedback by the Midvale team, the teachers from Dillingham and St. Clair suggested that they felt uncomfortable with the lack of teacher involvement in the decision-making thus far in the Midvale approach. To them, it seemed frighteningly reminiscent of many of the well-planned reform efforts of the sixties and seventies that arrived top-down and, in the long run, did not function as well in practice as they did in theory.

The St. Clair team described their effort since the Trek. Another school plagued by budget cutbacks, an aging staff, and an uncertain political climate, the faculty decided to put teachers and students together on academic teams in 9th grade for the 1991–92 school year. Each team would be built around a language, probably German, French, and Spanish. The language would form the focal point of the interdisciplinary curriculum work. The French team might study French and American history and literature, French scientists and discoverers, and learn math by solving problems the French face, contrasted with problems Americans face. The Midvale and Dillingham teams indicated that the language teachers on their staffs were very skeptical, believing that they did not have a place in Essential school work. The St. Clair approach was a hopeful one. The three teams dispersed—the Dillingham teachers to their classes, the other two teams to observe for the rest of the day.

Judd jumped two stairs at a time back up to his 10th-grade biology class—a double-blocked period—during which he intended to conduct a lab. The students had prepared their own labs. Knowing that they would look at three protozoa under the microscope, they had designed a series of experiments in order to see what happened to the organisms when various stimuli were introduced. One student's lab plan read:

1. Make a slide of amoeba
2. Make observations under low power and draw
3. Make observations under high power and draw
4. Check for movement, structure and streaming
5. Check for responses to:
   darkness
   low high food
   low high touch
   cold = 1   hot water = 4

Judd got out the little jars of micro-organisms and paper towels while the students settled into their seats, got their own labs, pencils, and paper out. Another announcement: "Mike Framson has been suspended. Teachers, please do not admit him to class under any circumstances." Judd asked the students why Mike had been suspended. Silence. He shrugged, stumped by their reticence because they usually told him such things. Judd reviewed how one prepared a slide, and then asked questions about their individual labs. One girl said she was going to feed apples to the micro-organisms, so he asked her how she was going to cut the apple small enough for the organism to get it. She hadn't thought about this. Another girl volunteered her necklace, which was a razor blade—drug-culture jewelry. Other kids were using salt and sugar and were asked to think about how they would dissolve these substances. One said with food color; another said with water.

He asked them what food color is. They didn't know. He asked them why they were doing this lab. "To see what happens."

"What will that information tell you?" Judd asked. They didn't know. The students appeared eager to do the lab but uninterested in understanding the purpose of it. Their answers were flat, careless. Still, they were friendly and casually attentive. Judd asked, "How many of you remember the scientific theory?" The students shrugged but didn't answer. "Yo, you guys. Did you forget everything I ever taught you? What have I been doing here?"

Finally one student said, "We're trying to experiment with various substances to see what happens to the organisms. It's how scientists work. They guess at things." Judd was relieved.

They moved into action preparing their slides. There were 17 kids in the class. The room was huge; each student had a microscope. The Re:Learning coordinator came into the classroom and strolled around, visiting with the students. He was well liked by teachers, administrators, and students. Fran walked in and said in a sort of general broadcast, "I just went into the girls' bathroom and there is a boy in there smoking with three girls." One of the boys responded, "Welcome to high school!" Judd moved from microscope to microscope. The students were having trouble locating the euglenas. A student photographer walked in and snapped a few photos of students working at microscopes. Several kids opened their science books to look up amoebas, paramecia, and euglenas. Because they were having difficulty locating the organisms, Judd had them make new slides. There was significant frustration. Gradually, students began making discoveries. "I got one! YUK! It's got little hairy things." Students nearby rushed to have a look. With each new discovery, students called Judd over to see.

The bell rang and a group of 9th-graders came into the room and sat around the other square of desks. Leslie got them going on a review of the district safety rules, then left to take another class. The students were encouraged to make safety slogans on construction paper. Several kids sat in a group and worked on a rap.

> Safety is the way to go
> Leave the gas on, it's going to blow
> Sound off 1, 2
> Sound off 3, 4

Other 9th-graders finished a series of bumper stickers quickly.

> If you play with fire, you may get burned.
> Wear eye protection in the danger section.
> First safety, second fun.

Two girls compared retainers, which they claimed they hadn't worn in months. The retainers looked like pink prehistoric fossils. The girls tried each other's on and burst into gales of laughter.

Judd attempted to get the 9th-graders to return to their seats so that the 10th-graders were not disturbed. Dannette did very simple drawings and described her observations:

> Food 1. Euglena surrounded the food near the head or top and then kept the food inside the system.
> Light 2. After every light change the Euglena would make like a circle or bubble then after a second it would start to move.

Very few students did the drawings or recorded their observations. More than half the class stopped working well before the end of the second period. Tom Michaels came in and sat up on the counter, and casually visited with two 10th-grade students about Desert Shield—would there be a war? Kids from across the hall popped in and then sneaked back out. The class was chaotic with high adolescent energy, but undirected to school work.

Judd cornered one of the students who had been absent lately. He put his arm around him and said, "Yo, Tony, where you been?" Tony said he hadn't been feeling all that well. Judd reminded him that he had to come to school; he was so close. Tony shrugged. Clearly school was not all that important to him. Judd dropped his arm and took another tack. "So, Tony, what's going on in your neighborhood these days? I was over there the other day visiting the Americos."

"Not much," said Tony. He liked Mr. Marshall and loosened up a little.

"You notice a lot of guys hanging out during the day on the corner?"

"Yeah."

"Are they old guys or young guys?"

"Both," said Tony. He rattled off a few names, guys he knew.

"How come they are there, Tony?"

"I don't know. A lot of guys hang out there."

"Do they have jobs? Is that why they are hanging out there? Don't a lot of them want jobs so they wouldn't be bored hanging out every day?"

"Yeah, but there's no work. There's nothing they can do." The tempo of the conversation picked up. Tony was a little irritated. Judd moved in closer, his voice softer.

"I know some of those guys, too. Some of them came through my classes. Most of 'em didn't finish school, Tony, and that is one of the things that makes it hard to get work. You're close, man. You can do it, huh?" Tony grinned and punched Judd in the arm.

"I'm in a band. You ought to hear us. We're pretty good—kinda." He moved off to his friends.

Judd reminded the kids to clean their slides before the end of the period. One student left, broadcasting an aphorism, "Leaders do what they have to do; losers do what they wanna do." The room was a mess—construction paper, paper towels, chairs over at the microscopes, science books scattered around. Judd felt gloomy.

> Too many things going on. Their performance level was somewhat like kids in a swimming pool in the summer: "Oh, mommy, look at this! Look at this, mommy!" I find myself trying to bounce from place to place to satisfy their show and tell. There isn't—to me—the required patience and intellectual curiosity about what they are doing. Now, there *is* that sense of wonderment; that's there; but once they've seen it, then it's all over. Maybe it's my lack of depth of expectations for them . . .

He moved to the Telemark room for a parent meeting. Two Hispanic women were seated at the table. Two small children were squeezed into a seat together. They sat very quietly. Judd greeted them all and sat down. The aunt did most of the talking as the mother did not trust her English. Dalinda was in the Telemark program and was getting a D. They wanted to know why. Judd went over the labs that Dalinda hadn't handed in. "Basically, she blew it. She's smart. She knows how to do the work, but she just didn't do it." The aunt noted that they had been helping her every day and that she knew that Dalinda had done the labs. The mother and the aunt speculated in Spanish about why Dalinda hadn't handed them in.

"You know, the kids say they hate working in groups."

Judd responded "Yep, I know—some kids. Most of the time, the majority of the kids like it more than they hate it."

"Dalinda says the other kids are lazier, and she ends up doing all the work. She feels like she ends up doing everything, and that the other kids make fun of her because she's Hispanic."

Judd leaned forward. "Dalinda needs to decide what's good for Dalinda. She's smart. She better not get caught in the minority thing. She needs to move forward and decide what's best for her."

"She loses her enthusiasm."

"I'm not aware that the other kids are using her, that she's doing all of the work."

"She's hanging around with Marta. Marta is a lost cause," said the aunt. The mother nodded agreement.

Judd said, "Marta isn't a bad kid. She's not as good a student and she doesn't care about school like Dalinda."

"Should we take Dalinda out of this Telemark program? Would she be better off?"

"No way. She's getting more attention here. We give the kids more support." He looked at both women. "Okay? You clear on the problem?" They nodded and said that they would keep track of the labs. Judd searched the halls for another parent meeting. To attend this one, he had to miss the confrontation with the parent who wanted to know about heterogeneous grouping.

In this meeting, both parents, all four teachers—including Jack who didn't like Telemark—and the student sat in a circle. The teachers took turns giving progress reports, none of which was very positive. They complained that the student was disruptive, had a short attention span. The kid looked at his desk and slumped lower and lower while the parents asked what they might do. The teachers made a variety of suggestions, all of which required that the young man conform to their procedures. Jack was the only one who pointed out that the youngster had made some progress and asked the student to acknowledge that. The mother yelled at the kid, "You get your act together or I'm gonna quit my job and I'll come to school with you every day. How would you like that? Would you like that? Having your ma round with all your friends? Answer me!" Her voice was shrill and angry. The father slumped, too.

When the conference finished, Judd returned to his classroom to clean up a bit before joining the visitors at the local pub. He picked up papers and moved chairs around. Fran came in to talk about how things were going. She felt discouraged because they seemed to have lost their focus on children. She also felt there was a lack of commitment to the program and that the faculty was too negative. Another faculty member, George, came in. Both Fran and Judd were surprised. He was not a Telemark team member, and almost no one who wasn't on the team ever came up to the third floor. George said hello and complained that the kids really drove him nuts today. Fran asked why. "I don't know. Just squirrely. Won't do any work. I'm going to start throwing the kids out of the class. I'm not going to deal with them."

"Then they'll be out in the hall," said Fran.

"At least I won't have to look at them."

"Do you see any solutions, George?" asked Judd.

"They are too far behind. They don't belong here. Throw them back. Send them back. The entire American public education system is lost, if you want my opinion. Can't be saved. Too far gone. To hell with it." He was a big man, over six feet, and the whole of him seemed angry and spent.

Judd suggested that they had made some progress, that they'd saved a lot of kids in the last few years. George responded by sneering, "Why didn't you save your favorite? What about Pedro, huh? You didn't have much luck with him!" Judd was silent—no answer to that one. When there was a lull in the conversation, Judd excused himself. He told George that it was nice to have visitors up on the third floor.

After a short drive to the pub, Judd plopped down on a bench with the Dillingham team and one of the visiting teams. "Can we just hoist a few beers, here? Give a guy a break?" The group laughed, feeling his exhaustion.

One of the visitors poured him a glass of beer and handed it to him. "We just wanted to congratulate you. You've got really nice kids. Your staff has done a great job of establishing a warm and caring climate."

"We got a caring program all right. We can say that much. We manage to keep a lot more of our kids in school. Although the average dropout rate in 9th grade is 44%, we kept everybody but three last year." He was at once ebullient and humble. "We have commitment on the team. Most of us. We get along pretty well. We've got great kids. But we don't know what we're doing. We don't. It's not that I want somebody to come in and tell us. We already had that. I don't want that. What I do want is . . . well, I guess I want our team to be teacher as worker and somebody else as a coach! Just a little time and a little guidance, a little coaching . . . you know what I mean?" The table rumbled with good, deep laughter; glasses clinked—a toast all around. "That's it! Teacher as worker, somebody else as coach!"

"But where do we get the coach?"

How the Kids Felt

Students in the Telemark program used almost the same language that the adults did in describing the program and its differences from the larger school—smaller classes, more personalized attention, harder work, more laid-back atmosphere. A majority of the students liked this program better. They were able to articulate what they liked without hesitation.

Jerry, a 10th-grader, expressed the most common sentiments. "We used to sit in rows and take notes. We had to be quiet. Here we're allowed to work in groups and have some fun while we work. We actually do more stuff instead of reading about it."

Lisa added, "If you're in the middle of something, like this lab, you get to keep going instead of losing your place after 40 minutes."

Toby, a 9th-grader said, "We get to know our teachers better. They are easier with us."

Sean didn't like it. He had recently transferred in from another state. "It's too much time in one place. I get bored. And they get on my parents, so I get in trouble at home."

Cheryl agreed. "I hate not seeing my other friends because we're stuck with the same kids all day." She did add that most of the time she liked what they did.

When pushed to explain what they meant about harder work, the kids were less articulate. They felt they had more to do, but couldn't be more specific. When asked to describe what they were learning, they gave content-based answers which suggested traditional lessons. One girl shared that she was better able to understand the history of the Middle Ages because she got some of the literature of the period at the same time that she was getting the history. When I asked them to give me examples that would illustrate the difference between the work they did in Telemark classes and work they had done in regular classes, the only concrete distinction they made was that in Telemark classes they were allowed to work together. Otherwise, the actual stuff—both content and process—of their learning seemed to be common to both programs in the school. The students were also aware of the divisions between the staff members. "Some of our teachers tell us that the Telemark team teachers don't deserve to be flying around and all that." Mary believed that it was jealousy that made the other teachers talk like that.

The fact that the kids could describe the program so well, using the same language as the teachers, was interesting. But whether that was because kids form quick loyalties, or because they were able to distinguish real, significant differences was unclear.

STEPPING BACK

Judd's team had a number of structures in place that provided support for the Telemark team. They had additional resources to help them with professional development and to pay for their time. They had a joint planning period for the entire team. Scheduling for their students was left to their discretion so that they had much greater flexibility. As one of the first Re:Learning schools, they also had the latitude to interpret school reform that later schools would not. The attention they received as a result of their new status protected them from some of the uncertainty that faced the rest of their school system. It also helped to bolster their own self confidence and their sense that in the face of enormous odds, they were really trying to do something productive, which was valued by others, for their students.

The team did a good job of establishing a more caring climate for students. Parents were more informed about their children's progress. The results from the first year were impressive; far more of their students had stayed in school. The adults on the team also felt that the work environment had improved in that they talked more and worked more closely together. Their membership in the Coalition made it possible for them to attend symposia and to meet and visit other schools.

The team had taken a big risk in accepting the challenge of devising a new kind of program in spite of the resistance of the larger faculty. In this second year, they had deepened their own commitment to change by establishing a second team and by moving forward with their students.

Challenges

Judd Marshall and his team members helped me to articulate the major challenges they faced as they attempted to overcome the apathy, the negativism, the low expectations, and the surrounding community forces that robbed their students of any success in school. They were fledgling members in Re:Learning and admitted that they had jumped out of the nest before looking to see how far they might fall if they couldn't quickly master the art of flying. Each of the challenges posed a thorny problem for the group—problems not easily solved in the midst of constant daily action.

Time to Plan

Time seemed to be the only resource they never had enough of, and the lack of it confounded their work in a number of ways. First, Judd and his colleagues realized from their critical friends how little time they'd had to work on planning the Telemark project. The other schools had a year and seemed to have some kind of comprehensive strategy. Telemark felt the absence of that sorely, but did not know where the time would come from.

Teaching new subjects took more preparation time. Scheduling two classes to run simultaneously posed time problems that seemed to serve no one well. Judd needed one fewer class and Maria needed the time to plan lessons in two unfamiliar disciplines.

Although the entire team did have a planning period in common, they did not use it for planning, claiming that it was hard to get together at the end of the day when their energy was low. In order to make that period productive, they needed either to use it as intended or to shift it to a more desirable time.

Skills of Collaboration

The group was finding it more difficult to work together than they had anticipated. After so many years of working alone, none of them was quite sure how far to push an issue or an idea. In their first year, the team agreed on a central theme: Power and the Individual. The theme provided them with a number of connections across disciplines. This year, Maria suggested Lifestyles as a possibility. No one picked up the ball, nor did anyone suggest any alternatives. She described how she thought it would work for them, but somehow the idea just floated out the window. Furthermore,

Jack Fisher did not want to work with them. The team was at a loss to figure out what to do in this case. They resorted to talking about him but not with him because they simply didn't have any experience with this kind of circumstance.

Judd described further dilemmas. "One of the new team members is different from the rest of us—more dogmatic, less laid-back. I'm not saying that's bad, just that it's different, and the kids notice it a lot. So how do we talk about that?" Another team member wanted to use the textbook as a curricular guide. Yet another team member did not believe that an interdisciplinary curriculum should be developed—wouldn't kids miss out and do poorly on important standardized tests? Maria and Tom were working together, but so far all they really had done was line up the historical periods between their two disciplines. Judd described their dilemmas in collaborative decision making, "We don't know how to make a decision. What are we going to do now? How are we going to run the schedule? When are we going to meet? What are we going to talk about? Do we have a theme? Are we going to have a theme? Are we going to teach our classes together? These are all questions we've raised, but we never resolve them. Can you believe it?" So far, they liked each other, appreciated the camaraderie, but recognized that they really were not working together in any significant way. They felt frozen and ill-equipped to know how to begin to undertake more substantive collaboration.

In a broader sense, the team needed the ability to work with the larger faculty. Everyone on the team talked about feeling isolated from the larger faculty. "Two or three years ago, we were isolated in our own classrooms. Just us—individually. Now we're isolated in our team room, the six or seven of us." The team believed that they did reach out to the larger faculty, tried to include them, but felt that those not involved just kept saying they didn't know what was going on or that they didn't want to be involved. The team felt frustrated, ignored, helpless—as if they were in a school full of deaf and blind people and didn't know how to communicate with them.

Some members of the larger faculty were bitter about what they perceived to be undeserved attention. They had, after all, taught next door to some of these people for years, knew their foibles, had listened to what they characterized as "sixties liberal crap" about schools. So far, they did not see any great changes in instruction—other than that the team had fewer kids and that they were more lax about noise and bells. Anybody could do better with fewer kids. Both the team and the larger faculty spoke disparagingly of each other, but neither side was attempting to bridge the gap or break the barriers, so the rift was growing and erupting in front of students.

The strategies the Telemark team tried with the faculty had not been successful, and yet, without their support or at least their partial support, the Telemark team would have difficulty expanding. Should bad feeling continue, they might eventually run the risk of losing important resources—human and otherwise—freedoms, and the support of the larger community.

Expanding the Team

Another problem emerged when they expanded during the 2nd year. Internally, the team had varying definitions of Re:Learning and what it meant to them. Not surprisingly, they had different views about what their work in the Telemark team should encompass. Some believed it meant that they should examine their teaching and search for new, more powerful methods. Others believed that it meant that they should continue teaching as always but deal more directly with families. Others believed it meant that they should divide the labor for planning for double-blocked periods. The one-year veterans wondered how they might share the insights they had gained from participating in Re:Learning activities. Most of those who had recently joined were experienced teachers; to suggest that they needed to attend a symposia on the nine Common Principles seemed condescending or simply wouldn't fit into busy schedules already full with the demands of certification requirements, family care, or master's degrees. To date, the veterans had not found a way to create a shared understanding about their program with the newcomers.

Changing Leadership

Everyone involved in the Telemark program felt that they were moving away from traditional hierarchical, authoritarian leadership to shared leadership. Andy noted that the faculty called it "his project" but that he'd given the team enormous authority. They had hired Tom Michaels. They had developed their own schedule within the constraints of the larger schedule. They had planned to use their time however they wished. He was confused about what his role was when he gave the team the authority to make decisions. For instance, Andy was unhappy that the team had decided to show a film on one of the days that visitors had come to see different instructional methods. Because he'd given them the authority to decide, he did not feel that he could comment. On the other hand, Andy wanted to control the Re:Learning budget. He liked playing the part of a wealthy uncle—making it possible for people to travel or to attend a seminar and having the freedom to buy educational books for everyone. Judd seemed to be in a similar bind with the students. He gave them the authority to build their own labs but was disappointed with the lack of depth. Still, because he had given them the authority, he did not make his discontent known to them. He did not feel that he could intervene. For both of them, the uncertainty stemmed from not knowing when to step in to share leadership responsibilities and when to share the problems of leadership as well as the benefits.

The team itself suffered from a lack of leadership. Although several members of the team believed that they contributed, in reality no single member carried enough weight to influence the actions of the others. Several of the team members raised issues that needed attention; everyone in the group expressed diverse opinions and the issue evaporated or was buried by a more pressing concern—a parent meeting, a new batch of visitors. In the absence of any clear leadership, both within the team and in the school at large, no one took responsibility for the overall quality of the Re:Learning effort in the school. Until some of the leadership issues were resolved, both inside the team and with the administration, progress would be hampered.

Essential Learnings

As Judd and I looked back on his case, we distilled several essential learnings important to the successful work of school change.

Insider/Outsider Dynamics

In psychology there is a substantial literature on insider/outsider dynamics. Whenever a select few—even if they are volunteers—choose to do something out of the norm of the larger organization, difficulties seem to erupt. Those doing something new are perceived as "special" by those not involved. Those involved perceive those who are not, as stodgy or resistant. In Judd's school, the dynamic between the insiders and the outsiders was particularly destructive. Both sides became competitive, each hoping that their side would hold sway in the end. Judd and his team needed to understand the dynamics at play here and to work harder to resolve them. If they let the nastiness flourish, it seemed certain at some point that the majority would exercise some effort to interfere with Telemark's work.

In analyzing the ways in which they dealt with the larger faculty, the team agreed that they had not enlisted faculty support but had made the classic error of innovators. When they described what they were doing to the larger faculty, they suggested that *they* were going to do something for kids that the larger school was not. "Humph," everyone else said, without missing the implied criticism. When the staff reported their first year successes, they announced that *they* were doing a better job of keeping the kids in school. "Humph," again. Insulted, the larger faculty muttered and returned the insults. If they had been invited to consider the implications of Telemark strategies or been asked to analyze the raw data on attendance rates, relations between the two groups might have been different. To combat insider/outsider dynamics, members of the Telemark team and the larger faculty needed real collaborative skills: the ability to confront, to deal with conflict and resistance, and to build shared understandings. Gaining these would have enabled them to build some of the bridges to connect the whole school.

Early Fame

Because the group was in one of the first four schools to join the state's Re:Learning effort, they received a lot of publicity even in their first year. In order to protect their program, they quickly learned to point out its strengths and its differences. Even the students quickly learned the rhetoric. Everyone's hope was that visitors would leave feeling assured that tax dollars were being well spent, and so far, so good. This attention was subversive to a certain degree, in that it took time away from potential planning and from careful scrutiny of their emerging practices. Describing the benefits of a program to visitors led the team to a false sense of their own sophistication. "If people are coming to see us all the time, we must be doing something good, right?" Talking so frequently about the strengths of the program seemed to convince the team of the program's effectiveness and to short-circuit their own critical development.

The early attention was also seductive in another sense. Judd had been asked to do a videotape for PBS and had been invited to be a facilitator for Re:Learning. These invitations allowed him to be a consultant for other school teams and to travel frequently. These new kinds of activities were far more alluring than sitting down with the faculty with whom he had worked for a number of years. Sharing new-found enthusiasm and experiences, despite the brevity of their project, was more personally gratifying than redesigning old lessons or attempting to solve persistent problems.

Andy was experiencing the same dilemma in a different way. He was being asked to do more and more in the central office. Because this was a new experience, it was much more exciting than facing the repetitive, seemingly unsolvable problems back in the school. He was involved in state organizations, working on his doctorate, and gaining recognition outside his own school for the Telemark program. This recognition simply was not forthcoming within the walls of Dillingham High. His absence and preoccupation with other responsibilities also affected the team's ability to engage in more serious work.

The Telemark team liked the recognition and appreciated the visitors, but they may well have benefited from devising a strategy for getting outsiders to help them, instead of feeling that their role was to impress the visitors.

Personal Agency

Almost everyone involved had trouble determining how much he or she could do to make things happen differently. Having spent years in bureaucratic, hierarchical systems, their tendency was to blame either those above or those below for problems. Judd blamed staffing problems on the administration and bureaucratic entanglements on the district. Andy cast around similarly, placing blame outside his sphere of influence. Several people felt cheated by unfulfilled promises made by those on top. The basic premise of the Re:Learning partnership was to reduce the barriers that lie in the path of changing practices; yet, as if hesitant to believe such claims, the participants seemed to maintain hierarchical patterns. Judd was also confused about how much additional work he should take on.

> Am I a professional or a salaried employee? What about extra pay for extra responsibility? Should I work all summer developing the schedule for no pay? It's a bind. I find myself constantly questioning why I'm doing what I'm doing. Why are these lessons so lame? Why do I cut a kid off just when he needs help? Why aren't we doing more experimental science? Why don't I lead discussions on the nine Common Principles with the team? I get a little confused about what I'm capable of and whose responsibility it is.

Breaking the norms of hierarchical behaviors is difficult. If the objective is to foster collaborative change, then each person is vested with responsibility for raising difficult issues, and for marshalling attention to them.

Shared Leadership

Because new leadership roles were demanded of everyone, it was important for teachers and administrators to think through what shared leadership really means. Certainly, sharing suggests that multiple parties are required. In bureaucratic structures, leaders delegate responsibility—giving others full authority for carrying it out. In shared leadership circumstances, it would seem that the leader needs to take a different stance, to participate as an equal party in the decision making rather than as a stronger, more heavily weighted voice or as one who has delegated responsibility. Such a shift is subtle and requires conscious agreement on the parts of all participants. The need for leadership in the team was evident. Rotating responsibility for organizing meetings or devising some system where each member would take major responsibility for some aspect of their work might have proved helpful.

Interpreting the Nine Common Principles, Expectations, and Shared Values

On reflection it seemed clear that the Telemark team, much less the larger Dillingham faculty, had not worked very much with the principles they were trying to implement. "Almost everybody thinks they do the principles already," said Judd. "I did in my first seminar. In reality, the nine Common Principles are so logical and they're so kind of sensible when you think about them in relation to kids, that you just say to yourself, 'Well, geez, I'm doing that.' What I've learned is that they have such depth to them that they require significant attention. I've got a long way to go in my own class-room."

Although the Telemark team had addressed personalization and had reduced student–teacher loads beyond the original figures, the staff had not begun to address the rest of the principles. The principles have embedded in them some suggestions about curriculum, pedagogy, and assessment which might have helped the team to forge a clearer sense of direction.

Staff at Dillingham, as at other schools, had a history of discussing students as if they were problems to be fixed. A good deal of sarcasm and ridicule directed at students floated through the air, leaving the sense that there was less than a tone of decency and neutral respect between students and teachers.

The staff as a whole seemed trapped, as many urban school staffs are, in longing for an earlier time, a time when their students were different and the school stood for something. It appeared that the staff had not worked together to forge any shared values about what this new/old school stood for since changes had taken place. They had not considered their responsibility in light of a changing student population. As a result, the lowered expectations for students, the undemanding work, and the surliness about students' capabilities conveyed a not-so-subtle but common brand of racism. A collective effort to determine what the school stood for, what the principles meant, and what its component pieces might stand for could have provided it with a strong foundation. From a stronger base, the entire staff might have built a more likely place in which children could succeed not only in coming to school but in learning while there.

In the 3rd month of the 2nd year of the Telemark program, Judd Marshall reflected on his original hopes in joining the Telemark team and Re:Learning. He had joined because he believed that maybe, just maybe, it might breathe new life into him professionally and make a difference for his students. Although he knew that their program hadn't had the most auspicious of beginnings, he also felt that it was perhaps better to have begun than to have thought about it for a year or two. It was entirely possible that they might never have begun at all. The teams were, after all, learning.

At the same time, he was torn by a number of contradictions. Although he believed that change was essential, he couldn't figure out how to move the team to address it in any serious way. Although he believed Andy had given them legitimate power to make decisions, Judd wanted him to be more involved. Although he liked working on the team, he didn't know whether he could actually work with some of his partners to build a shared vision because they were, in the long run, quite different. Although he wanted to change instruction, he found it easier to think about the problems he saw in his colleagues' classrooms than those he saw in his own. Although he could not turn the work tapes off in his head and he was reading more than he ever had before, he still found it exceedingly difficult to bring new ideas to his daily practice in the classroom. Although he felt renewed energy and more hope, he was exhausted, more disillusioned, and angrier than he'd ever been. Never had he experienced such a mess of contradictory feelings all at once.

> This has been much more difficult than I thought. I can't seem to think about anything else. I'm a little over-committed and under-experienced at this point—with 20 years under my belt, no less! I never thought I'd hear myself say that. But I am definitely committed, rejuvenated—like I found some kind of professional Geritol. I'm learning a lot and I talk about it with other people *ad nauseam*. Almost everybody agrees that we aren't helping kids in schools the way they have been for years. So the Telemark team jumped in. We've built a caring program. Not a great program, but a caring program. It's a beginning. We need to keep working on it, to tackle some of these problems—which only seem to get worse. Now the state is entertaining an early retirement program for which half the Dillingham staff is eligible. Imagine the kind of havoc that can perpetrate on our program!
>
> Truth is, this is a lot harder than I thought. I feel good that we are keeping more kids in school. I feel like we're committed to keep working at it. And that's a damned sight better than being burned out.

SINCE THEN . . .

After reading and reviewing the study, which seemed to them difficult but accurate, the team turned back to its work and tried to come to some agreement about what to do next. Partially because conditions in the school were still uncertain, they worked that next year somewhat unsatisfactorily with a teacher from another Coalition school who was to function as their critical friend. About that time, the state announced a new early retirement buy-out plan, which again threw teachers and administrators into turmoil. The principal and a number of faculty retired, and so did nearly 33% of teachers statewide. A new principal was hired for the fall, and the district superintendent decided to implement a magnet school approach to reform. Dillingham was named the Re:Learning magnet. Despite all of this, the team persisted, and, in fact, expanded to 12 members.

In the fall of 1992, a National Science Foundation grant was secured by the state and Judd left the school mid-year to become one of the coordinators of that project. A new state superintendent came on board with less enthusiasm for Re:Learning and began to rearrange priorities. The Re:Learning coordinator left and the state superintendent appointed a replacement.

At Dillingham, three magnet programs were started: a Banking and Finance Magnet, the Telemark school, and a regular high school component. The staff hired a separate principal to run the Telemark program and to lead the expansion of the program. Despite a massive turnover in staff and in the leadership of the school, the program survived. At the beginning of the 1992–93 school year, the staff finally felt that there was a promise of some stability and that they would be able to move forward in their hope to build an essential school. But in the spring of 1993, the state board declared that Telemark would not be allowed to take in any new 9th grade students because there were problems with the program. Team members negotiated with the board and were allowed to continue on the condition that the district would provide more support for both professional development and for evaluation. The team continues to demonstrate a willingness to look at itself and to strengthen its work.

4

Jennifer's Tale: A Math Teacher Generates a Formula for Making a Difference

J ennifer Rochambeau was an 18-year veteran math teacher in a large suburban high school. For the last 4 years she and her colleagues had been working to change the way they taught in order to make their school more engaging for students. What made Jennifer most unusual was that she worked in a math department that was very interested in change. Although many math teachers across the country suggested that current reforms, like teaming or integrated instruction, were fine for everybody else but not particularly useful in math, Jen and her colleagues had joined teams of teachers from other disciplines and had worked together to rethink the math curriculum and their instruction. In the spring of 1990, I visited Jennifer to find out what made her interested in changing her practices in math and to see what these changes looked like in the classroom.

A CHANGED JOB: "I SAID I'D NEVER, BUT I DID!"

Several years ago, some of my colleagues and I visited a magnet school for the Arts and Sciences to see what we might pick up in terms of our own programs. As a math teacher, I was interested primarily in the math and science classes. Well, kids were working in groups. They were lying on the floor, sitting at tables. Everybody was working and everything, but it just looked so informal to me. I told one of my friends that it looked real nice, but that I could never do it because it was just too unstructured. Besides, I felt like kids would be cheating on tests sitting around tables like that, and I just kept wondering how a teacher could keep these

kids' attention when they were all sprawled out. When we left, I let everybody know that that style of teaching was definitely not for me!

When I was a kid, my daddy used to say to me, "Don't let your mouth
write a check your body can't cash." I guess I did that very thing because
look at this classroom now!

We were standing in the back of Jennifer Rochambeau's Algebra I classroom. As I looked on, students were working in groups, some on tables,
some on the floor. Some were standing up, others were lying down. There
were no desks, only tables, no rows, and very little visible structure—the
very image of the classroom she had rejected just a few years earlier. Students were working together, quite absorbed, and paid little attention to the
two of us as we watched them work. Obviously, in the last couple of years
Jennifer had changed her pedagogy significantly. I wanted to know more:
What were these students doing? How had Jennifer taught before? Why had
she changed? What had prompted her to change? Did she really believe that
these students were learning better sprawled out like this than they did when
they were sitting upright in desks? What had caused her to change her thinking? While her students continued to work, she began by describing her
teaching practices and beliefs as a conventional high school math teacher.

Reflections on a Conventional Math Classroom

I've taught now for 16 years. For 12 to 14 of those years, I taught the way
I learned to do in higher education and the way that was modeled for me
as I grew up. My desks were in rows and my room was quiet. My classes
were 50 minutes long. I began by reviewing the homework assignment
from the night before. First, I'd call out the answers while they marked
their own papers. I'd ask the students to tell me which problems they had
trouble with; I'd work those problems for them at the board or, in recent
years, on the overhead. If they wanted me to work all 20 problems, I'd
work all 20. If they only wanted me to work three, I'd do three. I worked
the problems by copying them out, working the solution, then checking
my own work so they could see how I did it.

When I got all of their problems worked, we'd move on to the next
lesson. Following the book, I'd demonstrate the next kind of problem.
Then, I'd work a few examples. Finally, I'd assign homework and they
would spend the remaining time working those problems on their own.
For instance, in Algebra II, if I wanted the students to learn to solve equations by using the quadratic formula, I'd give them the quadratic equation on the board. I'd explain it, and I'd work a few examples—I'd plug in
a few numbers. Then I'd give them practice opportunities where they
plugged different numbers into the formula. Then we'd take the chapter

test. I tried to break everything down into little steps so that the kids could get it.

The pace in the classroom was very fast. In math, there is always so much to cover. I always felt I had to get through the entire book so that the students would be ready for the next level math course. As a result, there was always pressure to keep going, to move along. We moved through the textbook sequentially for the most part. I used the chapter tests provided in the book as a means to assess the kids. Every so often we had pencil and paper quizzes so that I could see how they were doing. I never had the students working collaboratively because I believed that they needed to know how to do this on their own. Working with someone else to me meant that one student would do all the work while the other goofed off.

Throughout my teaching career, I have received good evaluations from my principals. In more recent years, my principal has sent me letters commending good teaching—which I ended up not liking too much because they generally meant that he was going to ask me to do something else! Still, I have always felt that I was a good teacher. I went into teaching intending to be better than most, and I've worked hard to achieve that goal.

Maybe the most important indicators that I was doing a good job came from those parents who stopped me in the grocery store to say that their teenager really liked my class or that I'd made math come alive for once. Then every year I had some students who came back from college to say that they were doing well and appreciated the preparation they'd been given.

For years, I believed that I was doing the best I could, that not all kids were cut out to do well in math, and that that simply was the way it was. So I concentrated on getting the greatest number I could over onto the good side of the bell curve. I believed that my professional responsibility was to follow the principal's directives and to cover the material presented in the math curriculum.

Developing the Courage to Change

When I look back now, there were several events or activities that helped me to develop the courage to change the way I teach math. When I moved to this school, the math department was stronger than it had been in my previous school. The whole department ate lunch together and would meet in the mornings for a few minutes to drink coffee. In those conversations, I learned that some of my colleagues were really unhappy with the design of the texts and were skipping around in the books. Paulette, our department head, really helped our department to look at textbooks critically. Do you realize that every textbook organizes Algebra I, for example, differently? The order is different and the skills and concepts they cover are different. Gradually, through these conversations, they helped me to realize that the order of the material in the texts was more arbitrary than I'd always believed. I'd always believed that in math, there was some general agreement about what was to be taught and in what order. Then, they helped me to see that I could generate more complex tests, that the book tests simply asked the kids to plug in numbers but didn't enable them to really think seriously about application. So in our department, we did lots of talking and experimenting in order to find better ways to help the kids understand math. And eventually, I began to think that my own experience working with kids every day might count for something—like maybe I could think about how to do it differently.

Though I felt I was doing a good job, that I was a strong teacher, that I really cared about my students, I also felt I often moved too fast for the students, or sometimes I was impatient with the students because they couldn't keep up. After a few years of teaching, everything about math seemed so logical, so straightforward to me that I couldn't figure out why it stumped the kids so much. Then too, when I was fussing over coverage, I kind of ignored whether the kids were really getting it or not. The pace of the classroom was so fast, and I was so busy doing everything, that I didn't take much time out to think about whether I was satisfied with the quality of what they knew. And I felt frustrated. Every year, they'd get stuck in the same places. Every year, they really required more time on some chapters than the pace of the curriculum would allow. Most of us blamed the kids—they were lazier, didn't do their homework, or their families—they don't support education, don't keep up on what their kids are doing. Eventually, it became pretty hard to ignore that though my students could plug figures into problems they were familiar with, they couldn't really think their way through how to solve a new or unfamiliar problem. I had to begin to think that maybe it was the way we were teaching.

Then a few years ago, the principal was doing his doctorate. (We used to all pray for the day when he'd finish so he'd stop trying to get the rest of us to go to school with him. He was always putting articles about education and about teaching in our boxes.) He was invited to Brown University where he heard about Ted Sizer's work and about the Coalition of Essential Schools. He came back and started talking to the rest of us about what he'd learned. He'd had a major insight about our school. He said that when he'd walk down the halls of our school, he felt very good because all the kids were in their rooms, at their desks, and the school was a quiet, industrious place. Then he realized that he didn't know if they were learning, because they were playing such passive roles. This was a *big* learning for him, and he sure did not want to let it drop. So the next year he sent a couple of us to Rhode Island to workshops. I must admit I did not see how any of the techniques the presenters were talking about would work in math.

Finally, he sent another group of us off to a Coalition symposium in

Louisville, Kentucky. Now I have to tell you how I saw my role at this conference. I went to the symposium to get ideas to bring back to teachers who needed help in our school. I believed that the principal had selected me to go because I was a good teacher and I would be able to sort through all the garbage that was being said to bring back the good stuff to the teachers who really needed it. And I was prepared to do just that.

Well, I found myself in a session with Amy Gerstein on Math and Science. She started by asking us how we believed classrooms should be organized if kids were to learn well. The group yelled out all kinds of good and fancy stuff: fewer students, more real-world experiences, more problem solving or application of abstract concepts, that sort of thing—every teacher's dream. Then some of us proceeded to do the "Ain't it awful" routine. You've heard it: "We can't do those things because of this rule or that bell or the after-school schedule or the curriculum guide, too much to cover." She asked us how we dealt with the curriculum guide currently. We said not very well. And she asked why not. We got hot and said, "Because we don't have any decision-making power; we do what the principal tells us!" And on it went.

Over the course of a couple of days, Amy forced us to clarify where we experienced the greatest difficulty in teaching math and science. Sure enough, it was that we had too much to cover, we had to move too fast and the textbooks didn't help us teach the kids to use the concepts in fresh applications, nor did they present math in a very interesting fashion. Amy then got us to clarify what we wanted to do and then started showing us that we were the primary obstacles to teaching that way. You know, we'd never felt like we had the authority to make decisions like that. Well, I can tell you, our van was four feet off the highway with all the ideas we had on the way home!

There was one more thing that bolstered my courage to change. Though I was digging around with textbooks, I hadn't really changed the way I was teaching. It was an experience my principal provided that really enabled me to try some things out.

I still couldn't see how to apply a lot of the things people in the Coalition were talking about in a math classroom. Three years ago the principal asked us to do a kind of advisory group, which we called Forum. It was a place to cover current events, to get to know the kids better, and to help them get through school. It was a safe place for me to experiment because there were no grades and no exams to be taken. I had a small group of kids, and for the first couple of weeks I worked my tail off to keep them entertained. Finally, I stopped and told them that they were going to have to get involved. So, we set up a few projects, and the kids took charge.

We started investigating public education, which was being battered as usual by the local media. We went to a board meeting because the board was looking for a new superintendent. Then we read stuff—stuff from magazines and from newspapers. The kids brought visitors in. We went out to dinner. We had a great time that year. I really got to know those kids well and got to like them a whole lot, too. It showed me that personalization is really important to a kid's learning. It was in that class that I began to realize how detached kids are from school and how little they know each other. I began to notice how doggone passive they are. I put them into pairs just to see if I couldn't get them a little fired up. I had such a good time with that group and they liked the class so much that the principal asked us to share what we were doing with other faculty members.

Having all that fun with that group and then going back to my regular math teaching made me do some thinking. I began to hear the math kids a little better and noticed that they really did get stuck with some of the concepts over and over, but because we were in a hurry, I'd just give the test and keep going. It became apparent to me that the kids could not do a lot of thinking about what they were learning and that didn't seem right to me. They learned to survive, but they didn't learn to think. Now it irritates the heck out of me when some math teacher I am working with says, 'My students just don't think.' I want to ask, 'Well, do you give them a chance?' I didn't . . . I guess all of these things—working in the math department, feeling dissatisfied with the race to cover and kids' inability to transfer what they were learning, and having Amy confront us about what we could do about it—contributed to my gathering up the courage to change.

RIVERDALE HIGH SCHOOL

Jennifer began her career in an inner-city school in a Southern city of 350,000. In her 8th year, she transferred to a suburban high school that was part of the county school system. Riverdale High School served 11,000 students in grades 10 through 12. There was no busing, so the school reflected the community population: 90% white, with a small, mostly black, minority group. There were 60 members on the faculty, which had recently been influenced by 60/40 legislation that required all school systems in the state to have 40% minority teachers. To meet this requirement, white teachers from the school had been transferred into the city system, and black teachers had joined the staff at Riverdale. A new superintendent had been brought in the year before with a charge from the board to clean up the system. He was the first black superintendent in the county system.

Riverdale was a fairly typical American high school. Students had the opportunity to select from a smorgasbord of courses, from industrial arts to languages. They were required to take the core subjects (English, math, social studies, science), with additional requirements in the arts, physical education, and a few others. Students then chose elective courses to round out their program. They were tracked according to ability and, for the most part, attended classes with students their own age.

The school plant was filled to capacity. Four lunch sittings had to be scheduled because space was so limited, and expansion of the cafeteria was a constant topic of conversation. Built in the fifties along the banks of a stream, Riverdale was a big, sprawling place. A series of fields surrounding the school allowed a number of athletic teams to practice at the same time. All the buildings were clean, well lighted, newly painted, and graffiti-free.

The OTL Program

When Jennifer and her colleagues returned from that Louisville conference, they descended on the principal with a proposal to experiment with Coalition ideas. With his wholehearted approval, they established an interdisciplinary team of teachers—all volunteers—who agreed to take responsibility for 100 students who had done well in school up to sixth grade but then hit a slump, students who would typically be labeled "at risk." Jennifer developed a separate schedule for the students, and the team selected the kids based on their achievement scores. They called the program "Opportunities to Learn," which was quickly shortened to OTL.

The 1st year was very hard. The teachers found that the kids had tremendous needs and simply didn't feel good about themselves or their abilities. The teachers worked very closely with the parents, some of whom liked the program, some of whom were skeptical. The kids hated being different. Unlike the rest of the school, their schedule was double-blocked, and they were divided into four groups so that each teacher saw two groups every other day for 2 hours. They didn't like not seeing other students for a good portion of their day. And most significantly, they found it very difficult when the teachers asked them to work in different ways than they had been asked to work in school previously. The teachers were experimenting with the principle of student-as-worker. Students were required to play a much more active role in the classroom, whereas they had grown accustomed to relatively passive roles.

Although the teachers and students had persevered together throughout the year, they all agreed that some changes needed to be made for the next year. This year, the 2nd year of the program, two teams assembled. The 10th-grade team worked with 100 new students, and a new team was formed for a rising group of 11th graders. This year the teams agreed to select a heterogeneous group from among students who volunteered for the program. The schedule was single-blocked so that each of the team members saw each of the students every day. The 10th-grade team consisted of a biology teacher, a math teacher, a world geography teacher, an English teacher, and a life skills/health teacher. The students for the most part stayed together for five periods of the day. Jennifer developed the schedule for both groups of students and adults.

Jennifer and Her Role

Jennifer functioned as both teacher and coordinator of the program. She taught two classes in the OTL program, had two release periods to coordinate for the other OTL teachers, then taught two regularly scheduled math classes as a member of the faculty in the larger high school. Her schedule was:

7:30–8:25	OTL Algebra I
8:30–9:25	OTL Geometry
9:30–11:30	Program Coordination
11:30–12:00	Lunch
12:00–12:20	Lunch Duty
12:25–1:15	Geometry
1:20–2:10	Algebra I

Jennifer was asked to coordinate the program by the principal, Dr. Jamison, because she was both well respected by her colleagues and committed to change. During the double planning period she met with the two teams, ran interference for them, gathered materials, met with students and parents, and organized special activities—whatever needed doing so that the other team members could concentrate on their teaching. She also functioned as liaison between the team and the principal. She generally tried to find a few moments each day to share their plans with him, to ask advice, or to ask for his support in some way.

She had a very good relationship with Dr. Jamison and believed that he had done a tremendous amount for their school. He had recently announced that he would be taking another job the following year and she was nervous. Another principal might not be so supportive; she and her colleagues agreed that they had not been treated with so much professional respect by any of their previous principals. He expected them to carry the program and to solve the problems that went with it. They had become accustomed to making their own decisions.

Jen, like all the faculty members, attended one of the principal's monthly Quality Circles groups. Each group consisted of a cross-disciplinary section of the faculty. The purpose of the meetings was to exchange ideas about education and about the school program in small groups so that everyone's voice could be heard—an alternative to large, less productive faculty meetings.

Over the previous few years, as Jennifer heightened her involvement in changing her own instruction and in changing the school, she came to believe that her professional responsibility had changed.

> I think I have an obligation to work with my colleagues, to take a stand on what is good teaching and what is not. My job is to work to ensure that every kid gets the very best we can give him or her. It is my responsibility to make decisions about what should be covered, and when and how, because I am close to the kids and I know what they need. I feel more professional somehow because I am more involved in trying to understand what teaching is all about.
>
> I also feel I am involved in a very important movement to change public education. In order to participate, I want to read as much as I can; I want to find out and learn as much as I can. I think the kids in my classroom have benefited from that because they see how excited I am when I'm learning and how enthusiastic I get.

Jennifer Rochambeau was no slouch in the energy department; there were days when I thought she made the teenagers look slow. She was professionally energetic and then had a full family life once she left school. She held a Master's degree in Educational Administration and belonged to a number of educational organizations—the Association for Curriculum and Instruction, the Math Teachers Association, and a small cooperative math project at the local state university. She was certified at the top level of her state's career ladder program, something she had achieved before she became involved in the OTL program. In order to fulfill her responsibilities as a state mentor teacher, she was in the process of organizing an innovative summer high school staffed by interdisciplinary teams of teachers and attended by inner-city kids who were at risk.

In addition, Jennifer had just been selected by the Coalition to participate in a program through which teachers would assist other teachers in the process of change, so when she finished her local summer school, she planned to leave for the East Coast for a month. Over the next few years, she would be spending a portion of her time helping teachers and principals in other schools work toward school change.

In the course of very busy days, Jennifer was even-tempered, optimistic, and well organized. Her friends teased her that when she was excited she could talk faster than the speed of sound. The most remarkable thing was the speed at which she could talk and still sound like a Southerner. She had a good, easy relationship with her students, and a similar manner with her colleagues, although when the occasion required quick action, she could be brisk, to the point, and efficient.

Jennifer was fortunate to have a husband who was most supportive of her work. They had been married for 16 years. Although he had originally wanted to teach, they had found it too difficult to live on a two-teacher income, so he had gone to work for a local business. They had two small sons who took part in all kinds of sports, so the coordination of meals and schedules was quite a feat. Jennifer noted that she wouldn't have considered many of her activities if her husband hadn't encouraged her and worked with her to take care of the house and the boys.

In a moment of quiet, away from the bustle and immediacy of the school, she confessed her fears. "The three men in my life are my greatest blessings. Each time I take a step toward greater involvement in changing public education, I feel as if I am stepping away from them. I'm afraid of that; they are more important than anything else I do."

A DAY IN JENNIFER'S CLASSROOM

On this particular day, Jen started very early. She arrived at school between 6:30 and 6:45, grabbed a cup of coffee in the faculty room, and said hello to her colleagues in the math department. She then checked in with the principal, grabbed the daily pile of mail out of her box in the main office, and headed up to her room on the second floor. The room was brick, painted pale yellow. It had one window facing the fields, two blackboards, and an overhead projector set up midway down the room. The overhead screen covered the clock. On the bulletin board, there were questions in bright letters:

So what?
What does it mean?
Where have we seen this before?

As she arranged the materials she would need for the day, two visitors arrived with a video camera. They were from the state department of education and had come to videotape her teaching as a means by which to check the rating scale recently developed to evaluate teachers for the career ladder program. Originally, the rating scale had been devised to encourage teachers to use methods described in Madeline Hunter's Instructional Theory into Practice model. Jennifer had used those methods during her own evaluation but had raised questions about them immediately. She believed that some of the techniques she was regularly using were more effective with kids, but that the rating scale would penalize such teaching. The head of the career ladder program had come out and watched her teach, agreed with her, and sent this team out to video her class so that they could measure her instruction against their rating scale. One of the visitors was surprised that she had tables in her room instead of desks. Her response: "I just can't imagine how I could possibly have taught math with those piddly little desks!"

OTL Algebra I

The twenty 10th-grade students in Jennifer's OTL Algebra I class were in the room and at their seats when the bell rang. Jennifer started immediately.

"Coaches, please take roll for your group. The roll sheets are here on the desk. I'd also like you people to document your group's progress each class period for the duration of the project we are about to begin today." Students worked in teams of four. Each team had a coach—one student who took responsibility for group coordination for the week. They handled much of the paperwork, which had always distracted Jennifer.

"How is everybody? Y'all rested up and ready to go?" She stood in the middle of the room at the overhead and made eye contact with each student. The kids were spread around her at their tables. They groaned, grinned, and tossed out important comments.

"We won our basketball game on Saturday, Ms. Rochambeau."

"I'm real tired, Ms. Rochambeau. We didn't finish play practice till 11 o'clock last night."

Jen grinned at the student. "I don't want you falling asleep today in here, Rodney. Save your nap till lunch time."

The coaches picked up roll sheets (on which all the students were grouped by team with an asterisk next to the coach's name), filled them out, and sent them back across the room to Jen.

"Okay. We're starting a new project that will take up a week and a half. So, what day is your project due?"

They chorused, "Next Wednesday."

"I want you to plan a vacation. You can plan what you will be doing for spring break with your friends or you can help your folks plan the family trip this summer or you can make one up—whatever suits your fancy." She included the following requirements for the project: (1) a geographical description of the area; (2) a detailed budget; (3) a graph to report the percentages of your budget allocated in different categories; and (4) an oral presentation to explain your trip. She then handed out a sheet that described both the project and the ways in which they would be evaluated. The evaluation included the following:

1. A computational component to include your budgets, your graphs, and the work you do on how you'll get there and get home. This will be worth 100 points.

2. A visual component to include illustrations, diagrams, charts, and graphs to help us understand your journey. This will be worth 50 points.
3. A Self and Group Evaluation: Each of you will assess your own performance on a point scale of 1 to 10. The group will evaluate your ability to work together from 1 to 15 points. The group must reach consensus on the score. Both of these evaluations must come in with a briefly written description of the award.

"Any questions?"

The students began to talk among themselves about where they would go. No one seemed confused or dismayed. Jen recalled their attention.

"Okay. Let's work for a minute together. Where do you want to go?"

A student yelled, "Russia!"

"Why, Amy? Why is Russia interesting to you?"

"Because of everything that's going on there now. Like, everything is changing and it would be real interesting."

"If you were going to Russia, where would you think about going?"

Everyone chimed in. "The Kremlin."

"Red Square."

"Moscow."

"Siberia!"

Jen nodded. "It's a big country. What do you need to do to figure out where you're going to go?"

"Figure out distances."

"Figure out how much money you have."

The students were warmed up and seemed eager to get started. They had no difficulty answering the questions she tossed to them. Jen handed out a second sheet with a set of instructions:

1. List the resources or manipulatives you'll need for your project.
2. Construct a timeline to show how you will complete the project by the assigned date.
3. Identify the math skills or concepts you will be applying.
4. Estimate the total cost of your trip. Keep the estimate so that you can compare it to the actual cost when you've completed your work.
5. Construct a work schedule to show each person's responsibilities.
6. Design a method of graphically showing each of your budget categories.

"I want y'all to take the remainder of the class period today to plan how you're going to work on these tasks. Please work on the sheets of big paper which I'll bring around. We'll stop about 10 minutes before the end of the period so that the coaches can report the progress you've made. Do good work, now!"

As they began to work, she moved from group to group. One group of boys was unfamiliar with the word *consensus*. She worked to get them to extract the meaning out of the context by asking questions:

"How do y'all make decisions about rewards and punishments at home?"

"Dictatorship."

"Well, what is *consensus* then?"

"Democracy."

"How are decisions made in a democracy?"

"Majority rules."

"Does everyone agree when the majority rules?"

They eventually worked around to an understanding of the differences between a dictatorship, a democracy, and consensual decision making.

Another group discussed how you get to the Bahamas if you don't want to fly. Another talked about time changes in Australia, gaining and losing a day. Several of them had not considered this before. Jennifer circulated to each group. With some she sat down for a few minutes. With others she just leaned in to listen and to ask a few questions. The pace of the class was brisk and the atmosphere friendly. Near the end of the period she asked volunteers from each group to share their progress. She reminded the kids that it was okay for them to borrow ideas from another group. Three boys stood up to share the information on their big sheet of paper, which read:

To the BEACH in Florida:
1. Materials we'll need: poster boards, markers, road maps, pictures.
2. Jed will go to the travel agent. Mark will get road maps from the Shell station. Tom will figure out food and stuff.
3. Addition, subtraction, multiplication, division, DRT (distance/rate/ time).
4. Budget categories: 1/3 recreation; food is the largest chunk and lodging is a small chunk.

Jennifer asked them if they knew how to calculate all of these things. They said, "We'll talk to you after class." Everyone laughed. Jen noted that the whole class was going to have to talk about these calculations in class.

A group of girls presented their ideas about a trip to the Caribbean. Their graph included categories for food, airfare, lodging, car rental, and $450 for clothes shopping. Jed, the coach in the first group, said, "We don't need clothes; we're going to be on the beach the whole time." The class roared.

As time ran out, the pace of the class picked up. Jen asked each of the groups to put their worksheets up before they left. She reminded them of their homework—to make paper airplanes and bring in empty milk jugs. She told them to dress for going outdoors the next day and asked the coaches to write a few sentences about their group's work for the day. As the bell shrilled, the kids poured out of the room.

In the 5 minute break, Jen answered a few questions for the videotapers as they packed up to leave. She waved to her student teacher, who was working in another classroom for a few days. In between, she explained the sequence of activities that would take place during this project. The next day, students would learn to measure time, rate, and distance by flying paper airplanes outside on the field and by floating a few empty milk jugs down the river on the school grounds. On Wednesday, they would work on building pie graphs, review percentages, learn how to establish the vertex, and review what should be included in their budgets. On Thursday, they would have a day to work in class and to write up their progress reports—where they were and where they were having problems. She would give them two more directed lessons, one using maps to calculate distances and another on interpreting graphs. Then they would have one more day to complete their work in class. Their written report was due on Wednesday of the following week. On Thursday and Friday, the oral reports would be given.

Jennifer noted that it was more difficult for her to generate projects in Algebra I, where students were just developing the skills they needed. She felt that this particular project blended a little algebra with general math skills. Time, rate, and distance required algebraic figuring. Reading charts and graphs and understanding the use of axis all involved algebraic concepts. She believed this project was good because the kids reviewed some skills they had learned previously and picked up some new ones. She laughed as she described how liberating it had been for her when she discovered that she didn't have to go through the material in the order in which it was presented and decided she could legitimately pull material from different parts of the book.

Geometry

The next group rolled in, seventeen 11th-grade geometry students. This group was in the midst of a project in which they were to design or redesign a room or an area of their choice. One group was designing a golf course. Several others were remodeling rooms in their homes. Another group was designing a weight room for the school.

On the 1st day of the project, the students had done the same activity that the Algebra I class had just gone through. Around the room were their big sheets of paper describing their projects. They had identified the materials they'd need and the computational work they'd have to be able to do: figuring area, volume, and perimeter; working with fractions, decimals, and percentages; all the skills associated with budgeting. The sheets also described their time lines and who would do what.

On the 2nd day, she'd given them the "dog pen problem,"[1] which stated in part:

> Mr. Garcia has a new dog named Cosco. He wants to build a pen in his backyard in which Cosco can play. His neighbor, who works at a building supply store, gives Mr. Garcia 80 meters of chain-link fencing. Of course, Mr. Garcia wants Cosco to have as much space as possible. What is the largest pen he can build using the 80 meters of fence? (pp. 7–8)

The problem had several additional twists and turns once the students had learned to figure out the area. They had begun to see what happened to area when they chose different shapes. Each group had put its solutions on the board and had discussed the advantages and disadvantages. They had quickly begun to see why buildings are of such uniform shape.

The 3rd day of the project, students had brought in the problems they had begun to face. Jen had asked the industrial arts teacher to come in to work with her students while she worked with his. He had taken each group's problem and had worked it at the board for the students.

Today, she had prepared a graphing activity to help them develop interpretive skills when reading graphs. In their groups, students were given a set of statements and questions. For example:

1. Prices are rising more slowly now than at any time during the last 5 years. . . .
6. How does the cost of a bag of potatoes depend on its weight?

The students were given a set of 15 graphs (Figure 4.1.[2]). Their task was to match these statements to the graphs.

While the coaches for this class did the roll, Jen handed out the sheets they would need and gave them instructions. "All right, y'all. I want you to work in your teams to do this. But you must reach consensus on which graph belongs to which statement. When we're done, in about 20 minutes, I'd like you to be able to defend your choices and put them up on the board. The coach will appoint a spokesperson from each group. Y'all ready?" The groups moved right into the work.

Announcements came over the loudspeaker: "Fellowship of Christian Athletes need to pick up scholarship applications from Ms. Frank. All students going to Boston must meet in Room 202. Mandatory, but brief. Absence forms must be in by noon on Tuesday. Prom Committee meeting in Ms. Brown's room today. The boys' tennis match has been canceled. . . ."

The announcements went on for another 5 minutes. Students listened or worked quietly.

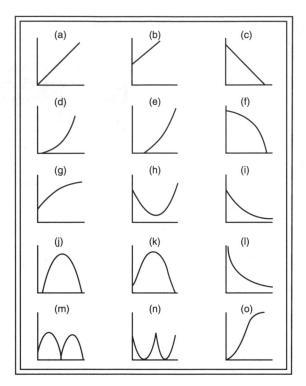

Figure 4.1. *Note.* Adapted from *The Language and Function of Graphs* (p. 82) by M. Swan, 1984, Nottingham, England: Shell Center for Mathematical Education, Dale Seymour Publications.

Jennifer moved from group to group. Three boys were hunched over the sheets. One wore an ROTC uniform and sported a crew cut. Another had an earring, a long ponytail, and sported a rocker T-shirt and jeans. The third was clean cut and dressed out of an L. L. Bean catalogue. They were working on statement #5, which read: "If movie admission charges are too low, then the owners will lose money. On the other hand, if they are too high, then few people will attend and again they will lose. A movie theater must therefore charge a moderate price in order to stay profitable."

"What about K?"

"Can't be; too high."

"What about O?" Silence while they considered.

"Nope, I think it's N, because if prices are too low, they'll lose money. And if they're too high, they'll lose money." They all wrote N on their papers.

One student groaned, "Where does she get these things? These aren't written in English; they're written in German!"

Jennifer moved around to every group. She stopped with some who needed help, just listened with others. After 20 minutes, she asked them to put their work on the board. There were seven lines of figures on the board when they finished. It quickly became apparent when there was consensus and when there was disagreement. Consensus was infrequent.

Jennifer asked them to resolve the disagreements. "Okay, y'all, find the two most common answers for #1. Then I want volunteers to defend each of the answers." The students engaged in a rousing debate. No students raised their hands. Jennifer did not interfere, as the students seemed well able to monitor the discussion. Her role was to ask, after each answer had been defended, "Which one is it?" and then, "Do we have consensus?" When the class did not agree, she asked additional people to explain the choices they had made so that the circumstances would become clearer for the whole group.

Toward the end of the period, she stopped them to ask a few questions. "How do you feel when you can't find the right answer?"

Tom replied, "I hate it. It makes you feel uncertain."

Jennifer grinned. "Are there more right answers out there in the world than uncertainties?" The kids debated that for a few minutes and Jen helped them to distinguish between factual circumstances and hypotheses. She shared with them that she was reading a book about decision making and that most "answers" are choices people have made based on the best information available at the time. She asked them what that meant for them. One of the students said it meant that they have to get good information.

As the bell rang, Jen reminded them that a progress report on their project was due the next day. The students said good-bye as they left. One student stopped to tell Jennifer that she'd loved the day's activity because she loved to argue.

Team Planning Period

Jen spent the next two periods meeting with the 10th- and 11th-grade teams. She met with the 10th-grade team three times a week and with the 11th-grade team usually once a week. She used the remaining time to organize the activities and materials they were all working on and to do the liaison work, the scheduling, and her own planning.

They met in the Commons area, which was also the cafeteria. The 10th-grade group consisted of four women and one man from a range of disciplines. As they gathered around the table, much of the talk was about grades: Who had failed what, how they were allocating their grades, whether they were done, and when the actual final deadline was. Many of them were disappointed with their students' work. Jennifer reminded them to put positive comments on each kid's report card. "We're trying to build these kids up, you know." She handed out a sheet listing the discussion topics for their meetings for the week. It also included important events about which she wanted to remind them.

They launched into the first agenda item: How were they going to organize next year's 11th-grade schedule? Did this team want to move forward with their students? Most did. Jen noted that the current 11th-grade team wanted to move forward with their students. She pushed them to talk up pre-registration for the program with their students because their plans would depend upon the number of students who chose the program.

They discussed a field trip to the state capital later in the week. Jennifer reminded them about the principal's Quality Circles meeting the next day. The whole school was considering experimenting with a double-blocked schedule, and that was to be the topic of the meeting.

They talked about grades a bit more. Jen again pushed for positive dealings with students. After several more announcements, Jen asked, "What else do we need to worry about?" They went back to whether they should move forward with their students and remain as a team, or whether some of them should stay with the 10th grade so the new team would have at least some experienced people on it. They couldn't decide. There were advantages and disadvantages both ways. They batted it back and forth until it was time to go.

Sam, the geography teacher, left first. The women noted that he had been down lately. They talked about why, and what they might do for him to perk him up. They decided to take him to a local restaurant for lunch on Friday and to cover his classes for him for two periods that day. They laughed about the fact that they had better go out to lunch while they could because the current principal was leaving at the end of the year. Jennifer wrote herself a note to swap lunch duty that day. As the bell rang, they raced off in four different directions. Jennifer walked one of the teachers to her classroom so they could discuss what to do about a difficult student.

The 11th-grade group assembled in much the same way. This team consisted of two math teachers, two English teachers, and one counselor—again, one male and four females. Jennifer handed them their own schedule with discussion topics for the week. They talked about registering the 12th-grade kids. One of the teachers noted that the school counselors were advising kids against the program; one student had been told that the program would adversely affect college admission. Jennifer's face absolutely fell.

The group talked about the fact that resentments among the faculty were still pretty substantial. People didn't understand the reduced student load; they felt the teams had been given special privileges. One of the English teachers reported that those teachers who were not supportive of their work were doing some lobbying among the other teachers. They were hoping that when the principal left, the whole program might be scuttled. It was apparent that the entire staff was concerned about the transition. Jennifer asked for volunteers to go with her to talk to the counselors. She noted that perhaps she had not done the very best job of preparing them for the registration proceedings and that they might use this as their opener.

The conversation shifted to how they might better communicate with the larger faculty about what they were trying to do and how they might build better support. Some suggested opening it up at the Quality Circles meetings, which all faculty attended. They considered an update memo, but feared that folks would be too busy or too disinterested to read it. Jennifer asked that they continue to think about this while she talked to the principal. She was visibly discouraged; she felt that they had worked very hard to keep the faculty up to speed and thought that they had reached the stage where their intentions and interests were pretty clearly understood.

The subject changed to which of the students might need credits for the 2nd semester. They generated a few names and split the responsibility for locating the kids and talking to them. Jennifer volunteered to check with the counselors about these kids and to contact their parents. One of the teachers talked about a student who had been depressed. The group agreed that a meeting should be called with his father because the boy seemed to be potentially suicidal.

Concerns about new interruptions to their class time surfaced—teen challenge and visitors from other schools. The time flew by. Jennifer added a few discussion topics to her list for the next meeting and they dispersed.

At lunch time, Jen grabbed a sandwich and went back to her room to complete her own grades before doing lunch duty. She managed to finish several before racing back to the Commons area to visit with students and remind others to put their trays away and to pick up their garbage. She confessed that this was the sole responsibility that she hated as a teacher. She felt that it forced her into a kind of relationship with kids that did not foster respect and understanding. "Teachers who are trying to encourage kids to believe in themselves and to work harder should not also have to play a policeman role."

Two "Regular" Classes

After lunch, Jennifer taught two more math classes. These were not classes in the OTL program and consequently were much larger, reflecting a more traditional student/teacher ratio: 28 in one class, 27 in the other. She noted that it was much harder with the larger group to do the kinds of activities she was doing with the morning classes. There were more groups to get around to. It was more difficult to keep track of who was doing what. The noise level was higher.

Still, she experimented occasionally. This week she was having these classes do the same activities. In general, she did not keep the two sets of classes on the same track, but she noted that her teaching with these groups, too, had changed. Instead of having the kids work individually, she paired them to do their homework, requiring that they both show the steps they had taken to arrive at the solution. Instead of working their homework problems for them at the board, she now asked them to demonstrate those that they had had difficulties with so that she could watch them work.

At the end of the school day, students streamed out of Jen's class, while a few stayed back with questions. She helped them until they seemed confident about their homework. Then Jennifer walked across the hall and poked her head into Paulette's room to see if they might work together for a few minutes. Several students came in, and it was difficult to know whose students were whose. Both teachers helped the kids with some questions they had about math. Once the students had left, Paulette showed Jennifer a new computer program she'd been using with kids to develop logic proofs. She showed Jen computer printouts—examples of the kids' work. They reviewed the sheets the kids had handed in. Jennifer, who claimed she didn't know how she had taught before there were computers, was excited. Jennifer showed Paulette the worksheet she'd found on graphing and told her how she'd used it with the kids. Paulette was delighted. "This is excellent. May I use this? You are a gold mine, m'dear! This is much better than that dry little set of activities in our book."

They moved on to Jennifer's concerns about the larger faculty and what should be done. Paulette sighed and said that they just had to be patient and to keep them informed. That was the best they could do. Then they talked about a student who wished to transfer into the OTL program. A counselor had sent the student to Paulette who had agreed to admit her. Jennifer wanted to follow that transfer up a bit more closely to find out just what was going on. Her concern was that students coming in mid-semester compromised the integrity of their program. She wasn't sure whether the counselors were using the class as a dumping ground, or whether they knew that the teams were trying different teaching techniques that required that they have fewer students. Paulette agreed to send the student to Jennifer so that she could do more investigation. She said, "You know, Jennifer, I have always been such a soft touch with the kids. I do believe that you are trying to save me from my own self, to protect me."

It was getting late, nearly 4:00. Jen gathered up her stuff, giving Paulette a kind of sheepish smile.

"Well, there's a little of that, but mostly it's that I think we could be working up a pretty good formula for making a difference with these kids. You know better than I do that we have to keep the variables to a minimum to figure out if it's a good formula or not! Now, much as I love you and your company, Paulette, I've got two handsome boys waiting on me. I'll see you tomorrow."

STEPPING BACK

Jennifer Rochambeau's math classes were lively and engaging, and they were very little like the math classes I had as a kid. In most math classes in which I have either participated or observed, students came to class equipped with paper, pencils, and the textbook. By contrast, Jennifer's students were bringing in things like blueprints for golf courses, carpet and paint samples, paper airplanes, empty milk jugs, and road maps from Seattle to Ft. Lauderdale. Her students were sitting at tables, working in groups, and engaged in projects such as redesigning rooms and planning vacations. They were preparing oral reports and visual and written materials to accompany their reports. I asked her to explain the changes she had made from past practice to her current methods, and then to think out loud about what both supported and challenged her as she engaged in these changes.

So What's Different Now?

Jennifer began her description of the changes she had made by noting the broad, structural changes the team had made at the outset of their attempt to provide better educational experiences for their students. They had formed a school within a school and built a schedule that allowed them to share a common group of students—fewer than the normal high school load. They had shared a common planning period during which they had worked together, planning their program and talking about their students. And they had talked frequently about changing their instructional methods.

These changes were inspired in part by their membership in the Coalition of Essential Schools and were guided by its nine Common Principles. Jennifer noted that it was within the context of these changes that she was able to examine her own instruction and to make further changes.

Projects and Problem Solving

Once we got all of these things in place—the schedule, the reduced student load, the teams—a whole lot of changes seemed to happen all at once. First of all, I want you to realize that I don't always do project teaching. Though I really love it and though the kids seem to do so well with it, I'm still learning how to do all this. For one thing, it's hard to figure out the projects and then to find resources. So I try to spend 2 to 3 days a week doing problem solving, a couple of days teaching basic concepts and skills, and then I try to build in a project every term. Projects usually take a couple of weeks, so one is really all I can fit in right now.

I've also changed the way I teach plain old concepts and skills. For one thing, I try to present new math concepts in terms of their application. I used to just move through the book: I'd show the kids a formula, I'd plug some numbers in; then I'd have them plug some numbers in and they'd do homework applications. I'd work their problems and then we'd have a test. Now, I start by giving the kids a real problem—say I want them to learn to do quadratic equations. I begin by posing a real-life problem where kids would need to know how to solve for a square. Then I ask questions like, "What do you need to be able to do here? Where else might you use this?" Then I go back and show the kids the formula. We work the problems together—usually a student demonstrates it while I coach from the side. Then I put them in pairs to tackle a set of examples. The kids seem to do much better when they are learning through problem-solving. They seem to understand the concepts better.

Cooperative Skills

And do you know another thing I have learned? These kids don't know each other. Even though they've been in school together for 14 years, sitting next to each other in little rows, they know almost no one outside their own small circle of friends. So I've found I have to do a number of ice breakers at the beginning of the year—activities to get them talking to each other. I have them line up by shoe size, or we tell number stories—where they ran into good numbers, that sort of thing. It might sound corny, but the truth of the matter is, it helps them to get ready to work together. While they get to know each other, I spend a lot of time diagnosing their math skills so that I know where each student really is.

When they work in groups, I'm better able to tell where they are really having problems because two kids are a lot more likely to speak up than one kid who doesn't want to look dumb. They feel like they've got some company. Their openness helps me a lot. I even do things like group or partner quizzes when we're learning new concepts. They think I want them to cheat! It's hard for them to get used to the idea of cooperating. I have to help them learn how to work together—like I ask them not to ask me until they've checked with all members in their group. When I ask them to reach consensus about the right answer, two things happen. First, I'm not the only teacher in the classroom anymore. Second, kids who get the concepts quickly reinforce their own understanding by teaching others. And, oftentimes, kids can explain these things to other kids a whole lot better than I can. So they do the teaching, and I have an opportunity to better understand each student's progress because I have more time to watch them. They work the problems at the board or the over-head, and I watch. You know, I used to be performing all the time. I gave all my attention to my own performance—demonstrating problems, explaining answers—and didn't have time to watch the kids. I know my students one whale of a lot better now.

Textbooks as Resources

Another difference is that I don't use the textbook like I used to. I've got-ten so that we use the textbook as a resource. It is a place where the kids can go to find out how to do the things they need to do. We skip around. I may think right triangles should be taught before other things, or I may decide in Algebra II that my group should go right to slopes of lines, which is in the middle of the book. When we do project work, I may cover three different chapters at once. I help the kids to see where the explanations of the formulas are in their book so they can use the book as a supplement to the classroom demonstrations. Kids tell me that I don't give them the answers. Ten years ago I would have thought that was an insult. Now, I think it's a compliment. Now, I want them to do the thinking.

Quality before Coverage

I also feel a difference in the pace of the classroom because we are making some discoveries about coverage. Coverage—getting through all the material in the book—used to be the most important thing to me. I believed that if I didn't get through it all, the people who were teaching the courses after me would be stuck. Well, we've been discovering that there is a lot of overlap in math texts and in math curriculum. I ask the kids a lot more questions these days. Whenever we start something new, I ask them, "Where have you seen this before? What parts of this formula do you know how to work?" I'm surprised at how often the kids can locate the parts they do know.

I want the kids to be able to take a math application and think through how to use it in new circumstances. To do that takes more time. Now I give kids a list of the skills and concepts we'll be covering during the course of the term, and they use that as a kind of checklist. I move through those skills and concepts, watching the students' understanding. If they don't get something, we slow down and come at it again.

The other math teachers and I are working on what things should be taught in Algebra I and what should be left for Algebra II. We're talking about what algebra skills the kids really need in order to do geometry. So we're trying to find ways to slim the curriculum down in each class so that we don't have to move so fast, and to help the kids learn more thoroughly. Once they know how to use a formula and can spot how to use it in fresh situations, they remember it better, so we don't have to do so much re-teaching. That's one of the ways we've been seeing that less is really more.

Teacher-as-Facilitator

All these changes have influenced the way I work in the classroom. I lecture a lot less—hardly ever more than 5 or 10 minutes—and the kids do a lot more work. I get them working in their groups quicker than I used to. Rather than me standing up there and going over things for them, I let them try it out so I can watch and see where they get stuck. I move from group to group, and I can tell you, there are days when I really wish I could wear roller skates or that I had some kind of a circular skateboard so I could get around that room faster! I spend my time figuring out how to get them engaged—through problem solving and such like, and how to get them unstuck when they get mired down—through analyzing how they are doing things and trouble-shooting. It really is a different way of working. Like I said, I concentrate on their performance now, not on mine.

Now, I have to say that I'm still learning, so I do spend a fair bit of time examining my own teaching. But I'm even looking at that differently. When kids didn't get something before, I used to look at the kids. What were they doing wrong? Goofing off? Missing class? Now, like as not, I look at what I did. Did I give them a good example? Was the problem too complex for the concept? Did I talk too long? Did I leave out a step?

I ask a lot more questions. Instead of giving kids information, I try to get them to give me information, so I ask questions. I also want them to make the connections, to see that one math concept builds on another, so I want them to see what parts of something they've worked with before. I want them to be able to use the concepts in real applications, so I ask those kinds of questions. And in order to ask all of these questions, I'm asking myself a lot more questions, too.

Support

Understanding that change is fraught with difficulties and challenges, I wondered what sorts of things helped her. Jennifer beamed and reminded me that she loved to talk about these things, especially because they were more positive, more uplifting. These were the things she thought about when she was having a bad day—just to keep her going. She talked so fast, it was hard to keep up!

The Kids

I have to say that the most important factor which keeps me going is the kids. The kids are sensitive, you know. They understand that we are attempting to change and they just seem to read our moods. If I'm having a bad day, they seem to know it and to give me a little space. Then they put some of my worst fears to bed. They let me know straight away that it was okay with them if I didn't have all the answers. I think it's a little comforting to them to know that teachers don't know everything and that they're still trying to learn too.

I can't tell you how many times the kids have surprised me. In problem solving and in project work, they end up tackling things I would never have thought they were ready for, and they do a good job—makes me feel a little guilty, like I've been holding them back all this time. Those kids can do things I never gave them the foundation to do, and it's just great to watch them do that kind of thinking on their own. Like the group in geometry who've decided to design a golf course. I told them that they'd have to do a lot more work because of the curves and angles, but they just said they didn't mind.

Another thing with the kids is that I think they are developing better leadership skills in my class now. Since they have been working in groups and since they've gotten used to helping each other, they know how to organize themselves, they know how to present their ideas, they know how to argue—all those kinds of communications skills that good leaders need. It's fun to watch them grow.

Finally, I have to say that I have not seen my students' test scores drop one bit in the 2 years that I have changed the way we've done things, so that has kept me going too.

Empowering Leadership

Besides the kids, if I look back at what made me want to change, three more things stand out. The first is the leadership we've had here at Riverdale, both in the math department and from the principal. Before the Coalition hit town, Paulette, as the math department chair, had us examining textbooks for coherence and such like. Well, that was a major breakthrough for me. Each text included some things that others didn't. Each put the content in a different order. None of them asked the kids to really stretch, to be able to think through another application of a concept. That exercise helped me to understand that there is more flexibility in math than I had ever thought about before.

Then, we talked about tests. I can remember when she told me that the chapter tests were too easy for the kids. I wondered where she was importing her students from! We started experimenting with different kinds of tests—stretch tests, tests kids didn't have to finish, tests where kids could select the problems they wanted to work on, group tests. All of this really pushed me to be more flexible—a quality math teachers are not known for.

Then too, Paulette treated me as if I were a resource to her. Here she'd been teaching a lot longer and she is just about the best loved and most innovative teacher in the school, and she would use the stuff I brought with her own classes. That made me feel as if I were really contributing.

Dr. Jamison has been a different kind of principal. He really trusts us. He has shared his own beliefs with us, as well as his doubts about what we're doing well and poorly here. He got us to experiment, like with the Forum groups he set up. He found money to send us to conferences. He provided reading material on current issues. He got us talking. When my colleagues and I went to Louisville and came back full of plans, he was all for it and let us know that although he would support us 100%, we should plan to run our own program. No one had ever given us that kind of authority, and I have to say that though it was frightening at first, now it feels right.

A Framework for Change

There's another factor that helped me out. Although the experience with the Forum showed me how I might try some of the principles in action, the symposium and the connection with the Coalition gave me a framework for my thinking. First off, the Common Principles are classroom-based. They deal with things that go on in the classroom—personalization, student engagement, student as worker, using their minds well. It was the first time anyone had said to me, "Look, the changes have to take place in the classroom. And it's got to start with the teacher. It doesn't start with the superintendent and work its way down."

That's what keyed me in, and made me think that I really had to do something myself. It made me want to read everything I could get my hands on. Now I'm putting articles in the mailboxes of other teachers and I'm sure they feel about me like we used to feel about Dr. Jamison when he was doing his doctoral work! The belief that changes must come from the classroom has led me to feel that I can make a difference. I feel that if I only change my own classroom, I have made a difference. Then, if I manage to bring a few other teachers along too, well, that's really making a *big* difference.

Challenges

Throughout our discussion, Jennifer mentioned frequently that these changes were difficult and that there were a number of factors that inhibited her progress. "There are a number of things which keep me from going 90 miles an hour. One is just my own fears. And the others are all about breaking old habits and beliefs about teaching."

Fear of Change

Sometimes I am afraid that I just plain don't know enough, that the kids will ask me something that I don't know, and that the whole thing will come apart at the seams.

I've also worried about the coverage issue a whole lot. I was raised to think that we had to cover, cover, cover, so there are days when I'm afraid that my students won't do well on placement tests. Also, I'm so new to this that I'm not sure yet what should be taught at what level and what can be left out one year to be taught another. I feel like these kids are on a journey, and if they don't get to where they're supposed to be, they'll be behind for the rest of that journey. I want to trust the instincts my colleagues and I are having, but I have a lot of years of training to contend with.

Sometimes I worry about my role as a teacher. I think, "I'm getting paid to teach. I should be doing the teaching." It is a funny fear and a kind of confusion about what teachers are really supposed to do and what they are not supposed to do. Since I am changing the way I feel about this, sometimes I am uncertain and it makes me nervous.

I am afraid about the principal leaving. My colleagues, the kids, and I have worked really hard over the past couple of years, and I think we are learning some very important things. If the new principal doesn't support what we're doing, our program could be scuttled in no time. I would almost have to quit teaching if that were the case. I don't think I can go back now that I've begun. Plus, we've gotten used to making a lot of the decisions. It would be hard to give that up.

Listening, NOT Talking; Watching, NOT Demonstrating

Then there are those things that are just plain hard. It's been hard for me to learn to listen to the kids and not to interrupt them. I have to hold myself back a lot of the time because the truth of the matter is, I like to talk. I've always liked to talk. It's hard to listen to the kids struggling and stumbling along. Sometimes I do not have the patience to wait, especially when I know the answer. I have to talk to myself constantly about this.

Then, I've been demonstrating problems at the board for half my life! I'm just learning that I can really find out a lot about the kids if I watch them demonstrate problems on the board or at the overhead or at their desks. So I've been looking for all kinds of ways to get them up doing the demonstrating so that I can watch to see what they're doing right or wrong. It's a lot easier if I demonstrate, but I don't think it's better for the kids.

Collaboration

Then there are days when I think the big difficulty is working with other adults. On one of our teams we have two people who just do not get along. Part of the issue is gender—one's a woman and the other's a man; the other part is race—one's black and the other's white. Also, we constantly struggle with the larger faculty—how to keep them informed, how to help them to understand what we want to do without making them feel angry or threatened. The AP teachers say we can do whatever we want as long as we don't touch their AP kids, and yet, I think the program would be real good for some of those kids. I think the kids are much easier to deal with than the grown-ups. It's hard to know how to get them to see eye to eye, and it makes me exhausted trying to figure it out.

It's also hard to get the kids used to working together—to get them to trust each other and to help each other out. The high achievers don't want to work in groups. They say that they've worked hard to get where they are and they think other kids should work just as hard. Then we have kids who don't believe in themselves, and it's hard to get them to open up to other kids who might want to help them. I think the kids also fought having to think. We felt like they were pushing against us with everything they had to keep from having to do any work. They'd all spent years perfecting passive participation, and they didn't like being asked to change.

No Models

And another thing. It's hard to do this when there aren't any models out there to follow and when there aren't very many materials. There aren't a whole lot of high school teachers who are trying to do these things and there are even fewer math teachers, so we kind of have to make things up as we go. Textbooks aren't organized to foster this kind of teaching so we have to generate a lot of our own stuff and learn to be even better scrounges than we were before.

Teaching as Continuous Growth

The hardest thing of all, though, was to believe that we were good teachers, and then to recognize that after a number of years at teaching, we might want to do things differently. We sort of felt that if we admitted that we might need to change, it would mean that everything we'd done before was no good, and the thought of that was just plain too painful. It held me back for a couple of years. Getting to the point where we didn't feel defensive, where we could actually believe that we were good but that there was more each of us could do was tough.

Since we got there, it has been difficult coming up with the courage to follow our instincts in the face of years of practice. Somehow or another, I think we as teachers do not believe really that we know what's best for kids nor do we believe that we have the authority to change long-time practices. I am constantly trying to dig up more confidence, more courage to believe in myself.

Essential Learnings

When Jennifer and I looked back at her case, we determined that there were four lessons which might help others in their consideration of change. Three deal with issues common to Judd's case and the fourth deals with mathematics in particular.

Resistance and Decision Making

In Jennifer's school as in Judd's school, there was resistance among the faculty about the changes that Jennifer and her colleagues were making. Although Jen and company hoped that their whole school would eventually become a teamed school, many of the faculty hoped the changes would go away when the new administration arrived. Looking back at the development of the OTL program may help explain why. The principal, very interested in change, made opportunities available to the faculty—articles, trips to Rhode Island and other conferences, and discussions in his Quality Circles meetings. For a variety of reasons, only those who were interested participated. When this group generated their plan for the original OTL program, they took it to the principal and he approved it. The larger faculty did not participate in any way in that decision. The original program served only those kids who were "at risk" and so the larger faculty and the counselors saw the program as designed for the less able, and not appropriate for "good" students.

As the program expanded and included a heterogeneous group of kids, it continued to be a process of negotiations between the administrators and Jen and her colleagues. Jennifer was hand picked by her principal to be the teacher leader for the program. Again, the rest of the faculty never had the opportunity or the responsibility for participating in the decision making about the OTL program. They could claim ignorance despite the fact that Jen and her colleagues believed that they tried to keep them informed. They felt, much like Judd's staff, like outsiders. It is possible that the development of a decision-making process that required their participation might have eliminated what appeared to be covert resistance. It is unlikely that, given the opportunity to participate, the larger faculty would have eliminated the

OTL program because they were generally interested in helping children. Debate about the need for change and discussion about the means by which to improve circumstances for students could have moved the entire faculty closer to shared values and beliefs.

Teaming for Personalization

The teams Jennifer both served on and coordinated included a number of disciplines, and yet the bulk of their discussions did not deal with cross disciplinary connections as much as they did with individual student performance and regular school business. During their cooperative team planning, they discussed students who were in jeopardy, grading procedures, and the possibility of field trips geared towards end of the year celebrations. In this case, then, the purposes of teaming were aimed at helping teachers know students better. Because these teachers shared their students, each of them could add a piece to the puzzle of a student's learning habits, potentially strengthening each teacher's ability to help individual students.

In many cases, the norms of a more personalized and caring environment for students run contrary to existing attitudes and behaviors towards students. As we can see from the discussion, Jen was constantly reminding her team to make positive comments about the kids, to build them up instead of tearing them down, and to use their time to figure out how to help kids. Although the staff members in the OTL program were moving towards a more decent and caring environment for students, they had not yet abandoned comparing how many 'F's' they had awarded and which students were the most problematic. The shift from seeing students as problems to be eliminated or fixed to seeing them as learning puzzles to be solved is difficult. Teams established for this purpose have their own habits to break which requires time, vigilance, and an openness to examining individual and collective practices.

Administrative Support and Teacher Leadership

Jennifer knew that her principal was leaving. This made her uncomfortable because she was uncertain whether she, in her leadership position, would be able to gather enough support to carry on. She was well aware that the work she and her teammates were doing rested on the strength of the principal's vision and on his support, and she was fairly certain that none of the other likely candidates would share the current principal's enthusiasm for change.

Jennifer worked to build a stronger base of support with folks at the central office and used the leadership position she'd been appointed to by the principal to garner that influence. Still, she worried about the reality of the circumstances: When he left, would she and her colleagues be able to continue? Would she, from her teacher leadership position, be able to protect and expand what they'd built? In her case, the question was a very real one because no structures, policies or procedures were in place that would ensure that the school wouldn't immediately revert to its general practices.

This is a lesson that has been learned too often in the past. Teachers' most committed efforts to make schools better places rest on the foundation of a hierarchical system that does not vest them with the decision-making ability, power, or influence they need to protect the changes they wish to make. Foiled by administrative turnover or by the withdrawal of administrative support, many teachers are cynical and resistant to change.

Mathematics and Change

The math department at Riverdale High School was unusual in that the teachers worked collaboratively to change a number of common practices that any one of them would have been hard pressed to make alone. The algebra teacher had to communicate with the geometry teacher so that they both knew of what 2nd year math students might be capable. Working together, they moved away from text centered work. They reached the conclusion that covering the curriculum was detrimental to students learning and appreciation of mathematics and so were reducing what was to be covered each year. By eliminating the repetition of review, they believed that they were able to gain the kind of time they needed to help kids understand the pertinence of math through practical problems like building a room or planning a trip. Because there were virtually no ready made materials that placed mathematical knowledge at the heart of a practical problem, they had to develop these. This was difficult because none of them were applied mathematicians.

These changes were no small feat for a group of teachers. At the same time, they were aware that the relatively new National Council of Teachers of Mathematics standards suggested that they go much further, that they integrate with other subjects, and that they consider mathematics a language which supports the development of logical thinking. The lesson here is that change takes time both within a discipline and across disciplines, and that no one discipline is more restricted than another. Jennifer and her colleagues realized that they were no more restricted by the discipline of mathematics than humanities teachers were by their discipline. The restrictions came as a result of their own beliefs and experiences, or lack thereof.

I asked Jennifer what she thought was in store for her and her colleagues, what she thought they would do next, and how they would proceed.

> Well, we'll add another team next year. The schedule is almost done, and the kids have signed up. The popularity of the program is growing so much that we might have to expand the 10th-grade team, and there are teachers who are willing to volunteer to work with us. We're all praying that the new principal will be supportive, and you can bet that we will meet with him right away.
>
> Truth of the matter is, I didn't expect to feel so energized by all of this. Earlier on, after I'd been teaching for 8 or 10 years, I felt more tired, more frustrated. I could see myself getting into a real rut. But that sure hasn't happened. I'm learning from my kids when they bring stuff in for their projects. I'm learning from my colleagues. I'm growing and so are my kids.
>
> Now, I don't want you to think that it will all be roses from here on out. I know that there will be more days when I don't think all this change business is working, days when I just want quiet, when I don't want those kids asking any questions. I've had a lot of days already when I thought that the kids were too social, where the room was a mess from all the materials, when nothing I did seemed to work. But the 2nd year has been easier than the first, and I'm sure that the 3rd year will cut those difficulties back a bit more.
>
> And it doesn't bother me to think that I've got a long way to go. I wouldn't say that I'm a strictly conventional teacher anymore, but I wouldn't say that I'm an expert teacher-as-coach either. I'd say that, to use a familiar metaphor, the biscuits aren't out of the oven yet. In fact, I'm not sure we're even *in* the oven! Still mixing the batter—trying to find the right ingredients—a little soda, a little baking powder. Trying to figure who to borrow from and who to loan a little of what we have extra . . .

In the midst of her reverie, Jennifer caught herself; her face spread into a great grin. "I can sure mix up metaphors, can't I? A little mathematics, a little science, a little home cooking. Any which way, as long as my students continue to come to class more willing to tackle problems, to work hard, and as long as they keep surprising me with what they can do, I'm going to keep working on my own formula for better math teaching."

SINCE THEN . . .

Since the spring of 1990, a number of changes have taken place in Jennifer's school and in her professional life. "A new principal has come to the school, a new superintendent and a new assistant superintendent to the district.

Though the staff at Riverdale are members of the Coalition of Essential Schools, the new superintendent is interested in establishing Padeia schools. The new principal, though well meaning, has not been able to generate support for the Coalition work either within the school or within the district. Originally, the plan was that the interdisciplinary teams would expand from one team at the freshman and sophomore level right through the upper grades." Jen was the coordinator of the Essential Schools program, and acknowledged that the entire faculty had never been united about change, and that many hoped it would go away with the new principal. In the first year of the new principal, the teams had expanded to three. In the next year, expansion had continued because all sophomores were assigned to teams. In the coming year, the staff would drop back to two teams, because too many staff had complained to the principal.

Despite the fact that the district's commitment had seemed to be waning, Jen had spent the summer of 1990 at the Coalition, training to be a member of the National Re:Learning Faculty (NRF)—teachers and administrators who work together to learn about facilitating change both in their own schools and as resources to other schools. In 1991, she had spent the summer teaching in the Brown Summer High School with two other NRF colleagues, designing integrated curricula and working with other teachers from Coalition schools who attended summer institutes. In the middle of that institute, she had wailed in her journal, "Why am I doing this? Why am I so far away from home, working with other adults who are stubborn? What am I getting out of this except aggravation for my family?" At the end, she wrote:

> Working with two other diverse NRF teachers over a period of 3 weeks has given me an experience of professional growth, unlike my previous roles. They helped me to learn more about assessment, exhibitions, tone and decency, and what's possible with the 9CPs. I taught them how to push people to look closer at the process of debriefing team building exercises. Listening to Ted (Sizer) speak helped settle me to the value of this experience. What we are doing is about kids and the voices inside each of us that push us to commit to the best for them. They deserve teachers who are thoughtful and reflective in their work.

As I talked with her in the summer of 1992, she was just on her way to work with math teachers in another state, and to teach a week-long course on curriculum integration. It appeared that her commitment to change her own practices and to hone her skills to assist others was very strong. During the summer of 1993, she helped to plan and carry out a new arm of the National Faculty for math and science teachers and was looking forward to continuing that work in 1994.

5

A Team's Tale: Four Teachers Experiment with Whole Day High School

*I*n the winter of 1991, Mary Tonatti, Paolo Cagayan, Enrico Ramirez, and Michael O'Brian experimented with a semester-long program for their high school students so that they could increase the depth of student engagement and provide closer, more personal attention to students' learning needs. They designed a course in which they would keep the same group of students all day for the entire semester. More time with the kids meant more time to coach and to diagnose knowledge and skill levels. Previously, all of the staff in their small urban high school had worked on integrated teams in the morning and students' selected electives in the afternoon. Because they did not feel they were reaching students, this team felt dissatisfied and so gained the agreement of the rest of their faculty to try a different approach. They agreed to provide work in the content areas that students needed through an integrated program that addressed the question: How does the environment affect our lives? Initially the plan was that all students would share a common seminar during which they read novels and articles and did writing assignments that helped the teachers keep track of their progress. Students would rotate through three projects: (1) videography; (2) animals and aquariums; and (3) the Ropes Course[1]. Each of the projects was designed to develop students' skills in several of the core disciplines like English, math, science, social studies,and p.e., among others. Interested in teaming and in what happens when teachers attempt something new, I joined the team for the first week of the semester and then visited with them again after its conclusion. I wanted to learn what kinds of changes teaming imposed on their teaching practices, what integration meant for their curriculum, and how these changes affected their students.

A CHANGED JOB

Monday Morning, January 1991

Early morning. The subway rumbled and swayed—hypnotizing, numbing. Several passengers had no shoes. Their feet were wrapped in rags. I had never seen this before in the United States; it seemed a grim portent of the kinds of problems the community that housed Cityscape High School faced. Cityscape High School was located in the middle of one of the nation's largest cities, in a black/Hispanic neighborhood where life was not easy for most of the people who lived there.

At the school, the principal, Adrienne James, was on the phone. "Yes, they had guns. No, I have not yet called the police, but I intend to. The security police have been informed, yes. Thank you. I would appreciate your help. Yes, we are worried too. Sure, call me if you need to." Three boys in a neighborhood gang had appeared on campus the previous day with guns, threatening to return today to kill two girls. Adrienne was enlisting the support of the gang members' parents. She had found often times that parents had little access to their children's lives and that they were grateful for any information local schools could provide. The parents were very helpful in solving problems such as these with the school. Violence, although it generally did not affect the school, was commonplace for many of the students.

Cityscape was a 5-year-old alternative school which housed some 360 students who came from 65 different city high schools. Adrienne described the school:

> Almost all of our students have been in some high school setting before or come from alternative junior high schools. All of them are considered to be "at risk." We have slightly more girls than boys. More Latinos than blacks. A handful of white students. One Asian. Officially, 75% of our students are eligible for subsidized breakfast and lunch. Last year we had a 6.7% dropout rate—a feat in comparison to the city's general dropout rate which is much higher. Eighty-four percent of our students went on to college last year. We have a daily attendance rate at about 80%.

As we talked, we walked through the halls of the school, which was housed on the grounds of City Community College. The main building was a tall, cement, modern structure. The school was on the second floor of this building and on two floors of a less interesting building across the way. Teachers and students shared auditorium and gymnasium facilities with the community college. The hallways were dark because they were interior spaces; windows were saved for the offices and classrooms. There were several bulletin boards displaying student work. A colorful unit on the Consti-

tution, "We, The People," displayed student essays about rights and responsibilities. These provided the backdrop for a food cart from which a woman
dispensed toasted hamburger buns, butter, jam, orange juice, and milk to
students as they wandered by. Students moved through the halls, talking,
greeting friends, and conferring with teachers.

We paused in a corner so that Adrienne could observe the flow. Tall and
elegant, she reminded me of the women on the cover of Vogue in the 1930s.
She talked quietly, describing the students and the school.

> These kids are not 'acting out' kids. They are passive resisters. When
> school does not work for them, they drop out. On average, they've lost a
> year and a half by not going to school. They describe themselves as
> addicted to cutting. So our job is to make sure that school works for
> them. That it makes them feel productive, good about themselves. Some
> of the kids come here because they're looking for a safe place. Others
> come because their parents are looking for an alternative to private edu-
> cation. The upshot is that they haven't felt successful in school, and
> haven't felt that they could negotiate. That's very important. Almost
> everyone needs to feel that they have some control over their lives.
>
> Most kids say they come to school here because the teachers care. We
> do believe that the relationship between students and their teachers is
> significant here. Kids work for their teachers. It is an intimate relation-
> ship, an important one.
>
> Although we have students who come from a range of backgrounds, a
> good share of the parents are in deep trouble themselves. Many had their
> children when they were very young and have a difficult time with non-
> conforming adolescents. I know. I had two boys like that myself. Some-
> where between 13% to 20% of our students have their own children.
> AIDS is a very big issue in this community; it has taken a toll already and
> will continue to frighten people and devastate families. Some 20% of the
> kids have been tested for AIDS. Seven students are HIV positive. Many of
> the kids are very angry—it is acceptable behavior at home for many of
> them, so they occasionally burst into flames. In most schools anger of any
> kind is unacceptable. We try to work with the kids to help them discover
> legitimate ways to deal with their anger. The truth is, if they were phleg-
> matic they'd be hanging out in their traditional high schools. Most of the
> kids are referred in by school counselors or hear about the school by
> word of mouth. In order to come here, students and their parents must
> come to the school to visit. Parents sign a contract; they have to under-
> stand what the deal is. We don't have an attendance policy. Kids earn
> credits for work done. The kids spend an hour a day in their family group.
> Each of the teachers has a small group of kids with whom they work until
> the kids graduate. We expect that the family group teacher and the bio-

logical family will work very closely together. Students take fewer classes—we have a core program which operates in the morning—teachers teach on integrated teams. Then the kids take electives in the afternoon—taught by individual teachers mostly. That is the usual daily profile. The team you will be working with gained approval from the rest of the staff to experiment with a whole day schedule for this semester.

Since opening the school, the faculty makes decisions by consensus. The whole staff must agree to any changes a team or an individual wishes to make. We meet for 2 hours every Monday night after school to deal with decision making. Over time, we have all gotten better at consensual decision making. We've developed the capacity to build what one book calls "united judgment." The point at which we make a decision has become far less formal than it was at first. I don't see people compromising so much as I see them learning more and more about how to consult with people as they're thinking about proposing something new. Everyone looks for win–win solutions. On the other hand, we still have trouble deciding when we should revisit a decision. It doesn't matter how closed an issue seems to some; for others it is brand new.

We walked down the stairs and into the central courtyard between the two buildings. Students were clustered in small groups talking, some smoking. Adrienne again found a corner from which to observe.

The team you'll be working with wanted to reduce their class size. One of the only ways we can think of to do that is to share responsibility for the students and to generalize—take responsibility for more disciplines. So the three teachers you'll be working with are teaching 57 kids all of their subjects. We tried this once before when we first opened, and it was not a positive experience for very many people. Mary liked it though and has been mulling it over ever since.

This particular group of teachers also wanted to keep the kids in school—to work on the attendance rate, to make school more involving, and they needed more time to work with the kids. So they thought about eliminating the afternoon elective seminars and offering the kids a semester-long project. Mary brought it up with the team leaders. (Each of our teams has a team leader. These people meet together once a week to coordinate the academic program and to think about instruction.) After trouble shooting it, the team leaders sent it to the policy board—our school-based management team. The adults raised some objections, but the kids thought it sounded wonderful. In the long run, the kids influenced the decision. So six teachers, one part-timer—a social worker—and a paraprofessional have been planning this since the beginning of the year. The design is very interesting. The kids sign up for Project Challenge and within that, sign up for either a concentration on family or a concentration on the environment. The team you will be observing will focus on the environment.

It was time for the morning faculty meeting. Adrienne moved upstairs and shrugged.

I've just managed a quick overview. I didn't get to the fact that we have a three-tiered academic program. Kids select the tier in which they wish to work. Tier one is a more modern curriculum and is geared to help students pass the state minimum competency tests that they need to pass in order to graduate. Tier two is a more traditional curriculum and perhaps a more conventional learning environment. Tier three is for kids who wish to do community college work earning college credit—while gaining graduation requirements. The tier three teacher provides them with help planning their time, organizing their work . . ."

In mid sentence, she introduced me to Mary Tonatti.

Mary was in her 7th year of teaching. She looked more like one of the kids in a short pleated skirt, sweater, and pony tail. She grew up in the city, second-generation American. She was educated in private schools, but knew from the time she was in 3rd grade that she was going to teach. She also knew that she was not going to teach like the nuns in her school—that she wanted kids to be active, to be Doing Things instead of just listening. Mary was brisk, direct, an impressive organizer, and intensely committed. When she smiled or laughed, everyone lightened with her.

The staff squeezed into a faculty room around a long table and waited for the meeting to begin. There was a refrigerator, a microwave, bookshelves, and a rack for pamphlets and articles. One woman blasted an Egg McMuffin. Others talked, read, or organized papers. Several talked with students. Martha, a math teacher with multiple sclerosis, was put into place by one of her colleagues. She had a mobile cart, but limited use of her hands. The faculty shared responsibility for getting her where she needed to be. A movie company was negotiating with her to do her life story; the faculty teased her about making sure they had starring roles. At 8:30 the meeting began. Adrienne handed out "Citysounds," a collage of information and musings that she wrote every day. While the papers went around, someone announced, "Don't forget. Several of our illustrious staff and students will be on TV tomorrow night—a special on inner-city schools." David, a tier-two teacher who doubles as the college admissions counselor, announced, "The first round of college acceptances came in." The staff cheered. "The first of many!"

The meeting clipped along at a fast pace. Volunteers to monitor basketball games. A class for raising babies. A discussion about the students' need to understand essential questions. Someone's husband in the hospital. Three visitors introduced. A family group breakfast with parents.

Mary yelled, "Okay folks. It's nearly 9:00. How about attendance?"

Adrienne asked them to call out their attendance rate for the day before. Those who had 100% attendance got cheers from the crowd. The meeting was like the squad meetings on *Hill Street Blues* except that information came from everyone—not just the principal. The door jammed with people moving out.

Mary stopped by her office for a minute. Staff shared three person cubicles—small offices. Each office had three desks, three bookcases, and a phone—a rare luxury for public school teachers. She checked with Michael and with Paolo, two of the colleagues with whom she was teamed that semester. Were they ready to go? Did they have everything they needed? Their conversation was funny, untranslatable to the unfamiliar. "I have the rings, the chicken in my briefcase."

"Good. I have the letters."

"Do we have paper, pencils, all that stuff? Nobody will have it today."

"I have the familiars. Enrico is working on the aquarium. What do you think about a boa constrictor?"

"Yuk! Get out!" in unison.

The activities for the 1st week were designed to do a couple of things. First, the teachers wanted to get the kids used to working together. Consequently, a number of the activities were designed around physically active team building exercises. Others were more academic, asking students to design the ideal school. The teachers hoped to use this information to help them design this program. They also hoped it would give their students a chance to work collaboratively. In addition, the teachers would introduce the students to seminar activities: videography, animals and aquariums, and the Ropes Course.

Today, because it was the first day of the semester, family group was from 9:00 to 10:00 so that family group teachers could welcome students back, answer any questions about schedules, and discuss family response to credits earned last semester.

Mary walked quickly over to the next building where her classroom was on the second floor. The room was very plain: chairs with desk tops on them, banks of florescent lights, and chalk boards. Several of her family group students were waiting for her, and as she unpacked her bag, others wandered in. She had 10 students all together. They sat in a circle. She asked everyone how vacation was. Acton, a short compact kid, vibrated energy, talked very quickly, and jiggled constantly. He wanted to change his schedule and was insistent. Acton had been kicked out of his last school for fighting. He had gone after a kid with a knife. His mother had made him transfer schools. He was 16 but had never made it beyond the 9th grade. Mary asked him to wait until she could at least get through the things she needed to tell them. Mary announced that one of the students would be leaving to go to a theater internship. Mary asked who would like to be on the fairness board. Students on this board adjudicated infractions of the rules. It was a big commitment. The students asked questions. Acton squirmed. Paul told him to cool it. "Fuck you, man," said Acton, and burped loudly.

"Acton, let's have some respect for others," said Mary. They wanted to know how the rest of the students in the school could be sure that the fairness board was really being fair and wasn't protecting their friends. The conversation boiled with students' examples of inequities. Mary suggested that it was important that they select students whom they thought would be the most fair. The group talked one of the students into doing it. Acton said he'd do it, but everyone ignored him.

Student senate representative was next. This was a more popular position. Several people were interested. The group selected one. Next was intake representative. Mary explained that intake representatives agreed to spend a day with students who wanted to come to the school. They took the visitors to their classes with them, ate lunch with them, introduced them around, and then worked with the family group teachers to decide if the student should be admitted or not. Their recommendations had to be grounded in their observations. The school was overcrowded and had more applicants than it had space. They hoped to select students who would flourish and finish school. The group elected a representative. The discussion became more general. Mary asked, "How did your families react to your reports?" Each student responded. Acton persisted about wanting to change his schedule; he wanted to join the other Project Challenge group because they would be going swimming. Mary clarified for him that he needed to stay put for the first day, but that she would check with the Project Challenge Family teachers to see what their numbers were. If they had too many students, he might have to stay. He groaned, writhed, swore—a physical embodiment of frustration.

Mary got the kids up playing a game. They had a new member who needed to learn their names. "Think of one word which describes how you are feeling today. It must be positive. Say the adjective and then your name. Excited Mary." The kids groaned. She cajoled them. "It's a good way to learn names."

"Come on, Mary! We know everybody."

"So what's her name?" Mary pointed to the new girl. "How do you think she's supposed to learn your names?"

"Okay Queenie."

"Happy Larry." Giggling all around. Mumbled swearing.

"Shit, man."

"Perky Patty."

"Vibrant Vince."

"Glad Rosen."

"Curious Tano."

She handed them a ball. They were to toss the ball identifying the receiver by name. The kids threw the ball listlessly. Mary encouraged them. She added in a rubber chicken, which they also threw. Two things at once. The energy picked up. After several minutes of lively exchange, they stopped. "Who can name everyone?" Several people did it successfully, including the new girl.

At 10:00, Mary moved to another room to meet her new project challenge students. There were 53 kids in the room—all shapes and sizes. Most were between 15 and 19. The teachers noted quietly that they had the whole basketball team in one room. They repeated the activities Mary had done with her family group, and she gave the directions. Paolo and Michael circled around and got people moving. The high energy of the smaller family group changed into resistant energy—a result of the larger group. The teachers decided on the spot to divide the group in half. Too many kids. Paolo took one group. Mary and Michael took the other. Students called their teachers by their first names, jostled each other, and swore a lot. Still, motivated by the force of Mary's "Let's Go!" and by the other teachers' quiet prodding, they participated. A new game was added: Under the Blanket. The purpose of the game was to get all of the opposing team's players under the blanket. The students again vacillated between wanting to be cool and wanting to play. Over time, everyone joined in. There was a great deal of laughter and yelling. Michael and Mary cheered them on from the sidelines. Mary was the umpire. When the game was at its peak—not yet won or lost, Mary asked them to sit down to debrief. She asked them to think about how they worked together.

"It was boring."

"It would have been better if everyone was involved."

"We could have planned our strategy better."

"How?"

"We could of agreed on how to get them all under the blanket."

"We planned! You just didn't pay attention!"

"Mary, why are we playing these baby shit games?"

"Yeah. This is kindergarten shit!" Comments roll through the crowd. "Shit!"

"This is stupid."

"I hate doing this shit."

"Come on. Respect for others, you know? I'm so glad you asked! When you signed up for Project Challenge this semester, we told you that you would be doing lots of work in small groups." She went on to explain that the purpose of the introductory activities was to help them build collaborative skills because they would soon be working in groups building collaborative projects. She went on to explain that the semester long course was based on the training the teachers had had at Ragneck Island from Project Challenge.[2] Their aim was to make learning adventuresome by inter-

preting different kinds of environments. She described the three projects the
students would be rotating through, and finally, asked them to write about
their expectations for the course.

The momentum dissipated again. No paper. No pens. The teachers
produced materials. Mary circled, asking students to be quiet. Kids in the
hall poked their heads in and disrupted things. The teachers handed out
a letter describing what they hoped for the course. They asked that the
kids write back with their expectations for the course and with any questions they might have. Michael was very quiet and silenced the kids with
glances. Eventually, what felt like an enormous cloud of resistance
passed over, and the kids settled into writing. They were quiet for 10
minutes.

Mary divided the students into groups of five by having them count
off. They moved sluggishly into various parts of the room to share what
their expectations were. The students exchanged their ideas with some
animosity. One of the groups spoke mostly Spanish. They generated a list
of questions, which the recorder wrote down in English. "Will we go on
field trips? Are we gonna work in the whole group all the time? How
many credits do we get in here? In what? Do we have to go outside to
play these stupid games? Because I am not going outside to look like
an idiot."

Mary answered their questions. "This is an integrated course. You can
earn credit in math, English, social studies, science, and phys. ed. Up to
eight credits." She had to stop constantly to get the group to pay attention,
to stop talking. By some miracle, it was 12:00 and time for lunch. The kids
handed in their papers and raced out. Mary spoke to two of the boys who
were the most troublesome. They left; Paolo came in and the teachers col-
lapsed for a minute. It had been a rough beginning. Each activity brought
with it a fresh force field of resistance from the kids. The teachers had
expended enormous energy pulling the kids in.

Mary wailed, "I want to go home! I'm exhausted. What's going on?"

Paolo noted, "Some of the kids know each other really well, but others they don't know at all."

Michael reminded them, "They've just been on 2 weeks vacation. The
1st day is always tough. We have three new students."

Mary was still despondent, "Half the kids wouldn't play the games."

Paolo countered, "Most of them got involved eventually."

"Maybe we need to explain this week to them more."

"Part of the challenge is working on things, sticking to it. That's what
they are supposed to get from this week."

They moved over to the other building for lunch. Michael disappeared.
He usually ate in the community college cafeteria. Paolo and Mary belonged
to the lunch club. Each day a staff member brought lunch for the other

members—now about 16. This way, they only had to bring lunch once every 3 weeks. Mary and Paolo joined Nathaniel, Peter, and Marilyn, the other Project Challenge teachers. The day was tough for everyone. They reviewed what they'd done and rethought the afternoon. Although they had an hour for lunch, the time evaporated all too quickly. All the talk was about their course, their students, and their plans.

At one o'clock, Mary, Michael, Enrico, and Paolo reassembled the kids. They asked them to count off by twos and divided them in half again. Michael and Enrico took one group and Paolo and Mary took the other. There were far fewer students in the room than there had been in the morning. Mary reinforced being on time and put a word game up on the board. The kids solved it—it was the word *environment*. More students wandered in while they were playing the game. She reminded them that they needed to be on time. She asked the kids to pair up, which they did with no fuss, but with low energy. Each group got a letter from the word environment. She asked them to generate a list of words each of which started with the letter they had been given, and that reflected an environment. Acton was in her group. He talked incessantly. Paolo gently reminded him to be cognizant of others, not to dominate. Acton and his partner generated words quickly. He had a good vocabulary and called out words faster than his partner could write them down. Their list: *ranch, road, reconstruction, reservoir, railroads, Russia, religion, rain, revolution*. They wrote their words on big paper, which Paolo and Mary had handed out. The kids shared their lists. Engaged, the students concentrated and discussed the task among themselves.

Once they got all the lists up, they were asked to categorize the words on the list. By this time there were 19 kids in the room. Students walked out and went to the bathroom at the end of the hall whenever they wanted and wandered back in. Acton interrupted the discussion constantly. Mary's voice became sharp when she spoke to him though she continued to ask him to be respectful of others, to think before he interrupted. The categories: places, people, traditions, nature . . .

Mary gave the next set of directions. "Using one of the words as a springboard, write about an experience you had. For instance, I might write about my dad who wouldn't let me go away to college because of family traditions." Paolo passed out paper and pens while Mary clarified the instructions. The kids settled into quiet writing and wrote for a full half-hour. Mary asked the kids if they wanted her to group them for sharing; they said yes and she had them count off by threes. They moved into their groups.

Tesa wrote about the time when she wasn't doing very well in school so her mom sent her down to South Carolina to live with her aunt. She liked it there and started doing better in school, but she and her aunt didn't get along so she came back. She came to Cityscape because her mom didn't want her grades to slip.

Imbu shared that he had spent his first 8 years living in Ontario's out-country with his mom, dad, and grandmother. They never saw anybody else. Finally his folks got a tutor for him. He wondered why they had to do so much moving around.

The teachers wrote questions on the board: "How does a change in environment change a person's behavior? How do your parents and your home environment affect your life? How does war impact on family and friends?" They had a lively 10 minute discussion that centered around the questions. At 3:00, the teachers collected the students' writing and the kids pushed outside. Two students hung back to discuss scheduling problems with the teachers. Those solved, Michael, Paolo, Enrico, and Mary squeezed into Mary and Michael's office. The afternoon had been better for everyone. They talked fast, laughed about the difficulties, felt visibly relieved that the first day was over, that the project was underway, discussed who would do what tomorrow, and hurried over to the faculty meeting for which they were 20 minutes late.

Faculty meetings ran from 3:00 to 5:00 every Monday. The staff tackled significant issues and were paid $25.00 per hour for attending these meetings. Everyone was expected to attend and participate. Adrienne had divided the faculty into four working groups around issues that needed resolution. Faculty joined whichever group was of greatest interest to them. One group was working to develop a policy on affirmative action hiring. The staff wanted more minority teachers. Another group was debating whether the students should be awarded differentiated certificates. A third group puzzled over decision making—specifically, when a decision should be reconsidered. Another group worked on health issues—whether they might switch from selling junk food to healthy snacks in the school store. The groups worked until 4:15. Everyone moved back into a large circle and a reporter from each group outlined their recommendations to the larger group. The affirmative action policy group liked the current policy but suggested that they needed to develop an action plan that made the policy a reality. The nutrition group noted that the majority wanted healthful snacks, but that there was resistance from one member who believed that they needed to make money in the school store. They recommended the issue to the steering committee for a proposal the staff could consider. The decision-making group recommended that a procedure be established for the review of decisions made. This would require closer documentation of decisions made so that they could track the actual process when a review was required. The differentiated credit group suggested that everyone needed to have a discussion with the students in their family groups about differentiated credit. The purpose of the discussion would be to gather student opinions. The group agreed to reconvene to consider student recommendations. Discussion followed. The faculty left at 5:15.

Tuesday

Tuesday morning dawned bright and warm. It was spring in the middle of January. The morning faculty meeting clipped along—announcements, introductions of another batch of visitors, questions, and reminders for coffee money. I joined Michael on his way to his office prior to class. Michael grew up in Ireland in a poor, rural community. He went to college and graduated with a degree in chemistry and mathematics. It was while at graduate school that he had decided to teach, although he had grown up in a teaching family. His grandmother and a number of aunts and uncles were teachers. Because opportunity was limited in Ireland, he had come to the United States and had been here for the last 4 years. At first he had taught science in a large comprehensive high school. One of the students whom he quite had liked dropped out and eventually transferred to Cityscape. "I listened to him describe the school and it sounded so good for him that I thought it might be good for me too." Michael was a tall, quiet man. He deferred to Mary's dynamism, but was watchful of the students. As we walked to class, he described the turmoil he experienced in the Cityscape structure. "The students here are really excellent people. Individually, I like them. I do find it troublesome at times, wondering if they are getting enough science and math. And then there are times when I'd just like to go off by myself to teach what I want."

At 9:00, in their classrooms, the environment group was divided into three classrooms. Michael quietly asked the students to write about a learning experience that was important to them. For the most part, they wrote. Some students wandered in late. Michael gave them the assignment. Three girls, all dressed in baggy, faded blue jeans, white T-shirts, black leather belts and heavy shoes, scarves, and rows of silver bracelets, did nothing. They talked sometimes in Spanish, sometimes in English. In either language they talked so quickly their conversation was hard to catch, but it was generally about what they did outside school. One of the girls had dropped out several times, but found school easier than work so she had come back. Michael stopped by their group frequently and asked them to attempt the assignment. They flirted with him. He moved off and gave the next step in the assignment. "What have you done with this learning experience?" Most of the students wrote again for another 10 minutes. Enrico arrived and joined Michael. He too circled the groups but was more insistent with the kids, pushed them harder. Enrico was short, compact, and had a lot of energy. He was a paraprofessional at the school, but was working on getting his teaching certificate.

> I can relate to these kids. I grew up here in the Cuban community. I know what it's like. I got in lots of fights. I know about drugs, about skipping school, about bad family life, about gangs. I want so much to help these kids. I like it here because the staff treat me as an equal. I help build the curriculum with my team, and I do lots of other things as well, like working in the computer room. I hope to get a job teaching here when I finish.

This term, he was taking 19 credits plus working—a heavy load. He spoke Spanish to the Hispanic kids, and English to those who spoke English.

Michael offered different shapes cut out in colored paper and students selected one. The kids moved into groups with others who had picked their shapes. There were no complaints about the regrouping. As one of the boys moved, a condom fell out of his pocket. The kids howled. He was unperturbed. "I am a safe sex guy."

The majority of the students seemed quiet this morning—resistance all gone. The three girls remained uninterested. Each group was to select one learning story and to role play it. Three boys role played a fight one of the boys had had at his previous school. One boy played a member in a gang. He threatened to kill the main character. The role play flipped to the counselor's office where the counselor suggested that for his own safety he go to Cityscape. The kids watched with interest. This sparked the interest of the girls. The three girls chanted "Buddha head, Buddha head," as the main character walked back to his seat. Enrico stopped them immediately for being disrespectful. They got up next and role played smoking weed. The dialogue: "Everybody is all fucked up."

"Yeah, fucked up." They licked their fingers and pointed at the other kids, then shrieked with laughter. The rest of the kids sat quietly, looking bored. The girls were engaged in private jokes. Michael and Enrico asked them to sit down. Enthusiasm for the role plays had vanished. No one else volunteered. The positive tone in the room vaporized. The teachers gave the next assignment, which was to characterize a good school, and moved students back into working groups. The lists the kids generated were charged with sexual innuendoes. Nothing was too embarrassing to talk about. One of the boys kept dropping his pen in a very obvious way so that he could look up the short skirts of the girls sitting near him. They ignored him. Enrico entreated the kids to work—to stick with it. He moved from group to group. They told him this was really boring. He told them to persevere. He was like Mary in that he exuded good cheer and confidence in the kids. He told them that it would make sense to them eventually. Michael quietly listened to individual groups and then asked the whole group to make a master list of the qualities of a good school. As students wrote their lists on the board, Enrico eliminated the inappropriate comments while prodding the kids to keep going. By 11:00, the effort to keep the kids going was enormous, and the kids burst out of the room. The teachers again looked spent—as if they'd been moving concrete blocks uphill.

Everyone moved down campus to a large auditorium for the academic awards assembly. The kids were very rambunctious. The place felt like a basketball stadium during half-time in a play-off game. The crowd yelled, whistled, and jostled. The students switched seats repeatedly. Eventually awards were given for excellent grades and for earning enough credits to graduate. While the spectators thumped and cheered wildly, the kids who had received awards seemed pleased.

In the faculty lunch room, the teachers talked about engaging kids in consensus activities. They agreed that the morning's activities had not engaged the kids. They decided to stick with their plan—part of the design of this first week was that the kids would persevere through difficult activities to accept major challenges. They saw this first week as a sort of metaphor for the rest of the semester—facing challenges.

After lunch, the group was again divided into three. Paolo took one group to introduce them to the physical challenge part of the course. Mary took another third to introduce them to the videography work. Enrico and Michael introduced the animals project. Enrico was clearly excited about this activity. Despite the fact that it was January, the temperature was in the 70's, and so their group agreed to go outside. Once they were settled on the bleachers, Enrico explained that this assignment represented the kind of work they would be doing in the 6-week seminar on animals. During the rotation in which they studied animals, the students would be solving problems related to animals and their environments. They would be expected to do some writing—perhaps some brochures to inform the community. Today's activity was representative—if not as closely focused on animals as their later work would be. It was a problem which dealt with the environment. Everyone was given an egg, ten straws, and two pieces of tape. They were asked to create a structure that would protect their raw egg when dropped from eight feet. They must also advertise their invention. They divided into groups and set immediately to work.

Three boys and one girl gathered around their materials. The girl, Candy, removed herself and looked pouty. The three guys sat looking at the materials for a while. Imbu asked how many points they were going to get for this. Enrico jollied him along. Tony began bending the straws around the egg. Paul said that the Marine recruiter was coming to his house on Saturday. Considering the military was more critical since Desert Storm was underway. The other two guys rejected the Marines right away.

"The Marines brainwash you, man!"

"My cousin went into the Marines because he thought he was going to be real brave. He cried every night. He hated it!"

Tony said he'd figured the problem out. He was going to build a structure like a goal post.

"Not with our straws you're not!"

"That ain't gonna work."

"Well, an egg won't break if you drop it on its end," said Tony. "I learned that somewhere."

He explained his idea and drew a picture. They were hunched over the drawing, thinking. Imbu and Paul made some modifications. Imbu shouted at the girl to get her ass down there to help them. She responded by walking off. Tony told him to lay off her. She just found out that her new nephew was dying of some disease and probably wouldn't live to be a year old.

"Big deal," said Imbu. "School work is school work. My old man got shot and I was depressed, but I did my work. My grandmother died, and I still did my work." No sympathy. All three boys, while talking, had their hands involved in the building of the design. They ran into a problem trying to figure out how to close up the end of their structure. They sat back and looked at it for a while. They talked about whether they were going to go to college, when they would graduate, and whether they thought kids should be kicked out of the school if they didn't do their work. Enrico told them that he intended to test their contraption by dropping it off the bleachers. They teased him, "Enrico, man, what you been smoking?" As they finished up their egg basket, they began to do their advertisement. Imbu did the writing while the other two suggested ideas. The groups worked steadily for an hour and a half, designing and redesigning.

Bringing the whole group back together, Enrico dropped the eggs from midway up the bleachers with great ceremony. Half broke. The kids cheered wildly. Those whose eggs broke shouted explanations. Enrico asked the kids to debrief. What skills had they used? How had they figured this out? How had they worked together? What prior learning had they brought to this activity? An esprit d'corps developed—an opposite tone to the morning's work. The kids noted that they had really enjoyed this activity and would like to try it again, now that they've seen what happens. Everyone left in high spirits.

Michael and Enrico were jubilant as they met Mary and Paolo in their offices. Despite the fact that somebody else had developed this lesson plan, they loved it and found it had easily engaged the kids. Mary and Paolo had equally positive afternoon sessions. They reviewed attendance. A student came in to use the phone to check on her daughter. The teachers talked over why the morning activity was such a bomb. Should they scrap tomorrow's activity? Tomorrow they wanted the kids to work in groups to build consensus about ideal teachers. After some discussion, they decided to stick with it even though they knew that the kids were not responding well. They reviewed the rest of the week's activities and left Mary muttering to herself about the afternoon attendance. "Damn, damn, damn. Don't take this personally." She took the list to Adrienne on her way out of the school. If they created this all day thing to keep kids in school, they needed to do some more work.

Wednesday

Paolo's morning routine followed the familiar pattern: faculty meeting; then stop in office to check with team mates. Paolo Cagayan was in his first year of teaching. He was young, Asian, and always dapper in a comfortable sort of way. Although he had known for a long time that he wanted to teach, his family wanted more for him. Finally, despite their dismay, he had decided to follow his inclinations to teach. He saw it as a political act, an act of participation in a democracy. His undergraduate work had been in political science, and he had completed a masters-in-teaching degree at a prestigious eastern university. During his masters program, he had been introduced to the Coalition of Essential Schools and set off to get a job in one. He was very calm with the students and carried himself with uncharacteristic self confidence for a first-year teacher. He loved his students, loved teaching, and found that he could be so much more—a big brother, a teacher, a friend, a counselor, a champion, and a coach. He was committed to staying in this school at least until his original family group graduated in 3 or 4 years.

The students were divided into the same groups they had worked in yesterday afternoon and simply rotated to one of the other two activities. Paolo's group took a stress test as an introduction to the kinds of physical challenges they would be undertaking in the Ropes Course. The kids were stressed about money, college, graduating, and their home life. After the students had finished filling out the stress test and sharing the results, Paolo made the connection between stress and physical exercise as a means of release. To demonstrate, he got the kids up and moving around. They played Pass the Nickel, a pattern game, and did a challenge. Each student walked through two lines of students without laughing—or tried to.

The students moved from one activity to the next with no fuss. They debriefed about the morning by discussing the connection between stress and physical activity. They talked about teamwork and trust. The kids noted that even though the school was small and their classes were small, they didn't really know everybody in the class well enough to trust them. At 11:00, the group moved off to a lecture delivered by Students Against Drunk Driving.

Some of the teachers attended; others used the time for additional planning. Paolo zipped into his office to look over the kids' stress tests and to get ready for the afternoon. At lunch time, he attended a new teachers' meeting in the principal's office. Each new teacher in the building was paired with a mentor. Every Wednesday, they ate together to talk about things that were confusing to newcomers. The discussion ranged from how teachers could get computer time, to writing process training, to how to get classroom repairs done, to grading policies, and on to a discussion of essential questions. Adrienne did not dominate but moved the conversation back to students' intellectual and physical well-being at every opportunity.

In the afternoon, the Project Challenge Environment group was divided into two groups. Somehow, between 11:00 and 1:00 the kids had become wild. The weather had changed from beautiful and uncharacteristically warm to cold and dreary. The kids were to work in pairs to describe their fantasy school. They were to identify five teachers, outline five courses, and think about five rules that could guide the school. Paolo and Mary worked together with their group. Many students were late. Mary reminded them that it was important to arrive on time. Other kids got up and walked out. It was difficult to get any sense of the flow of the activity because there was so much moving around. The kids were rebellious; without being specifically rude to the teachers, they worked just on or over the margin of acceptability. After the two described their school, they were to join with another group of two. After comparing their schools, they needed to reach consensus about the kind of school they wanted. In twos their work was fairly serious—although disrupted. As the groups got larger, the descriptions of the schools became more riddled with sexual innuendo or the ridiculous: a topless school, a school that lasts only one hour per day. Paolo and Mary were busy policing the halls and keeping the groups working. They asked the kids to take this seriously, to no avail. Half way through the session, Mary looked angry, irritated. Paolo continued to prod the kids.

At the next step, the kids merged into three large groups. One group of particularly rowdy boys described their school to the group who joined them: They could smoke anywhere and anything; girls don't wear any clothes.

"Yeah, man. It's a school for safe sex."

"Where a man can come." They hooted; one of the girls rolled her eyes, looked extremely bored, and left the classroom. Mary went after her while Paolo asked the guys to be more creative, to move beyond the locker room stuff. The boys told the remaining girl to take notes. She ignored them and worked on the assignment by herself.

Mary got the three groups to share their findings toward the end of the period. Their work reflected a mixture of sarcasm and seriousness. The kids left disgruntled. All four teachers gathered together, frustrated, irritated.

Paolo yelled, "I felt like a monitor!"

"The kids were not serious."

"The kids were out of control."

"Why were there so many people out of class?"

"Was it the activity that was useless?"

"Maybe it was that the weather changed?"

"Who knows?" They were all talking at once. Mary reminded them to listen to each other. The group slowed down. They decided to consult a student or two and located Nancy. She had walked out on her group because the boys were ridiculing women. She looked as if she were about to be sent to prison. They asked Nancy why the lesson was so badly received. She said it was boring and ridiculous—creating a fantasy school. "Why should we do shit like that?"

"But we're going to use it," said Mary. "By the end of the week, we want to take the information you all have generated this week about good schools and good learning experiences. That information will form the basis for our challenge—the teachers' challenge for the remainder of the semester. We hope that your work will guide us—both in how we behave and in the subject material you want to cover over the next semester."

Nancy said, "Don't give me that. These activities are useless!" She was very direct and angry.

Enrico kidded her, "Would we lie to you? Come on, we're asking for your honest opinion."

"Then why didn't you tell us what you were going to do with the information?"

"For instance, we can add a unit in on sex ed if everybody wants it. It was on everybody's list," Mary said and added, "She's right, though. We should have told them what we were going to do with the information."

"But it would have wrecked the challenge part of the first week." said Enrico. "They need to understand that you have to tough some things out to get the rewards."

"Why were so many people walking in and out today?" Paolo asked Nancy.

"Because half of the kids weren't doing their work. I'm not going to sit around and listen to those guys talk about a topless school."

"So should we have intervened?"

"Maybe it would have helped to know that we were doing this for some good reason." She did not recommend that the teachers intervene. Nancy was calm now and thoughtful. They thanked her for her time.

They spent the rest of the afternoon discussing the activity, how they might have approached it differently, and how they would begin the last step tomorrow. They agreed that Mary would tell the group how they intended to use the information gained and that Enrico would tell them how he had felt during the afternoon session—like a cop, not a teacher.

They moved onto talking about Friday's activity. They had planned a large group challenge, but were unsure as to whether it would work. They reviewed the rules, what they needed, and who would do what.

The other Project Challenge team joined them at 3:30, looking just as exhausted. Mary had an agenda on the board: 1. How's it going? 2. Class lists; 3. Plan Friday; 4. ???? Nathaniel continued to talk about the lesson they had done today. Mary asked him to turn to something that concerned them all. He continued. She stopped him again. Peter asked Mary why she didn't just tell them what she wanted them to do? She acknowledged that they were all having a tough first week, but if they didn't work together, they'd never get through it. They moved on to a general review, comparing and contrasting how things were going with the environment group and the group focused on family. It was clear from their discussion that building new curriculum was difficult and required more hours than they could find in a 24-hour stretch. They continued to work until 5 o'clock.

Thursday

Thursday arrived cold and nasty. At 9:00, Mary, Michael, Paolo, and Enrico brought the whole group of Project Challenge Environment students together. The kids were quiet and passive. The teachers described how they had felt yesterday afternoon, why they were doing the activity assigned, and asked the kids to make a commitment to their work and to be serious about it. There was no time allocated for discussion. Several students muttered that they had no choice about the commitment, but did not raise a general rebellion. The task for the morning session was to revise the work they had done yesterday for their fantasy school, select a name, select a location, design and draw the school, establish an agenda, and flesh out any details they felt were incomplete. They were also to make a presentation at the end of the period. The kids complained that they should not have to prepare presentations for the whole group because they wouldn't have enough time to get their work done. The teachers agreed, suggested that they could just report progress, and the kids moved into three groups.

Four boys looked at the teachers they'd listed yesterday. "Who is that child psychologist? Dr. Spock?"

"Na, get somebody real."

"Dr. Spock is real, man!"

"Let's design the school first and come back to the teachers." Someone else jumped to naming the school. "What about Michael Torres School?"

"Reach for the Stars School?"

"Yeah, Star School, and the logo will be a star. The outline of the school could be a star."

"Yeah." Tim started writing, taking down suggestions, and reviewing the rules they'd need. All four boys huddled into a circle, thinking hard. Michael visited their group. They told him they were revising what they did yesterday and turned back to the task. Tony got out a pencil, some paper, and a ruler and began to draw the star. Tim told the other two guys to do something. He listed a number of tasks: somebody needs to keep track of the buildings; somebody, to draw the place; and somebody else, to work on the logo.

"Where we gonna put this school?"

"Fort Lauderdale."

"Yeah, on an island. We can get a boat."

"Put it in California."

"The star outline should be of the whole campus."

"No, it's of the whole school."

They added dorms, a football field, saunas, and swimming pools. Tim told one of the guys who was still brainstorming to make a list of the buildings and to make it neat. The conversations flipped back and forth over their individual tasks.

"We should have a planetarium—with laser stuff."

"I've never been to one."

"They are real cool—you can look right up into the galaxy . . ."

"Sigmund Freud taught psychology."

"How big is the gym?"

"How do you multiply width times height?" Mary showed them the equation. They worked the problem. They spent considerable time thinking about the athletic facilities. Then they added a large lab, a library, and argued that the library should be bigger than the gym. They added a museum of natural history, a concert hall, and practice rooms for musicians. The last fellow to join in drew the school's logo and name in bubble letters.

"Damn, we are running out of time. Who is going to do the presentation?" They reviewed what they had done and who would do what. An hour and a half flew by. All the students worked hard. There was none of the chaos of yesterday afternoon.

During the reporting, teachers and students alike were amazed at the detail and the thoughtfulness that had gone into the reports. Most of the groups developed mission statements and rules, and selected teachers consonant with the mission. One of the groups called their school "Intelligent Young Minorities." Their charter read, "IYM is a school designed to fulfill the needs of our nation's intelligent young minorities. Our classes are preplanned to allow our students to identify with successful minorities from which our students can learn to be aggressive, dominant individuals with extremely promising futures. Although IYM classes are aimed towards educating minorities, we do not deny applications from other races. We do not discriminate. We educate." A big debate ensued.

"This school is against everything Dr. King was trying to teach us."

"Yeah, it's a segregated school."

"But maybe we need a school focused on minorities. We didn't exclude whites."

The teachers pulled them back to listen to the next group's report. The schools the students had designed revealed a good deal about how they thought schooling should be done. They did not eliminate academics— rather, they suggested facilities that would allow them greater hands-on activities. In addition, students in all the reports were more involved in the decision making in their schools.

At 11:00, all the students moved off into their family group sessions. At 12:00, the eight Project Challenge teachers ate together noting that they felt as though it should be the end of the first semester. The 1st week was tough. They discussed students who wanted transfers, the balance of numbers, and their attendance rates.

During the afternoon session, the three groups of students rotated through the third introductory session. Mary's room was temporarily occupied by the photographer who had come to take school pictures. She punted and moved the kids down two floors. She wanted to introduce them to the video camera so that they might get a sense of the videography unit. First she put them in pairs and handed them blindfolds. One person was the camera, the other the cameraman. The blindfold was lowered from the camera whenever the cameraman wanted to take a shot. The kids moved through the halls while doing this and rotated roles. They debriefed after a few minutes, and the kids talked about how limited the scope of the camera was. Mary divided them into groups of three. They generated five interview questions. She reminded them to generate acceptable questions. What was acceptable to them was not always acceptable to her. That done, she gave them a brief overview of how to use a camcorder. Each student took three roles—the cameraman, the reporter, and the interviewee. The kids moved off with two cameras to tape their interviews. Igar came in 20 minutes late. She told him to catch up from the others. He was 6'5" and was dressed completely in red. He moved in with a group. The kids found a space in the stairwell. The interviews began and the questions quickly blended into a standard set: How do you feel about the war? (Desert Storm had just begun.) What are your plans for the future? What do you like to do the most? How do you feel about sexual intercourse? The answers varied.

"I think the war is like kinda stupid, but I think we should bomb them up and get it over with."

"I think the war is a stupid thing because we are shedding blood we don't need to be. Shedding blood for oil when we got enough already. We should get out."

"I like sex."

"I think people should practice safe sex."

"I will not answer questions about sexual intercourse. It's none of your business."

After everyone had been interviewed, they returned to the classroom and watched each segment. The kids were very attentive even though there was a good deal of repetition and not much action. They laughed about the funny things and clapped at the end of each one. Mary asked them what they would do differently.

"I'd come up with better questions."

"I'd make sure the light was better."

"I always thought I was more handsome than that!"

"You are!"

"You're uglier than that!"

"I'd get a better mike and pay more attention to what I was doing with my hands and things."

Mary explained that for 6 weeks of the term, students in videography would work in small groups and would develop a question about some environmental issue. They would put together a short, 10 minute feature. She explained that it took a lot of footage to come up with 10 minutes and that the editing took enormous amounts of time. One of the students volunteered that she had taken a class with Mary last year and they had filmed a hooky party (a party held during school hours) where all the kids were drunk or high. But they had never finished editing it. She had hoped they would be able to finish because she thought it would be good for kids to see. The kids playing hooky looked pretty down and out. Students asked questions until past the time to leave—about topics, cameras, teams. Enthusiasm for the project was high as the kids left.

Mary, Michael, and Paolo left school almost immediately to go to Mary's house not too far away. They needed one extended block of time per week to review what they'd been doing and to plan forward. Sometimes they stayed at school till late; other times they met at someone's house.

First they talked about a student in Paolo's section today who had completely blown up after the stress test. He shouted that he masturbated every day, that it was the only way he could reduce stress, and that he hated "these fucking stupid activities." Paolo talked about feeling stunned first, angry second, and personally attacked third—then just wondered how he might best support the student who was clearly troubled and more often than not an outcast. They talked about how varied the kids' responses to activities had been during the week—mornings bad, afternoons good or afternoons bad, mornings good—like a roller coaster for the teachers. Generally, the kids had not liked most of the activities related to creating the perfect school. The teachers agreed that they should have made the purposes for the first week's activities explicit to the students. Still they were not willing to abandon their original plan. They wanted to do a large group activity with the whole 50+ students on Friday. It was a blindfolded activity that they had done during their Project Challenge training, and they all loved it. They were not sure the kids were going to like it, but if it worked, the kids would learn about team building, trust, and problem solving. They decided to try it anyway, but to talk to the kids about why they wanted to do this, what their experience had been like with it, and to give it a real try. They moved on to their integrated curriculum.

"Okay," said Mary. "Let's see where we are overall. Environments, the home, the city, the state. We're going to read *The Family Installment,* by Edward Rivera. It is his memories of growing up Hispanic. I loved the book, but it has two trouble spots. The grandfather commits suicide and there is another scene where several young men have sex with cows. The author teaches at a local university, and I might be able to get him to stop by. I think we also have to deal with sexuality. These kids think about it and talk about it every day. Maybe we should do a survey on sexuality."

Michael paled. "Just ideas, you know."

Over the next couple of hours they downed two large pizzas that Mary's husband had picked up. The course, as they envisioned it in their introductory week, had two components—a seminar and the rotational projects in videography, animals, and the Ropes Course. In math they wanted the kids to get ready for the statewide exam and so wanted to cover fractions, decimals, percentages, and graphing. They searched for integrating hooks—surveys, problems that could be related to the environment. Math could be covered in the seminar, but maybe they could do it in the animals section, too. Phys Ed was built into the Ropes Course, which was being set up in their gym. The kids would do family histories as a result of their reading—part of a history requirement. Each of the groups would produce a video tape that centered on some problem having to do with the environment. Each group would decide the focus of the video. They'd have to do research, some interviewing, some script writing, and some editing. Then they'd have to get the reactions of others. The kids would do substantial writing—but not many finished pieces—a problem to be solved. The kids would read two novels and a number of articles—many of them about environmental issues. English would be covered in both the seminar and in the research and writing done in the rotational projects. The biology requirements would be covered in the animals project—kids would be building and studying various animal environments. Field trips were planned to a local aquarium, the zoo, and a museum of natural history. Paolo noted that they should deal with enculturation—another topic in their history curriculum. They agreed to consult with the art teacher. The students would create their own environments with her; the teachers needed to know how much time the art teacher needed and when she needed to get started. This project would come out of the seminar time.

The challenge was to ensure that in the midst of their integrated unit, kids were gaining the skills and knowledge they needed to function in a discipline-centered system. Credits were still awarded in subject areas. At the end of the year, the kids had to take minimum competency tests required by the state. Considerable discussion circled around whether kids were getting what they needed to succeed.

After checking to make sure that they were covering important substance in English, history, science, math, p.e., and art, they went back over the schedule for the next week, blocking in what would happen when, and who would be responsible. Each of the teachers needed time off to do some additional planning. Michael needed to generate the survey, contact the zoo, and build part of one aquarium. They found time for him to rotate out of the classroom to do those things and did the same for Mary and Paolo.

They turned to an assessment measure they had learned at Project Challenge. In order to set expectations at the outset, the teachers decided they would do "full value" projects in each of the three rotational sessions. That meant that kids established goals at the outset of the project and drew a representation of the project—a metaphor or a being or something. Their goals went inside the drawing. At the end of the project the kids came back to their goals and put red or green dots indicating where they felt they had succeeded and where they thought that they had stopped. They wanted the kids involved in self assessment as much as possible.

Late in the evening, their energy flagged. They were excited by the heightened flexibility they had gained by having the kids all day. They were a bit dismayed that the plan they had developed so carefully during the last 6 months still seemed to be a skeleton—requiring flesh and bones in a hurry.

Friday

Friday morning, the teachers divided the group into threes. Each group wrote about yesterday's activities—what they'd done, what they'd gained. The kids settled right into writing and wrote for half an hour in complete quiet. The teachers facilitated a sharing session.

The rest of the morning was spent in the gym in a big challenge activity. All three groups of students were blindfolded and told they were part of a color group—blue, green, or red. The object of the game was for each color group to reassemble and then to form a leg of a complete triangle. The teachers, who had loved this activity during their training, believed that by trying to solve problems without sight, by attempting to find group members, and by working together, the kids would learn about cooperation, concentration, and other skills they needed for their rotational projects. Two boys got in a fight during the directions. Several of the girls sat out because they didn't trust the boys. Nearly all of the kids fiddled with their blindfolds so that they could see a little. The debriefing was not revealing because the kids simply weren't into it. They dispersed to family groups at 11.

At lunch, the two teams of Project Challenge teachers ate together again. Nathaniel wanted to review the rules to the challenge that Mary's team had done in the morning. They all warned him that it hadn't gone so well. They decided that the kids in their group simply did not know each other well enough to enjoy the activity. Nathaniel persevered. Mary thought, too, that maybe they just hadn't given the directions well enough. They reviewed the rules. A family group teacher cornered Paolo. She was the family group leader of the student who blew up in his class yesterday, and he mentioned the incident to her. She explained a little about the quality of the kid's home life, which was violent and abusive. He was a sensitive, talented kid who was very angry and worked hard to shock people. She said she would talk with the kid about the encounter.

All three teachers worked with the large group in the afternoon. Although there were supposed to be 57 students, only 26 showed up. The students listed all of the activities they had done during the week. Then they wrote about the purposes of the week, how everything fit together, how useful the week had been, and how it fit into the larger scheme of the whole semester. The students were asked to evaluate their own participation. Mary reminded them that although kids were used to giving evaluative feedback, they would be asked to do more of it because this was a new course. The kids wrote begrudgingly. The next task was to write the headline and a short newspaper article describing the first week in Project Challenge. A group of five had a serious conversation about several genres of music while they coached one girl who wrote their article. The energy in the room was again rebellious. The kids wrote only derogatory things about the course and a negative momentum escalated. They shared their work toward the end of the period. Because of the negativity, the teachers sagged but carried on without censoring the kids' work.

Mary explained the point value of the course and asked the kids to fill out a goal sheet—how many points they hoped to earn each week. Paolo asked them to add the characteristics of good partners in group work. He asked the kids to think about who they would work with on their projects as they began the rotation next week. At the very end of the period, Mary got everyone standing up holding hands to affirm the fact that they had made it through the week, to affirm that they were committed to working together, and to working things out so that the kids graduate. She asked for a moment of silence with eyes closed so that everyone could make their intentions for the next week. Although a few were still rebellious, their friends brought them into line and the day ended on a nice note. Many of the students wished their teachers a good weekend as they streamed out the doors.

Once all the kids were gone, all three teachers burst into laughter. They laughed over the activities that didn't work. They howled over these, gasping and sputtering. They laughed at some of the things the kids had said. They laughed at their images of all those giant, tough kids holding hands. They laughed in relief over a beginning completed.

They retired to their offices where they divided up all of the written activities the kids had been doing all week, assigned points to each, read through some of their work, and headed off to drink beer at Mary's house with their other four teammates—to commiserate, to celebrate, and to refuel for the next week.

Eighteen Weeks Later

By the end of the semester, much had happened for the four Project Challenge Environment teachers. As they packed up for the summer, they reviewed their first semester of whole day integrated teaming. Michael was absent from the discussion. The Ropes Course had proved too difficult to do in the gym for extended periods of time, so after the 2nd week, they had made it part of the seminar time and had developed a third rotational project: Kids were to investigate the culture of their community. In working on this, the students had to strengthen their observational and interviewing skills, and then learn to develop field notes and final reports. The teachers' discussion moved quickly:

MARY: We don't know whether our attendance was better yet or not; we haven't had time to compare this semester's records to last. But we do know that the kids who stayed really liked the program and recommended it to others.

PAOLO: And we did keep good track of the kids and published regular records of who was cutting. Some of the kids didn't like the fact that we could hold them so closely accountable.

MARY: All in all, I think three of the four of us would at least say that this was a much better way to go. I was able to finish three video tapes—one on pregnant teens, another on the life of a neighborhood park, and a third that was the school's video yearbook. We've never had enough time to bring things to completion.

PAOLO: We took a lot of trips and we also had some pretty amazing days— breakthrough days. We did a kind of Foxfire project[3] with the kids in Seminar. They generated a bunch of questions about landfill and garbage and then we went on a field trip to a landfill place. Because the kids had been working on interviewing techniques while doing their family histories, they fanned out over this garbage dump and started interviewing people.

MARY: When we came back, they decided to start a recycling project here for the school. We didn't get it finished, but we got it started.

ENRICO: They went for walks along the local river, too, observing conditions of sanitation along the river. That made them think. We went to the zoo and the aquarium; then we made mini-environments in tanks here at school. Some we purposefully polluted. Others were polluted by outsiders—because we had trouble locking the room. Made 'em think hard then when we went to the landfill!

PAOLO: Other things happened, too, in the classroom—which the others tell me don't happen all the time. The kids really got into the descriptions of their community. They yelled for more time, started asking us to rearrange the schedule so they would have more time. Tim wrote this shell of a piece on discovering a kid who was dead—knifed on his street. We asked him to flesh it out—to write more detail. He looked at us like we were sick, and said, "To do that, I'll have to relive it."

MARY: But he did it. He kept working on it and working on it. We all decided that he should not have to do everything everybody else was doing in the family history unit because he was really doing something worthwhile . . .

PAOLO: When he was done we wanted him to read it, but he was embarrassed and said no. Mary finally got him to let her read it, and the kids were really awed by it. They said in their final evaluations of the unit that they hoped they would be able to write as well as he could.

MARY: Then, I had an amazing day with one of the groups in the video project. We were talking about what makes for a good environment. In October, one of the guy's best friends died of a drug overdose. He has never talked about it at school—but everybody knows that they were really tight. He started to cry and talked about friends and how important friends are and how he is dreading summer because his friend won't be there for him to hang around with. One of the other guys in the class put his arm around him and everybody started to cry as he talked about how hard the year had been and how he would never have made it if it hadn't been for his family. Everybody was sobbing; those two big boys with their arms around each other was enough to send anybody off, but, geez, it was time to go, so I asked them to hold hands for a minute to acknowledge the experience we'd shared. A new kid said, "Fuck you, man, I ain't holding hands with nobody!" and the kid who'd been talking, who complained like crazy at the beginning of the semester about doing baby shit stuff, yelled, "Listen asshole, we hold hands in this school, so you better hold hands!" and grabbed his hand. That new kid held hands without a word. I never would have predicted that this group of kids would get so tight. That was a very powerful experience.

PAOLO: We got to know the kids much better working with them all day long every day. That made a huge difference. We also had a number of kids who made major strides in the Ropes Course—kids did things they never thought they could do. Cheri showed the whole group how to do a rope climb that was very difficult. She said it was the first time in her life that she knew what it was like to lead other people.

MARY: And we had to deal with the fact that the three of us did not believe that Michael was pulling his weight. We established a number of conditions for working together at the outset of the term like: you can't talk about a team member to other team members unless you've been honest with the one who's driving you nuts first; everybody has to agree to work together for the full semester—no quitting midstream, which means we have to work out our differences; if a team member asks for help the rest of the team has to pitch in; any team member has the right to ask questions about another team member's performance and responsibility.

PAOLO: Michael was hard to work with because he is so quiet, and he didn't do anything to help us integrate math or science much either.

MARY: The group set meetings to help him figure out how to integrate math because Enrico helped him with the science. We made a lot of suggestions like charts and graphs and surveys. But he just didn't follow through. So, in the long run, we had to tell him that we wouldn't team with him again because he didn't hold up his end of the bargain.

PAOLO: We made a lot of changes too. What we thought we were going to do in that first week was not what we ended up doing!

Furthermore, the teachers had developed a new report card that focused on anecdotal records of a student's performance, and then provided space for both the student and the parents to make substantial comments. They had wanted something that would give parents better information about their child's work, while acknowledging the integrated nature of their curriculum. They admitted that the new report card was tough on the parents—they wanted more traditional information—how their student was doing in each subject. The teachers also acknowledged that they hadn't prepared the parents well enough, and that they had more work to do.

In addition, the faculty made two changes as a result of the Challenge teams' experimentation. One month into the semester, they agreed to move the family group period from 11:00 AM to 9:00 so that the Challenge group could have more flexibility. Then, at the end of the year, based on reactions from the staff and students, the whole faculty decided to go to whole day teams. As a result, they dismantled the three tier system they'd spent 5 years constructing.

STEPPING BACK

After some time to reflect, the teachers described what was new for them in this experimental semester. Issues of subject matter integration, teaming, and experimenting all took on new dimensions.

What's Different?

Issues of Integration

The Cityscape teachers had been working on integrated instruction for a long time. When the school first opened, the teachers agreed to work in teams, and so for 6 years had been gathering experience. Paolo explained, "We want to integrate because we believe that we provide a more coherent learning experience for the kids—more life-like. In the everyday course of events, I don't experience things as English, history, or geometry. I have problems to solve that require that I read, think about past experience, and then do some figuring. So that's what we want for the kids." When the school began, the teachers tended to stick to their disciplines and to divide the labor of a unit along disciplinary lines. Gradually, they came to feel that the divisions were artificial, and so they began to experiment with essential questions and to plan their curriculum together. Each team member was respected for whatever disciplinary expertise he or she brought, but was not limited to it.

Paolo summarized what they would like to shoot for now: "We'd like a seamless curriculum—where all of the subject areas are blended into the projects we've chosen to work on. This term we made progress, although there are still some very obvious rough spots. I don't think the kids were aware that they were doing English when we were reading the two novels we used. Nor were they aware that they were doing 'art' when they worked with Alice, the art teacher, to make city environments. In this way, learning becomes enmeshed in the actual work students are doing, so they learn through application. It's much more powerful."

Mary continued Paolo's train of thought, "This term, we made progress with English, art, science, and history, but we have a ways to go with math. Science could have been more strongly connected, too."

"Building integrated units gives kids more time to work on exhibitions—real demonstrations of what they know and can do. Like Tim's piece on finding the murdered guy or Igar's video on teenage pregnancy," added Enrico.

"Two other things," said Mary. "Teachers come fresh to the subject when we integrate. Because the essential question is usually new, we come at our subject areas from a different angle. I think that helps to prevent burnout. We also have come to recognize that the kids retain stuff better. Though they might not be able to spout dates and facts for a college bowl game, they do remember what they learned from year to year, and it crops up in discussions."

"There were difficulties, too. It takes so much TIME." Paolo's comment was close to a wail.

"The more integrated we get, the more time we need. We have to plan together because there isn't any good pre-packaged material. Then we have to grade papers together because we have to be consistent. We have to debrief daily so that we can attend to homework and requirements." Mary sounded strained from the effort.

Enrico pointed out another fear, "We are not sure that it is prepping the kids for college. Believe me, I just finished college. You have to remember facts. And you don't have a group all the time to help you understand things."

"And this particular change has been hard to explain to the parents. They need to understand why kids aren't taking discrete subjects."

Paolo spoke thoughtfully, "I have mixed feelings too, because I got a lot of factual information in my own education and some of that has been valuable. But, on the other hand, I think that exploring specific themes and topics in depth gives our students a better grasp of what history is, who it affects, and who makes history. Perhaps they won't know when the Emancipation Proclamation was signed, but they can talk about the civil war and how it affected blacks, the South, and how it affected ordinary people in ways that I think students who get the traditional curriculum can't. I think that is much more valuable. Much more useful."

Then, there was the issue of math. Michael was not as committed to building integrated curriculum as the others. All along, the team had believed that they were being very clear with Michael about what they expected, and individuals were talking to him regularly. Later in the term, he had the students doing math worksheets during some of their project time. Although his reasoning was good—that the kids needed the practice before they took the statewide exam—his actions belied his original commitment to integrate. Mary, as the team leader, was forced to confront him at the end of the school year.

And there were systemic hurdles to jump—the state-mandated leaving exam, for example. This year, they stopped at the end of the year to prep the kids for the exam—something they do every year, but do with irritation and disgust. They were in constant discussion about whether they should try to integrate the test material or whether they should just set up tutorials to help kids cram.

Issues of Teaming

The integration of instruction is doubly compounded by the fact that teachers worked on teams. Typically, teachers work alone and are used to working alone in schools. "When we decide to integrate curriculum and instruction, we end up working in teams. We've learned a lot about teaming—both its value and its problems." Mary described further, "I am much stronger when I work with others, and as a result, I get further with the kids. Teaming lends a richness to the classroom that just isn't there when one person works alone. It's impossible to know whether what I am doing is good or right when there is nobody else to check it out with."

Paolo nodded, "There are serious limits to 'one teacher/one classroom'; I keep running into examples of my own individual limits. When you are working with one or two other people, you have so much more to draw on—a larger knowledge base, more resources, different styles. As a first-year teacher, I think everybody should be paired. There were times in my sessions where I was working alone when the kids asked me a question that I just couldn't answer. Sometimes the silence turned weird because I just didn't know what to do next. When Mary or the others were in the room, they could help me out. Sometimes, they leapt in to save the discussion. Other times, they were able to talk it over with me so I could see what happened."

Other benefits percolated. These teachers got to know each other better and became much closer than they would have ordinarily, which made work more fun. They troubleshot for each other, validated each other's expertise, and provided better support for the kids because they hired fewer substitutes and because they had multiple perspectives on the kids. Adrienne believed that teaming was the best staff development available. These teachers were conducting their own workshops on new techniques, then trying them out, revising them, and trying them again.

Teaming also required special commitment. Mary, Enrico, Michael, and Paolo outlined several working conditions made explicit between them from the outset. They learned that they had to think in advance about the ways in which they would work together. They forged a kind of contract, which they all had to agree to in advance, that they believed helped them to stick together and to work things out. With this agreement, they hoped to forge a culture of honesty and greater trust, while admitting that conflict was likely to arise.

Teaming meant that all of them, at some time or another, had to teach out of their disciplines, and they also had to teach lessons generated by someone else. Functioning as generalists was not as big a deal as others sometimes make it. It happens all the time within disciplines. Paolo illustrated, "I had to be a generalist in my first history class. I assigned an essay, and the kids said, 'What's an essay?' I was taken aback. I thought everybody knew what an essay was even if I didn't know how to explain it. I thought, 'I don't know how to do this!' but to the kids I said, 'Well, you start with a topic sentence and then support, support, support.'" Echoes of his high school English teacher . . .

All of the teachers taught out of their areas of specialization during their experimental project. Most of them loved the opportunity to branch out and enjoyed the things they learned. Paolo taught P.E. in the Ropes Course. Mary taught algebra in the middle of the seminar. Michael coached kids through work with a novel. Enrico helped kids do role plays to understand their neighborhood environment. When they knew they would be teaching out of their disciplines, they learned how to organize the work so that they felt adequately prepared. Lessons prepared for the group had to be reviewed well in advance of the actual teaching time—not handed out 10 minutes before class or even the night before. The teachers needed adequate time to make the lessons their own, to review them, time them out, and think them through. Then they needed the opportunity to review them just prior to teaching and immediately afterwards. New lessons can often be confusing simply because they are a dash through the unknown. Group talk often helps to clarify difficulties and iron out wrinkles.

In addition, at each of their weekly meetings, the teachers had to swing back and forth between discipline centered requirements and their integrated project to ensure that kids were getting what they needed to pass standardized tests and to move forward. Although they were, for the most part, satisfied that the kids were gaining rich knowledge and skills, the teachers worried about whether their students would be able to cope in college where integrated instruction was not the norm.

Issues of Experimentation

The four Environment teachers spent the entire spring semester field testing the new curriculum and new instructional techniques in the new daily structure. Experimentation is, to a certain degree, the norm at Cityscape as teachers struggle to search for better ways to work with their students. As with everything else, both benefits and dilemmas arise. "Almost every term, we build a new curriculum. Part of that is so that we can stay fresh. Part of it is so that we can deal with topical issues. We also have a transitory student population—here one term, gone the next—so we need a flexible curriculum. It's also part of the fun of working together—to create something new," explained Mary.

"But we sure learned our limits," added Paolo. "We had this grand vision at the beginning of the semester. Planned to do a lot of things. 'Less is more,' we kept saying to ourselves, to quote one of the nine Common Principles. Every time we'd get together for a group planning session, we'd dream up more possibilities. We have to learn how to trim things down to a manageable scale. This term, many of the projects we started were never brought to closure. For instance, the kids in my ethnography unit were scheduled to do a magazine of their family projects. We got everything onto the computers and edited, but ran out of time just when we should have begun laying the magazine out."

"It's a problem, assessing the amount of time a project takes. It's not only tough assessing how long the kids will take, but how long it will take us as teachers to get everything together." Enrico had spent enormous time rounding up old tanks so that the kids could use them in the Animals and Aquariums project.

"It's also tough to deal with the uncertainty," said Mary. "That first week, we knew that the kids were not wildly enthusiastic about designing a school, but we knew that it was an exercise in team building, and so we persevered. It's hard to tell whether they benefited from our persevering, or whether we should have changed direction. We know for sure that we should have told them why they were doing what we wanted them to do."

"Then, the kids who complained the loudest about the games that we played the first week asked why we quit doing them later on. And we all agreed that the group of kids who had the Ropes Course unit during the first 4 weeks jelled into the most cohesive group," Paolo added.

The conversation went on ranging over what they had done, what they could have done, and what they should have done. Already they were planning for the next year. Mary, Paolo, and Enrico would teach with Nathaniel, one of the teachers from the other Project Challenge team. This time, the course would focus around a history of their city, and of course, they would have their students for the whole day.

Support

In a school like Cityscape where things were different already, this group of teachers kept pushing. I asked them what conditions or circumstances enabled them to keep going. They agreed that decision-making structures, the culture of directness, and shared leadership enabled them to push ever harder on behalf of their students. They also noted that teaming, the ability to integrate, and greater control over their schedules were powerful supporting elements.

Decision-Making Structures

Adrienne had started the school a number of years previously and had ensured from the outset that the school would be run by consensus. That meant that everyone had to be involved in decision making, whether they liked it or not. Over the years, they had developed a number of management strategies so that actually reaching full consensus didn't hang them up. Mary's team's interest in whole-day school was a good example. Although the whole faculty had not been willing to agree to move to whole-day school, they were willing to allow two teams to experiment as long as they made weekly reports about what was going on and what was problematic.

Adrienne noted that this structure had made the rest of the faculty much more interested in what the teams were doing, and had changed the nature of their resistance. The larger faculty had been engaged in problem solving with the experimenters and had been expected to critique it openly so that the experimenters could be more thorough.

Because everyone had been involved in the decision making, they had developed a much stronger culture of discussion and analysis. Someone in the group would invariably ask whether the proposal they were considering blended with the goals of the school, or whether a new instructional or assessment technique had visible, tangible, positive effects for kids. Once the positive potential of a particular innovation had been determined, the whole staff had been genuinely interested in the results.

Another aspect of their decision making structure was that the staff handled many of the major decisions frequently left to administrators or central office folks in other school districts. The Cityscape staff determined how they would spend professional development money. The Project Challenge team had elected to go all together to a week-long seminar that demonstrated how to make school much more adventuresome. This week together had given them some techniques and materials that had helped them to integrate for whole days. The staff had also elected a hiring committee that oversaw the hiring of new staff. Most recently, they'd determined that team members should hire their own colleagues.

In another way, their group decision making required that teachers take more responsibility for difficult decisions in the school. Michael had been told by several teams that he was not a team player. Although the staff had originally hoped that Adrienne would get rid of difficult people, she was adamant that they had to act together in these decisions too, or in no time, a subversive culture would develop around decisions she had made that some others didn't like.

A Culture of Honesty and Directness

The decision-making structure they had chosen fostered a culture of honesty and directness. Mary noted that in her previous school experiences, the administration had set policy, staff had disagreed in private, and as a result, little was accomplished. In this school, everyone was required to take a stand. Mary learned that conflict did not have personally embarrassing consequences and that confrontation did not involve shouting or disparaging comments. She had learned over time to consider the views of others as helpful and had come to see confrontation as necessary to her own personal growth and that of her team members.

Shared Leadership

Cityscape was a school that had very strong leadership, though the behaviors and strengths were quite different from those in traditional, hierarchical schools. Adrienne set the agenda for meetings with input from others, established processes that involved everyone, and then participated as a single voting member of the group. When the group deferred to her or tried to give her voice greater authority than their own, she pointed that out to them. She continuously pointed out that if the school depended on her voice, it would not succeed beyond her tenure there. She established the team leaders' group through the staff decision-making process and then worked with them for several hours each week on issues of leadership.

Mary was supported in establishing meeting agendas, sticking to timelines, keeping people on task, confronting troublesome team members, and establishing team rules. The team leaders' group also were vigilant of each other to ensure that none of them were operating hierarchically. The modeling that Adrienne provided for the whole staff was repeated by the team leaders so that time was well used, and all participated.

Challenges

Like every staff engaged in change, these teachers had encountered several challenges that confounded them and caused great frustration. Although they had experienced many of the same challenges that Kathryn and others had, their unique circumstances raised several others.

The Difference Between Support and Willingness to Participate

Despite the thoroughness of their pre-experiment agreements, their team had not agreed thoroughly enough about the importance and the power of integration. Michael, all along, had believed that the kids were not getting enough math to get them through the competency tests. He had believed that the kids needed skill and drill practice, and, although he could not counter the force of the original commitment, he had slipped a few worksheets in during seminar periods and had ignored the group's suggestions about how he might integrate math into the Project Challenge focus. Michael's unwillingness to integrate had belied his attitudes towards mathematics and teaching and learning. Although it was likely that Michael himself had not known how strongly he felt about this at the outset, their mutual discovery of his beliefs had made the term difficult for everyone. The question they still asked themselves at the end, and had not answered satisfactorily, was how they might avoid this circumstance in the future: how they might better determine the difference between general support for their approach and real willingness to participate fully.

Finding Time to Experiment

Preparing and field testing a new unit or course takes much time. There is the curriculum to gather, develop, and prepare; teaching techniques to consider; assessments to match to both; and schedules to set, among other pressing needs. Although this team had had the capacity to free people up to run errands, to gather materials, and to make arrangements, and although they had had mutual planning time each day, they had still found the time inadequate. Because they had enjoyed working together, they had set up another meeting each week to work at someone's home or after school, and still they had been pressed for time. They had come to understand that time is one of those resources that is always in short supply.

Dealing with Uncertainty and Ambiguity

Mary and Paolo both pointed out that they always had a tough time knowing when to change things and when to hold steady to their plans. When trying a new curriculum for the first time, they had floated in a sea of ambiguity and uncertainty. Did the kids get what they were trying to do? Was their work what the teachers had hoped for? If not, why not? Should they go back and do it again? How many of the problems could be attributed to teachers' miscalculations? Although they had learned to ask students to help them understand when things weren't going right, they had also been unsure whether what they were encountering from the kids was simple resistance to change or whether there were serious problems. Fortunately, because they were working on teams, they had had multiple perceptions to draw on. This, however, had not eliminated their own confusion.

The Question of Rigor and Quality

Kids in this school were generally given points for doing work. This did not necessarily ensure that they did their work well or that they learned to distinguish between a fine effort and a weak effort. Sometimes, the work they did had been inspiring. At other times, it had seemed less than acceptable: the kids had not treated the assignment thoroughly enough to gain skills, knowledge, or competence. In addition, because much of their work was experimental, kids had not managed to complete all the things they had started. Although some of that is acceptable, students also learn important lessons when they complete projects and receive feedback. "What is rigor anyway?" asked Mary. "For our kids, is it just getting to do the work? Is it getting them to complete things? Is it getting them to pass the competency tests that make us all so mad? Is it getting them to perform at the level of the kids in other schools? We talk about lofty things—like self esteem and motivation—but are they really gaining the ability to think more clearly, to solve their own problems?" During one of these discussions, the group looked back into the work students had produced. Quiet, the shuffling of paper the only sound, each of the teachers seemed to be looking for the answer to the question of rigor, and how they might change things to deal with it more thoroughly next year.

Essential Learnings

When we looked back at this case study, several lessons came clear from its unique context. Again, these lessons helped to shed light on what happens as teachers progress towards better schools.

Whole School Culture

Like Kathryn's school, Cityscape was a school that was recently started from scratch. As a result, everyone hired from the original staff to the new staff was given information up front about the school, how it ran, and what it was attempting to do. Structures like their decision-making process, their early morning meetings, the daily schedule, and teaming were all in place. Their weekly staff meetings were used to discuss current practices and new developments and to make decisions. The family group structure was also an integral part of the school. Teachers coming into this school were encouraged to change their practices by those with whom they worked and by the structures already in place.

The fact that the whole school was moving in the same direction and that it was small enough for people to meet to make decisions helped to ensure that teachers who chose to teach there would share similar values and beliefs. The expectations for openness, honesty, and shared decision-making helped to protect the school from splintering into factions going in different directions. These norms also suggested that until the staff were really ready for everyone to accept a new direction, those interested in doing so could do that in a respectful climate. What was perhaps most interesting was that the staff continued to look for structures that worked rather than settling for their first fresh approach. Cityscape developed a whole school culture that was analytical of its own practices, self-reflective, and self renewing, and that encouraged innovation promising better support for students.

The Tension Between Experimentation and Student Expectations

In a place like Cityscape where experimentation was the norm, there was a tension between the need for new courses and materials and the expectations for students. Universally, when teachers try things for the first time, their timing is often faulty. The support that they give students in the completion of first time tasks is often short circuited—as we saw in the new school activities. These general conditions held true at Cityscape. When students didn't understand why they were doing what they'd been asked to do, the quality of their work suffered. And when timing was off, students weren't expected to bring things to closure. The message kids got when encountering new material was similar to the message they got when teachers focused on covering the curriculum. That was, "Not enough time to do this thoroughly, to see what you can really do!"

On the other hand, a second generalization applies. New material is refreshing for teachers and students alike. It means that teachers are learning right along with their students, which builds a more collaborative climate. It keeps teachers more focused on students and their reactions as a means by which to evaluate new materials. Students are flexible and tolerant when they know teachers are trying new things on their behalf.

In schools like Cityscape, the staff had hoped for both at once: the ability to experiment and to stay fresh, and to maintain high expectations for their students. Although it would be overly simplistic to suggest that one is more important than the other, it is also detrimental to ignore the consequences of a predisposition toward one over the other. Finding a balance between experimentation and expectations for students is an important challenge.

Team Works

Mary's team believed that teaming adults was beneficial to students. In order to ensure that their team worked well, they had developed a series of guidelines and required activities. Each team had a leader selected by the group. The team leader attended regular meetings with other team leaders and the principal to build his or her shared-leadership skill. Within teams, the group had established agreements about their working relationships, which they had adhered to during the semester. Within teams, members had learned to value confrontation of other members as a means by which to build a stronger team. They had learned that confrontation worked counter to their initial fears; it had made them stronger rather than weaker. They had learned how to confront difficult issues—to deal with them as soon as they appeared problematic, to describe the problem as clearly as they could, and to work as a team to find a mutually satisfying solution. They had also learned that when their best efforts backfired, they needed to be as direct and as honest as possible when cutting their losses.

—

Michael joined the team to clean up their offices, to sort student work, and to bring some closure to their collaboration. Because of the honesty which had prevailed in their relationship, the atmosphere was surprisingly friendly and straightforward. They read excerpts from kids' work, and despaired over the bulletin board they could have done if they'd had more time. Eventually the conversation turned to a discussion of what the kids had gained from their integrated experiment: whether it was rigorous and whether it met the teachers' expectations. Paolo mused, "The trick for us as teachers is getting students to think about themselves as learners, to recognize that they do it every day. They are locked into believing they can't learn. We have to find the key to unlocking that vault they are in."

"I think of it another way," said Michael, in his soft accented voice. "I think of learning as having two parts. In the first part, the learner experiences something new. In the second part, that new learning has to be connected somehow to what I already know and what I am doing. That is the tough part—making those connections."

"Here's what I want for kids," said Mary, tilting the focus of the conversation. "I want kids to make progress in the development of their intellectual, personal, and emotional processes. I want them to be amazed at how much they learned. For me, I want learning to be much more involving for them. The kids *were* more involved in their projects this term than they were in my class last term; they started telling us how to schedule the day and what to cut out because they wouldn't have adequate time to do deeper work. I LOVED that, and I want it to happen regularly."

"What I want for these kids from the inner city is self esteem. The courage to feel good about themselves because they've accomplished meaningful things. I want them to see themselves as integral to this society, and to believe that they can bring about change." Paolo stood a little taller in the course of his comments.

"I want to help them learn the things they want to learn," said Enrico.

"We want them to be able to navigate their own ships," said Michael.

"What we want and hope for . . . well, is it what we got?" asked Paolo? And off they went, comparing goals to actions, real accomplishments to hopes.

SINCE THEN . . .

Nearly a year later, Enrico, Mary, and Paolo gathered in their disassembled office—the school was moving to a new location—to look back at their experiment, and at the process of being studied while in the midst of such an experiment. Since the initial study in 1991, so many other things had happened. Enrico, an aide during the study, had completed his education degree and was a full time teacher in the school. Paolo, now a veteran teacher, saw his family group graduate and moved to a new coatlition school in another state. Mary and her husband had had a son named Theodore. She was scheduled to return to her team leader position after maternity leave. She felt that the full-day structure and the curriculum, now twice refined, was much stronger, tighter. Michael took a year's leave 2 years ago after his team mates had suggested that he had not upheld his share of the responsibility for teaming and for integrating curriculum. Just recently, he had returned and had indicated that he'd like to return to the school. No team had been willing to work with him, and so the faculty hiring committee had suggested that he look for a position elsewhere. Although according to the contract, he could have returned to the school if he chose, he, too, had thought it better to find another school.

The whole staff had shifted to whole day teams. Everyone had been excited about their move to a new building—the whole school was now in one building and each team had its own floor. In the fall of 1993, they had added 7th and 8th graders to their school; this had been just a first step in what they hoped would eventually become a K–12 school.

During the past 2 years, the staff had been developing their own criteria for performance-based assessment to be used as a requirement for graduation. In preparation, at the end of the year, students had been presenting some aspect of their work from their seminars in a series of round table discussions attended by other teachers, their family group leader, and community members. After each series of round tables, the staff had revisited their newly developed exhibition requirements to ensure that they were preparing kids for these kinds of performances. The first class to graduate by demonstrating competence in the domains and standards developed by staff would be the class of 1994.

6

Elizabeth's Tale: An English Teacher Grapples with Her Feeling of Uneasiness

> lizabeth Ehlers was in the midst of changing the way she teaches as she moved towards her 16th year in the classroom. When I first met her in the winter of 1990, she and three other colleagues were just beginning with a new group of students whom they shared in an interdisciplinary block at Newline High School. They had recently graduated a group of 70+ high school students with whom they had worked for 3 years—carrying the students from 1 year to the next. They were hopeful that they would keep this new group for the same length of time. During the time I spent with Elizabeth, she taught me about how important it is to know students really well if teachers are to help them develop as fully as possible. She also showed me what it is like for kids to be asked to change the way they "do" school. Used to treaties[1] that allow them to be passive and to pick and choose, Elizabeth and her colleagues concentrated on knowing both the students and their parents very well, so that the students found themselves unable to be passive. The transition was not always a comfortable one for students, their parents, or the teachers. In addition, Elizabeth and her team taught me about the critical necessity for system-wide support and for a shared vision of what a reconstructed school might look like.

A CHANGED JOB

"Twenty to eight." Elizabeth Ehler gripped the steering wheel of her large van with determination. I could see that she was concentrating, thinking

146

hard as we sped down open roads that divided the rolling fields of the Ozark foothills. We were on our way to Newline High School where she had worked all of her 14 years as a teacher.

> Now where was I? What happened to prompt my changing as a teacher? . . . I think it came from within. For a long time, I had had a feeling of uneasiness. Even before Phil Manor, our former principal, started talking about the Coalition of Essential Schools, or before I met Ted Sizer, I had this feeling that something was wrong. Things just were not right in my own classroom. My students were asking me, "Why do you always stand up here and say, 'This is important'? *Why* is this important?" They were frustrated and bored. And I felt it. It was hard to live with that feeling of—of uneasiness.

She was quiet for a moment, moving back into the midst of those unsettling feelings.

Originally, Elizabeth had been hired at Newline to teach French and English, which she did for 10 years. Three years ago, she volunteered to join an experimental interdisciplinary team, four teachers who were to start a school-within-a-school serving 80 students. She had volunteered because she felt discontented with the way students were responding—with a sort of half-hearted presence in school. Inspiration for their experiment had come from the Coalition of Essential Schools. Their project had come a long way in 4 years. The original name, School-Within-a-School, had been dropped. A second team of teachers and students had been added. The first set of students had graduated after 3 years in the program, and the original team was beginning with a second set of kids. In those 3 years, Elizabeth's role as a teacher had changed significantly.

Elizabeth spoke softly, with a lilting, gentle, Southern drawl. The softness of her voice belied her intensity, but the rapidity with which she spoke dispelled any questions about it. Her gaze was very direct, forthright, and clear. She had a marvelous sense of humor and was constantly poking fun at herself.

Elizabeth had been married for 15 years and had three sons. Her husband ran a successful business from their 80-acre farm. Elizabeth laughed easily as she described the gargantuan task of shuttling three boys to their various sporting events, lessons, and schools—a full-time job in itself. Her family life was very important to her, and the juggling of home and career provoked a number of challenges. Frustration showed as she mentioned that her husband often commented that she expended the best of her energy at school; he would have liked her to stay home. She didn't think that would be possible for her, nor could she see how she might do less as a teacher. "You can't do it half way! I can't, anyway."

Reflections on a Conventional Classroom

As we sped along past stubble-strewn fields and occasional farmhouses, I asked Elizabeth about the kinds of changes she had made as a teacher. To clarify her changing role, she launched into a description of herself as a very good "conventional" teacher during the first 9 years of her career.

> A typical lesson in French—we would go over the chapter vocabulary. I would say the word to the students and they would repeat it. I usually had a group of 30 or so students. It was my show; I did most of the work, and at the end of the class I was very tired because I had done all of the speaking. I worked hard to generate interesting, active lessons that moved along and that incorporated a variety of different types of activities. They would, on command, repeat for me. We would do vocabulary, and then we would cover a certain number of pages, say one through five, in the book. That work usually included reading passages in French, studying a little French history, or looking at another grammatical form. Then I would assign seat work, exercises A, B, and C. I moved about the room to answer their questions and to give them individual attention—as much as was possible. Occasionally I asked questions: 'What is *je suis?*' Sometimes we played games. Oftentimes I brought in little bits of French culture. Then, when they started the seat work, it was my time to go back to my desk. Because I have always liked teenagers, my room was always a comfortable place to be.

Elizabeth went on to articulate her early philosophy. She had worked hard to maintain an orderly classroom because she had believed that it was needed to support a good learning environment. Her shelves were neat, the desks were in rows, and the students worked quietly so that they could concentrate. She had thought long and hard about how to reach her students, how to make the subject matter more alive for them, and how to maintain their interest. Like many of her colleagues, she had not felt that her teacher-training courses had been particularly rich in preparing her to teach, but because she was conscientious—and curious—she had constantly evaluated what worked and what didn't in order to expand her repertoire of skills.

Her classes varied, and she had developed a range of techniques that could be used depending on student moods and outside influences and interferences. Sometimes she had lectured. Sometimes they had discussed. Other times the kids had done role-plays or given demonstrations or reports. They had taken field trips to films and plays when she had found something that was particularly appropriate.

The textbook had formed the basis for curriculum planning. She and her other French and English colleagues had cooperated in planning what should be taught and when. Students who took French I had covered what they needed in order to be ready for French II. In her English classes, she had assessed where students were having difficulty and had attempted to give them the skills they lacked. She had worried about whether the kids were getting what they needed. Did they understand what paragraphs were? Could they write with depth, correctness, and precision? She had often felt frustrated by their lack of skills, by the diversity of their problems, and by their sheer numbers. In order to ensure that she was at once a good colleague, a good employee, and a good teacher, she had abided by the rules of the school and had been very task-oriented with her students. They had wasted little valuable instructional time.

My idea of a professional was one who supported the rules, who arrived on time, who listened very attentively in faculty meetings but did not necessarily offer an opinion and, if she did, not an adverse or dissenting position—generally because I did not think that to do so was appropriate. I filled out my lesson plan book, and I did the things that were expected of me so that I could be labeled as a good teacher. My professional responsibilities were to teach my students to the best of my ability and to be familiar with my course outline so I could cover all of the topics. In addition, I thought it was my professional responsibility to interact as little as possible with the administration, that I was doing a good job if I did not have to be in their offices, talking with them. They had huge jobs, and I did not want to complicate their lives further.

I knew I was doing a good job from the number of Commendable's and Exemplary's on my evaluation. I knew I was doing a good job because I kept close tabs on absenteeism in my room. I knew I was doing a good job when I kept the noise level down and the chairs in a straight line. If most of my students passed, and if I didn't have any parent complaints, I knew I was doing a good job. I can tell you, I did things by the book.

Previous Attempts to Change

I experienced frustration right along, and as a result I constantly tried to figure out better ways of working. In the seventies, I built individualized learning packets. It was a start, you know, because at least I felt that I was giving them the opportunity to go at their own pace. The problem with that method was that I ended up with students who had finished and were ready to go on to the second packet and students who were still just beginning on the first packet, and I didn't know how to deal with all of that. It was too much; I had a large classroom and a large number of classes.

Elizabeth had also struggled to find ways to engage her students, such as developing a reward system that she had believed would provide them with heightened motivation. Although she laughed at these earlier attempts to deal with her own uneasiness about schooling, she recognized that she had always been working to hone her skills. At this point in her musings, we pulled into the parking lot at Newline High School.

In the Midst of a Comprehensive High School

Newline was a large comprehensive high school sprawled out in eleven buildings. The master schedule was a huge and complicated masterwork that coordinated all 100 teachers and 1602 students through a seven-period day. The facility was filled far beyond capacity; there was no room that was not used every period of the day. Many teachers had their materials on rolling carts—transients because of the lack of space.

Four years previously, Phil Manor, then the school principal, had gone to a national symposium and had heard Ted Sizer speak about the Coalition of Essential Schools. Elizabeth remembered the beginnings of their current project.

> He came back with pages of meticulous notes and he shared these with the faculty. He suggested that we read *Horace's Compromise*. Because a good professional did what she was asked to do by the administrator, I read *Horace*. I was afraid I was going to be tested! I thought he was going to tell us to put our gradebooks under the tables! Anyway, he suggested that he would like to try out the Coalition principles at the high school. I was not exactly sure what all of this involved because he was saying some pretty strange-sounding things for our school—like I would have to work with other teachers, like I would have to relate what I was doing to other teachers, and like it would probably be good if we had a multicertified staff. But I'm a risk-taker, and so I volunteered.

A four-teacher team was subsequently assembled, and the team then devised the following courses as suggested in *Horace's Compromise:* Inquiry and Expression, Literature and the Arts, Mathematics and Science, History and Philosophy. The four teachers were to share 80 students for 4 hours a day, from the second through the sixth period. This instructional time was divided into four 2-hour teaching blocks over 2 days, with each teacher taking 20 students per block. In addition, they were given two planning periods: one was used for planning their own courses; the second was for collaborative work. The teachers had control of the instructional time so they could double-block periods if needed or work all together in a large group. Students volunteered for the program in the 10th grade and stayed with those four teachers for their remaining years in high school. The project was funded in part by a grant from a local foundation, which enabled the teachers to attend Coalition symposia and to do curriculum work.

The district office had agreed to a 3-year plan. In the middle of the first year, the principal had resigned and an interim principal had been assigned. The next year, Gordon Smith was assigned to the building, the third principal in less than 2 years. Still, the project had remained intact.

Three students who had been in the program described their experiences to me. They talked so fast that their comments piled up on one another.

"We really got to know each other well. We got to be good friends with the teachers so that we could really talk to them. We had to do a lot more school work, rather than having something handed to you. We had to develop our own point of view."

"In School-Within-a-School, you have to work on things that interest you and really go after it."

"They didn't teach out of books."

"We did more hands-on stuff, rather than having one person stand up there and lecture."

Katie was a freshman at the biggest of the state's universities.

I learned to think for myself in School-Within-a-School. I didn't have to learn that when I walked into college. In School-Within-a-School, we got a problem and were asked to look at it from all different perspectives. We constantly got topics which didn't have a right answer. In School-Within-a-School, we had to think about all the old authors—Plato, Socrates— and we had to understand why they said what they said, and then we had to connect it up with everything else we were studying. We focused on our own uniqueness. We did things in art, in music, and in writing so that we could discover our own uniqueness, our own talents. The group helped me to discover that I wanted to be a writer.

One of the boys said, "I always did have talent, but the group refined it for me!" His friends groaned. "And our teachers were always there for us. We all came back to see Mrs. Ehler because she's our friend. Many of us were inspired by our teachers."

Katie recalled that it had been hard to be in the program at first because no one liked being different. "I thought my teachers were trying to stunt my social growth forever. I thought I'd never get a date hanging around with the same kids all the time!" The other students agreed. By the end of the 3 years, her feelings had changed. "It was a privilege to be in that school because we were treated so well. When I am comfortable in my environment, I learn more. I felt more confident. I'm shy and would never have spoken out, but I did here and felt confident. I feel that they gave me the gift of my mind."

Another student, a junior who had been in the program for 2 years but had to leave in order to get the science courses he wanted, described his experience. "I developed more critical thinking skills. I learned to think about why things are the way they are instead of memorizing facts. I can't remember a lot of specific facts I got in there, but I have skills. I feel differently about myself. I think of myself as a scientist in a lab instead of a kid in a class. The other thing was that we felt like a family unit. We came from different social groups and yet we meshed into one. The teachers took that diversity and turned it into a melting pot."

Now in their 4th year, Elizabeth and her colleagues were starting over with a new group of students. The principal had changed the courses back to English, science, math, and history, against the teachers' recommendations. He claimed that in order to institutionalize and expand the program, it had to fit into the regular school. Elizabeth taught two eighty-minute blocks of English per day and one study hall. She had two planning periods, one planning her own classes and one for team planning.

Elizabeth 's Role

Elizabeth attempted to describe how her role had changed in the past 3 years. She saw herself as a facilitator of student learning and noted that this stance required quite different behavior from that of conventional teacher. She reviewed her new behaviors.

> Most of the time, I move from group to group; I rarely sit down. I'm moving about constantly, asking questions. You know, that's difficult because I don't think we as teachers know how to ask good questions. I work hard to try to formulate questions that will cause the students to think and to respond. Most of my questions recently have been "why" questions. Yesterday, for instance, I was working with a group of guys who were very excited over the mini-Exhibitions they are just beginning after reading *Of Mice and Men*. First, I asked them what they were going to be doing. They were going to make a parody of the book. I asked them why they wanted to do a parody. There was just dead silence. Finally, one of them said, "I don't think anyone should feel sorry for Lennie. He was mentally deficient and why should you feel sorry for someone who can't do anything anyway?" So my next question to him was, "Why do you feel that way? Are you saying that a person's worth in society is determined by what he can contribute?" He said no, and we were off into a good discussion.
>
> I have certainly changed my notions about my professional responsibility. Now I think my responsibility is to become a learner again. I need to do that whether it means interacting with other teachers, participating in workshops, or whatever. I feel it is my responsibility to stay in touch with my administration. I keep them informed as to my opinions about some of the things that are going on in our school community.

She smiled and looked sheepish. "Sometimes I'm successful, sometimes I'm not. Sometimes I push the wrong buttons . . .

My responsibility with the students is to get them to the point where they are confident enough to take that first step in using their minds well, and then, having done that, I need to nurture them as their confidence develops. I am no longer a dispenser of information, and I like that. I see myself as a facilitator. I think that I still run the show, but it's not quite as obvious. I have been learning to ask good questions and am training my students to ask good questions. I spend time convincing them that they want to take responsibility for their learning and then guiding them while they do that.

As we left the faculty room and headed for Elizabeth's classroom, she noted that she used her time differently now. She spent far more time working with her teammates and far more time with her students because they were in her room constantly. She spent less time grading their work and more time assessing it as work-in-progress and coaching the students to practice.

A DAY IN ELIZABETH'S CLASSROOM

Elizabeth's classes met in the school committee boardroom. She had volunteered to take the room because of the lack of space in the rest of the school. Seven long rectangular tables were lined up in the room with four chairs at each table. "What I really like about my classroom is that we have tables that lend themselves to grouping and interaction. My students are forced to look at each other and to notice each other's expressions. My desk isn't really noticeable there in the back corner; and because I rarely have a chance to sit at it, it has a different function." The podium at the front was a reminder that this was a boardroom. There was also a big-screen TV, which Elizabeth's team frequently found useful.

At the back of the room, sets of textbooks were neatly stacked in bookshelves: *Adventures in Appreciation, British and Western Literature,* and *Scene Seventy.* Student work—illustrated poems and stories about fall—decorated the walls. This bit of reflection was centered in a student's fall collage: "When I think of fall, I think of cold, stormy nights and deep sleep where the sound of rain fills our heads with dreams. I think of brilliant colors jumping from tree to tree and falling to the ground to be collected up in bags. . . ." Elizabeth remarked that a mother had called the principal to complain that high school students shouldn't be doing 3rd-grade work.

Elizabeth had done a poster entitled "The Basics of Tomorrow." It listed the skills students would need to succeed in the 21st century:

Evaluation and analysis skills
Critical thinking/synthesis
Organization and reference skills
Problem-solving strategies (including math)
Decision making
Application
Creativity
Communication in a variety of modes

Two large triangles, suspended from the ceiling, floated above the classroom, each asking a question:

What is a scholarly attitude?
How does one develop a scholarly attitude?

Elizabeth explained that students often had stereotypical ideas about questioning and about scholarly attitudes. Kids thought that if they questioned their teachers, they would be accused of rudeness. They thought of scholars as bores, as people who have no friends. The students believed that it was an attitude to be assiduously avoided.

To combat these stereotypes, she and her students spent a good deal of time discussing the two questions. They had progressed to the understanding that scholars are comfortable with questions that do not have answers and with circumstances in which there is no right answer. They were working now on understanding the behaviors of scholars. A list of characteristics of a scholarly attitude, in student handwriting, was posted in the room:

1. Asks good questions
2. Good study habits
3. Willingness to learn
4. Patience—takes time to learn
5. Good attitude towards school and learning
6. Good listener
7. Accepts that teachers don't always have answers
8. Reads
9. Has charisma
10. Has self-confidence

Two 10th-Grade English Classes

Twelve 10th-grade students arrived gradually and took their places around the tables. Books spilled over the table tops, coats were draped on chairs, everyone greeted everyone else. The tone in the room was friendly and easy.

The day's agenda was written on the board:

1. Good/bad discussion
2. Journals
3. Groups do two tasks
4. Individual work

Elizabeth moved to the side of the room, welcomed everyone, and asked how they were doing. Some moaned and buried their heads in their arms; others said, "Fine." She asked them to get their learning logs out and to review which learning techniques worked for them and which didn't. She also asked them to think about identifying the kinds of triangles the scholarly attitude questions were on. The students leafed through their notebooks. One student said the triangles were isosceles; someone else said that they were not because the angles weren't right. After a bit more discussion, Elizabeth asked them how they might find out precisely. Another student said she'd ask Ms. West, their math teacher.

Someone asked Elizabeth to explain again what a mini-Exhibition was. She answered that it was a demonstration of their understanding of John Steinbeck's *Of Mice and Men*. Because they would actually demonstrate what they had learned, they needed enough time to do the assignment very thoroughly. They would be working on these demonstrations for the next 2 weeks. She reminded them that she had suggested several options: they could make a film of a particularly moving or pivotal scene; they could write a seventh chapter in Steinbeck's style; or they could develop a scene that was mentioned or alluded to in the book but not thoroughly described.

Elizabeth inquired how the kids' parents had responded to their grades and whether there were any surprises. More moans.

Elizabeth asked the students whether they had any more questions about the work they had done the previous week. Because there were no responses, she asked them to write in their journals for the next 10 minutes, a regular classroom exercise to develop fluidity. "You can free-write or you can write about any current event that might be of interest to you. The Berlin Wall came tumbling down this weekend, and there were also two important rallies right here in our town. You may wish to write about those." Elizabeth discussed the assignment privately with one student back at her desk. He left the room. The rest of the room was quiet while the students wrote.

After 10 minutes, she asked them to stop and to review the homework assignment she had given them for the weekend. They were to have chosen one of the mini-Exhibitions from the list she had given them, or she would entertain their ideas if none of the options looked appealing. They were to have planned their use of time and generated a list of the things they would need. The response was slow, lethargic. Only one student had done it. After a little investigation, it appeared that the students felt uncertain about what she had asked them to do. They had never done a mini-Exhibition before, and they had never been asked to plan their time. They didn't know what such a plan should look like. Elizabeth concurred. She reviewed the assignment and the nature of a mini-Exhibition and then gave them some clues on working in groups. "You-all have not done mini-Exhibition work before, so this is new to you and is genuinely complex. You should expect some problems. You may wish to appoint a facilitator for your group who will monitor your schedules and keep you on task. The facilitator should appoint a recorder. The recorders will hand in the time schedules and your—"

Announcements burst over the intercom mid-sentence. "Homecoming pictures can be picked up in the counselors' office. Students can order their video yearbook in the main office. Today is the Great American Smoke-out, and we hope everyone will participate. The Foreign Friends Club is meeting this afternoon in room 503. Please bring 50¢ as your contribution to the up-and-coming language fair." The students talked quietly right through the announcements.

"Where was I? Oh, yes. The recorders need to hand in your schedules and your daily evaluations. I know you haven't devised an evaluation before either, but you'll get better as the days progress."

One student asked, "I don't get the evaluation—we're supposed to tell you what we did during each day, right? Can we use a scale from 1 to 10 to rate how we did?" Nodding, she told them to use whatever method worked best for them and reminded them that they could revise it over time. She asked them to work on the two tasks for the next 30 minutes. She walked to the girl who had actually done her planning schedule, looked it over, and congratulated her. She then asked her to put it up on the board as a model for the rest of the class. Other students dispersed. One boy moved to a table by himself. The rest worked in groups of two, three, or four students. Elizabeth moved around the room, stopping to check with each of the groups.

Two boys worked together quietly, hunched over their notes, sitting side by side. Their list read: "Go to the library. Finish reading."

"I think we should switch them. Like we should go to the library after we've done some writing."

"Hmmm," considered the second. He was the recorder.

As several students left to go to the library, Elizabeth moved to another group of two boys. These two had planned to use their study-hall time. They told her they'd agreed to write a seventh chapter. Their schedule read:

Monday: Reread Chapter 6. Study it carefully.
Tuesday: Outline Chapter 6. Begin discussing ideas for Chapter 7.

Thursday: Make small rough draft. Begin Chapter 7.
Monday: Go to library to research Steinbeck's writing style. Finish Chapter 7.
Wednesday: Turn in completed assignment (typed).
Evaluation: Be graded on a scale of 1 to 10 on the amount of progress and quality of work we completed that day.

They discussed whether they knew how to use computers and whether they would read Chapter 6 together. Elizabeth asked them to be more specific about their evaluation. She suggested a variety of possibilities. She moved off to join another group.

After 30 minutes, Elizabeth asked her students to talk about how they felt about doing the planning. One boy noted that he felt very rushed. She laughed and said that they should clearly begin to see that they had little time to waste. She resumed her roving for the remainder of the first hour. The tone in the room was relaxed but serious.

A group of girls said that they were looking forward to their report because they were going to select a topic they were very interested in. "Can we do this like a report to the class instead of as a paper?" Elizabeth said yes; they must use the same procedures they used in Mr. Daley's room— bibliography and note cards.

At that point, most of the class filed out for their 5-minute break. Several students stayed back to visit with Elizabeth. She talked animatedly with them, admired pictures, and listened. When the class returned, Elizabeth returned to working with the groups.

The two boys, Todd and Bryan, skipped to generating ideas. Elizabeth joined them to review their progress. "Todd, tell me what you two have done so far."

He began to explain, then looked at her and said, "Do you want me to read what we've got so far?"

"Whatever you want to do."

He read. Curley had gone on a kind of shooting spree, killing his friend and several others. She interrupted, saying, "How can that be believable?"

They grinned at each other. Bryan said, "I told you she'd think that."

Todd explained their rationale, with Bryan interrupting when important details were missed. Elizabeth persisted in asking questions.

"Why would Curley want to do that?"

"Because of the rape."

When he'd finished with his explanation, Todd looked at her and said with experimental certainty, "There's irony in this."

She was clearly delighted and agreed. "You're right. That's very good." Again, she moved among the various groups, answering questions, asking questions, never sitting.

Toward the end of the hour, she sat down with me to share her own beliefs about the benefits of teaching in this way.

> The advantage is that the students begin to realize that they are individuals, that they each have strengths to contribute. I have a lot more time to engage in face-to-face interaction with my students, so I have more time to get to know them, to know what they need to work on. And because we teach in teams, the students each have four teachers who know them well. I think they have a much broader base of support.

Elizabeth talked about the complexity of the Coalition ideas, the set of nine Common Principles that guided the work in which she and her teammates were engaged. For instance, she felt that the concept of teacher-as-coach and student-as-worker demanded a great deal from teachers.

> It requires that both teachers and students make a commitment. And there is a paradox that happens when teachers think about making the transition. When they move to coaching, teachers are afraid to give up old ways for fear that they will be losing something. The paradox lies in the fact that you get a lot more than you give up, because students are so much more involved.

As the double period neared an end, Elizabeth called for the students' plans and for their evaluations of the work they'd completed during the day. The students handed in notebooks or papers and moved out of the room quickly; they had only 20 minutes for lunch.

Once the room had emptied, she explained the difficulty these concepts presented for her students.

> This group is new. We've only been working with them for 9 weeks, so they are not 100% comfortable with the notion of student-as-worker. They still want 'right' answers. We have been working on their understandings of scholarly attitudes. I started off gradually trying to convince them that they have at least 50% of the responsibility for their own education. This mini-Exhibition exercise is their first opportunity to develop their own stuff.

While she was ruminating, her 20-minute lunch period disappeared, and her next group of 10th-grade students began to wander in. Elizabeth turned around to find a student at her elbow who wished to make a phone call. Tina wanted to call a famous Southern gospel musician, a pianist, to interview him about whether he had a "life dream" and how he fulfilled it. She had picked this assignment because each of the characters in *Of Mice and*

Men had a life dream but not one of them ever fulfilled that dream. She wanted to interview someone who had actually pursued his dream and had gone forward with it. She liked this assignment because "it's better than just sitting in class looking at books all day. It's hard, though, because it takes so much work to get a hold of him." She had called twice previously and had been directed to different numbers and then told to call at a particular time. Elizabeth left the room, telling the rest of her students where she was going and asking them to review their notes from the previous week in preparation for a "good/bad" discussion when she got back. She took her personal phone credit card because the school couldn't afford calls of this nature.

During the 5 minutes or so they were gone, the rest of the students settled in to work. They leafed through their journals and talked in their groups. When Elizabeth and Tina came back to the room, Elizabeth opened the good/bad discussion, an opportunity for the students to review and to reflect on the class and their own work. She asked them, "What did you do in class last week that you enjoyed or that you gained from? Could I have been more helpful to you in any way?"

There was silence for several minutes. One girl responded, "We were supposed to have an open-book quiz on the short story we've been working on." Elizabeth gasped. "Why, thank you. I completely forgot. I'll get going right away on that." The other kids yelled at the reminding culprit.

Another student said, "I finished the book, and I thought it was real depressing." Others nodded.

"What depressed you?" Elizabeth asked.

"Well, it was just such a gray book. And while nobody seemed bad, nothing good ever seemed to happen." As the student was talking, Elizabeth walked over to another student whose head was on his arms to see if he was okay. He looked up sleepily and said, "I'm just readin'." Everyone hooted.

They returned to reviewing the day's work—a clarification of their mini-Exhibitions, the evaluations, and the planning. Elizabeth concluded the review by suggesting, "If you can do these mini-Exhibitions in one day, then we need to talk. Maybe we haven't designed it right. You should think about the mini-Exhibitions as a way to help you answer the question on why Steinbeck wrote this book."

This group was livelier, less prone to work cooperatively.[2] They talked louder, were wormier, moved around more. One group of boys described the violence they would do as a team to Lennie and to George as they reconstructed the book. A group of girls looked through their homecoming pictures. Elizabeth worked individually with a girl who wanted to do a baby book for Lennie as her mini-Exhibition. Elizabeth pushed her to clarify the purpose of the baby book. What would it teach her about Lennie? She suggested that the girl go back through the book to find all of the passages that refer to Lennie's aunt and to his earlier life. Without discouraging her or retracting the choice the student had been offered, Elizabeth wanted to ensure that the work would be substantial and serious.

She moved quickly to the next group. While she worked with them, another group of four boys concentrated on making animal noises and began bopping each other surreptitiously. Two of the boys became very uptight, repeating that they needed to figure out what it was they were going to do. Eventually, they agreed to do the film. One described a series of violent scenes they might do—giggling all the way. As if in a refrain, one of the others continued to ask for seriousness while another told the story of how his brother had starved his hamster. They talked about rewriting the whole book; half of the group laughed hysterically as the other half grew more tight-lipped and more frustrated.

Three girls were engaged in an intense conversation about which scene they would do. They talked about Aunt Clara and how much they knew about her. Maybe they could do a scene between Aunt Clara and Lennie. The facilitator yelled, "You-all!" to bring them back on task. One of the girls suggested that they find the scene where Curley's wife was with Lennie. The facilitator read aloud while they all leaned forward, listening.

The bell rang for the mid-period break. The students moved out into the halls. Elizabeth read a note handed to her by a student; she hugged the student and thanked her. One of the boys asked her if it would be okay for him to come by her house that evening about 8 o'clock because their group wanted to film their scene on her property. She ran through her own children's basketball schedule and countered with 8:30.

Mr. Daley, one of her team members, came into the classroom to observe.

The kids trickled back in and resumed their work. Elizabeth got the giggling group looking through their notes to see what they did and didn't know in order to do a final chapter of the book. She moved to the next group, handling four questions from other groups while working in the midst of this group. One boy was treating *Of Mice and Men* as a tragedy, so she directed him to clearer definitions of tragedy and maybe some comparative possibilities. Two girls came back in from the library with a stack of note cards. They had found too many resources and were despairing. Elizabeth suggested several strategies for sorting through and eliminating some of them.

Elizabeth moved to work with another boy who had done his homework and who already had a draft of the seventh chapter. He explained that he had tried to maintain the tone of hopelessness that pervaded the book. He had written seven pages but needed some suggestions for the reworking. "When I finished the book, I thought there should be more to it. I just started writing and it evolved. I think I'll keep most of this stuff. Does it sound like Steinbeck?" He read, "The frost on the barley ricks sunk deep into my hands." Elizabeth appreciated that sentence as Steinbeckian and suggested he examine his dialogue and compare it to Steinbeck's. She hugged him and told him to keep pushing and that he was doing fine work.

She conferenced with another group, who read what they'd done so far. She asked, "Where is it going from here?" The recorder responded, "I don't know really. I think I'm gonna have the cook wagon fall on Cookie's leg and then I might have the three of them move off together. I don't know from there." The rest of his group argued with him.

Across the room, a girl took out her compact and checked herself out— a serious examination of teenage beauty. She took lip gloss out, put it on, and sent it around her group. Everyone dipped, then glistened. Next, they all sprayed Binaca into their mouths.

Elizabeth moved to the front of the room as the 2nd hour was nearing an end. Slightly modifying part of the assignment she had given them to think about earlier, she said, "I'd like you to take out a half sheet of paper and answer the question, 'What have I accomplished today?' I'd like you to think through what it was that you had to do and what you did. Please be as specific as possible. This is an individual self-evaluation." The room was silent. Elizabeth stood at the front of the room and gazed outside. The sun was shining on the bleached, winter-white football field; the temperature had dropped 30 degrees in the course of the day.

After 5 or 6 minutes, she asked them to stop and share. The spokesperson for the Binaca group quietly admitted they had spent some of their time looking at homecoming pictures. She said they didn't do a very good job. Elizabeth confirmed that it was very easy to get off track but asked her to clarify why she believed they hadn't done a good job. The girl blurted out that she was working with a group that was doing an assignment she was not really interested in. Elizabeth suggested that that was an important insight and that perhaps the student might want to work alone.

She asked the divided table of gigglers what they had accomplished. Sam, who was so frustrated, said that it was really hard for them to get anything done once they picked a topic because it was hard to get the others to concentrate. She asked him how he would rate their use of time given a scale of 1 through 10. He said they would rate about a 5 because they talked too much. He could think of nothing positive. She listed the work they had accomplished—they had selected a mini-Exhibition topic, narrowed their focus, and brainstormed a list of possibilities, playing them out—and reminded them that the difficult part about group work was that everyone had to take responsibility. She encouraged them by suggesting that tomorrow would be more productive.

The two girls who'd been to the library reported that they had planned their week and made up an evaluation, which they had filled out already for that day. Then they had chosen their mini-Exhibition, gone to the library, and found too many resources. They were just now identifying what they would use. They sounded very efficient and clear about their own productivity.

As the bell rang for the end of the sixth period, Elizabeth wished them all a good evening and told them that she looked forward to working with them the next day.

As the students left the room, Elizabeth shared her perceptions with Peter Daley who had been watching.

> This group is my challenge. I had two possible approaches: I could have lectured them or I could have stuck to my original plan to give them the opportunity to evaluate themselves. I would have lost them completely if I hadn't turned it back to them. Did you notice how the room changed when I asked them to get out a piece of paper? Like I was going to give them a pop quiz. I used to feel so sick when teachers asked me to take out a piece of paper—like I was about to be stripped naked! These kids are just taking a little longer to trust me and each other.

Just then a former student walked in to visit. Two more arrived as Elizabeth's two other teammates assembled for their team-planning period. Elizabeth looked momentarily exhausted as she faced both the visitors and her colleagues who needed to get on with their meeting. She took a deep breath, threw her arms around the students, and walked them toward the door, saying, "How are you-all? I am so glad to see you. Will you be around after seventh period? I have a meeting right now." The students exchanged greetings with some of the other teachers as they moved out into the hall.

A Team Planning Session

The four team members gathered around a table in the middle of the room: Tom Whitman, the science teacher; Peter Daley, the history teacher; Sally Watkins, the first-year math teacher; and Elizabeth. Peter's student teacher, Elaine Martinson, also joined the group. Sally was the COW—coordinator of the week—a responsibility they rotated. The COW's job was to keep the agenda for their daily planning sessions. They began slowly, visiting among themselves and comparing notes on the day. The tone was friendly and easy. They reminded each other of things they needed to deal with until Sally recalled that they had already postponed talking about a student whom she wanted to transfer to another class. They reviewed his schedule and made the adjustments. Peter asked how the filming had gone—both Elizabeth and Tom had been videotaped the day before. They recapped their feelings and the kids' reactions. Elizabeth checked with the team to see if anyone would cover her classes for her on Friday so that she could attend an important meeting. No one was particularly receptive. Elizabeth said that she would try to get a substitute. She inquired about a work space during first period since the boardroom was in use by one of the language teachers. Everyone who had a room invited her to share their space.

They moved on to other issues on the agenda. Elizabeth reviewed the latest request to visit their program from a superintendent in a neighboring state. The others marked their calendars. They marked in Tom's trip to Tennessee to another conference at which he was presenting. Peter said he felt a need to work on ways they might integrate disciplines as he began to cover the ancient Greeks. They discussed who was doing what and when. Sally thought she would be able to switch to Pythagoras when Tom was ready. They listed the resources they had available to them, including books on mythology and copies of *Oedipus Rex*. Tom suggested that he could do classification and offered to check on other possibilities. Peter wondered whether everyone should read *Oedipus*. They laughed and noted that the kids still really liked it because it was a mystery, convoluted and "weird." Peter asked everyone on the team to reread *Oedipus* so that they might have a more in-depth discussion of the possible uses. They agreed.

Continuing, Peter waxed eloquent for a few moments on the importance of "connections" for kids. He really wanted them to see the interrelated nature of the disciplines because he felt that it breathed more life into what they were doing. He asked whether they might have a more serious session to brainstorm connections. Tom suggested they might use, as the central focus, questions about the influence the Greeks have had on contemporary life. Perhaps they should begin with a walk through a neighboring town to see its Greek revivalist architecture. Elizabeth questioned Peter about myths, fables, and the recent PBS series with Joseph Campbell to see how they might cooperate.

Although they appeared to be warming to the subject of possible connections, the topic shifted when Peter mentioned that Elaine had been very frustrated with the reports the students were currently doing. Elaine verified that she could "just as easily have pulled their teeth" as get them to revise their work. Elaine and Peter agreed that the idea for the reports was good but that the results were dismal. Elizabeth asked for a description of the problems. "Is it that they can't get the information that they need? Or is it that they don't know how to extract information from resources? Or is it that they don't know how to organize it once they've gotten it?"

Elaine looked chagrined. "I don't think that they even know how to write paragraphs, really—with a topic sentence and supporting ideas." Peter chimed in, "The kids just have not written much. They are not used to doing what we are asking them to do. If it means that we do less world history while they get it, that's the way it goes."

Elaine continued to analyze the problem. "The topics are too broad. Maybe I didn't give them enough of an assignment, but even given that, I don't think they could do a very good job. The kids are tired of it." The group went back and forth in an attempt to diagnose the problem and figure out how to salvage the assignment.

Elizabeth asked, "Is there tension between you and the students over this, Elaine?"

Elaine said, "It's really hard not to blame the kids, but it is simply not their fault. They need to be taught. But I don't think I can salvage this assignment." Various solutions were suggested: a trip to the local university library to beef up their research skills; one-on-one conferencing about their writing skills; some plain old grammar work. Elaine said she would bring some of the reports over for Elizabeth to read, who in turn agreed, once they had determined what was to be done with these reports, to rearrange what she was doing to help build the skills the kids needed.

The discussion turned to Peter's exploration of his students' curiosity. He felt that the students were not curious and did not demonstrate any personal motivation to learn. Tom reminded the group that they had only had these students for 9 weeks and that they needed patience. Their discontent stemmed from comparing these students to the students with whom they had worked for 3 years. They all felt cheered by Tom's comment and agreed how genuinely likable the kids were.

They then moved into a discussion of a particular student, which led them to a greater understanding of the seriousness of the student's problems. As a result, they agreed to set up an appointment with the student and to follow that up with a meeting with the parents.

Sally raised the final issue. The principal had suggested that he would like to administer an evaluation of their program to their students soon, to be given in the gym without the teachers present. They pushed to determine what the evaluation would be used for, but since they couldn't clarify that until they talked to Mr. Smith, Tom asked that they consider what they, as a team, would like to know from an evaluation. They brainstormed:

Which of your classes is most like ninth grade?
Are you asked to write more than you were in ninth grade?
Describe your best learning experience so far this year.
Are you comfortable with the way your classes are scheduled?
Are you comfortable with the ways your classes are organized?
Are you being challenged to think? If so, how? If not, why not?
Describe your favorite class activity.
Do you enjoy your classes? If so, why? If not, why not?

They went back and forth among the questions, prodding for clarity and for differences. Each of them agreed to think of several questions that would really help them serve their students better and to bring them to the next day's meeting. By the time they broke up it was nearly 5 o'clock, and everyone was exclaiming about being late to pick up children, spouses, and groceries, and complaining that they had papers to grade.

Elizabeth crammed a set of class learning logs into a bag and rushed out to pick up her son at basketball practice. She called to the former students who had come to visit: she was so sorry. Could they come back? How were their parents, siblings, boyfriends, girlfriends, classes, jobs? They trailed her out to her car. Katie showed her a paper she had recently written for her toughest journalism class at the local university. She'd gotten a B, the highest grade in the class. She wanted to share her rich delight with Mrs. Ehler.

Elizabeth stopped in the parking lot, hugged Katie, and said, "You're gonna be a famous journalist some day. I just know it. We all will be watching you on television, reading your own stuff. Keep pushing yourself." Stuffing bags and books into the van, Elizabeth hopped in, while Katie yelled, "Barbara Walters, LOOK OUT!"

STEPPING BACK

What Changed?

A day in Elizabeth Ehler's classroom did not reflect the kind of teaching she had described as characteristic of her first 10 years in the profession. She laughingly described it as her type of personal make-over. In the course of the past 4 years, Elizabeth had stopped using standardized textbooks as her basic curriculum. She had moved her desk from the front of the room to the back and now used it as a place for conferences with individual students. She had developed different relationships with her students, asking them to work in different ways, and changed her own role as well. In addition, she worked closely with three other teachers, joined a much larger network of teachers nationally, and spent more time with her students' parents.

Elizabeth made all of these changes because she believed they were important if she was to provide a higher quality of education for her students. Elizabeth indicated that many of the changes she had made were the result of her team's attempt to put the nine Common Principles into practice.

Teacher/Student Ratio: 1:80

"When we began School-Within-a-School 3 years ago, we worked to implement all the principles from the beginning, so the ideas and concepts have been with me for a while and it is difficult for me to give one a higher priority than another. They are all interrelated and each affects the others. I suppose, though, that it all starts with the 1:80 ratio."

Elizabeth was referring to Principle Number 4, which proposes that no secondary teacher should have responsibility for more than 80 students per term. Reduced student loads allow teachers to know their students well, so that the course of study can be tailored to individual student needs. Reduced loads also allow teachers the time to plan more complex curricula designed for heightened student engagement.

"Although many educators adamantly believe that most of the principles already exist in classrooms across the country, I do not agree. When I taught 1:150, I was not the same teacher and could not engage students in the same way."

Personalization

I believe that I have come to understand the concept of personalization because I have had no more than 80 students, and because I had the opportunity to work with those students over time. Because my classes are small, I find I am able to do some of my instruction through writing personal notes, comments, and letters; the students and I communicate in their learning logs. In addition, because I know my students better, I see them as whole people as opposed to students in an English class. I am able to help them and to grade them more holistically.

Student-as-Worker

When we began, the district supported us by putting the 1:80 ratio in place and by providing us with common students and common planning time. They did this by telling parents and students about the program and by allowing students to volunteer. Once 80-some students volunteered, they were scheduled with us for 4 periods of the day. We four teachers discovered that our first task was to teach the students that they *could* use their minds well.[3] They literally panicked when worksheets were replaced with less familiar ways of learning. We had most of those students for 3 years though, and, by the end, they were excellent critical thinkers.

The notion of student-as-worker has been a hard one for many of my students, as has the concept of mini-Exhibitions. I think, though, it is change that frightens them. But their fears diminish over time. In addition, some of the students' apprehensions have been fueled by their parents' concerns. One parent told our principal, "I don't want my child in a class where he has to do all the work." Initially, my students had difficulty with the idea that we trusted them, period. That, too, developed over time. We have not tackled the question of diplomas awarded by Exhibition because our state regulations seem so prohibitive. However, we have begun building mini-Exhibitions so that our students develop a greater familiarity with them.

Teacher as Generalist

I have also changed in that although my course is called "English" this year, I also teach geography, history, some French, a little art, and current events, among other subjects. In fact, I perceive myself differently. I feel more like an elementary school teacher, and I try to model this approach to the interconnectedness of things so that students will consider this a natural characteristic of learning. Another ramification of this change is best expressed by my husband. He says, "Liz, before you were a part of the Coalition, you didn't seem to come home nearly so exhausted." He's right. I determine curriculum, juggle and revise schedules, encourage, and discipline. And I find that because I have the time to know my students well, there develops a strong bond between them and me. They are quick to tell me their successes and their sorrows. I am constantly interacting with my students.

Parents as Essential Collaborators

One important thing I've learned as a result of trying to put these principles into action is that parents should be treated as essential collaborators. Most of our School-Within-a-School parents became our champions, but we spent time educating them as to what we were trying to do. Now, starting over again, I am finding it necessary to educate my parents again.

In Elizabeth's school, the nine Common Principles were not posted anywhere, nor did the teachers talk about them daily in their meetings together. However, the principles appeared to undergird the decisions they made, leaving them free to choose their own structures and their own descriptive language.

Support

Elizabeth believed that a number of other factors, in addition to the nine Common Principles, were in place to make change possible. Those factors were varied and complex.

A Champion

Elizabeth declared that their first principal had functioned for them as a champion for change, both by inspiring them and by enabling them to take the risks, and then by giving them the freedom to experiment. "Change is so difficult; it is such hard work. People need to realize that somewhere in all of the crowd, there has to be a champion. That champion needs to speak loudly and clearly for those who are trying to implement Coalition principles, because without that champion, people just feel in the dark." Although he was not at the school very long after the program was put into place, everyone on Elizabeth's team agreed that nothing would ever have been started without his initiative and support.

The Network

A new kind of relationship—the Coalition network—also helped Elizabeth to change. The partnership with Brown and with other schools across the country that were struggling with the same sorts of ideas was extremely beneficial.

> When I first met Ted Sizer in Cleveland, we had decided that my course would be called Inquiry and Expression, one of the courses Ted had suggested in *Horace's Compromise*. I had no idea what that meant or what I was going to do. I asked him for suggestions. I thought that since he wrote the book, he would know and he would tell me. He said, "You know, I'm not exactly sure; let me think about that and I'll get back to you in the morning." I was very shocked. I thought, "What do you mean, you have to think about it?" The next day he told me that he intended his work to be interpreted, that it wasn't by any means ever intended to be a model, so he really had to do some thinking. Between us, he and I hashed out a couple of places from which to begin. Over the summer, he and my colleagues and I talked through what I had done. Initially, I think, we all needed reassurance, since none of us really knew how to get started.

In time, Elizabeth realized that Sizer's initial response provided her with an example of the kind of relationship she wished to develop with her students: co-explorers, thoughtful people who were comfortable knowing that there are very few right answers. Over the years, Elizabeth developed a number of connections with other experimenters—teachers, principals, and professors—and together they discussed new approaches, compared interpretations of the Common Principles, and critiqued each other's work.

Teammates

A second kind of relationship was also new to Elizabeth and remarkably helpful. Elizabeth indicated that her relationship with her Newline colleagues was her major source of support.

> My relationship with my teammates is a whole new relationship. The level of interaction we have—the support, the encouragement—has been extremely positive. I concentrate almost all of my energy on these people. I think I mentioned before that I was so afraid of working with them; there is such irony in that fear! I keep a file for each of my team members. I have folders full of ideas they have shared with me, letters we have written during the summer, and examples of their students' work which taught me something. We are constantly teaching each other.

Elizabeth noted that she and her colleagues discovered one characteristic they all had in common. They were all curious, knowledge-seeking people, investigators—interested in learning. Although she felt that the term was overused, she believed that they were "risk-takers." "I know that's been talked about till we're all sick to death of it and, at first, I didn't understand it, but a lot of the work of change you do alone. You really do, and you just have to be willing to test the waters. We have all been willing to do that."

Time, Money, and Autonomy

Other support came in several forms. The group had received a grant to help them get going, which allowed them the time to experiment and later to gain the support of their school board. Of greater symbolic importance, the grant had given legitimacy to the experiment because it demonstrated that outsiders agreed that the project was important. The grant, which totaled $30,000, allowed them $10,000 per year. Elizabeth noted that the grant had helped to win the support of the central office.

Time was another aspect of systemic support. The fact that they had been granted 3 years in which to work at the outset of the project increased the likelihood that significant change might take place. Then, the teachers had been given an extra planning period each day so they could make collective decisions about their use of time during the school day, and so they could generate the necessary curriculum. In addition, they had reorganized their instructional schedule so they had longer blocks of time with their students. Each reconfiguration had allowed the teachers the opportunity to try out new techniques and arrangements, to revise, and to try again.

The autonomy they had been given to rearrange their time and to redesign their curriculum had also been important. Although they had frequently felt they might be the blind leading the blind, they were also clear that the autonomy had pushed them to ask questions they had not previously asked and to design experimental units they later refined and reworked. Elizabeth summarized, "Practice, practice, practice. That's what we did!"

The Motivation to Continue

Elizabeth and her colleagues were also motivated to continue. This motivation was drawn from several sources. Elizabeth was very clear about the primary source of motivation. "The response of my students has helped me more than anything to know that I am on the right track. They come in eager to solve problems; they grow in curiosity. They work harder and are much more engaged."

Another motivation for Elizabeth was the expansion of her own knowledge and understanding.

> I've thought more about who we educate and why. I've thought more about schedules and the use of time and the organization of time. I've thought more about materials, what's quality and what's not. In fact, in a sense, I value my colleagues who are working in traditional circumstances more because I realize that we're all struggling to do what's best for our students. I feel that I understand more clearly the difficulties they face because they have 5 classes, 30 students a period, 150 students a day. I think I value them more now.

Peter Daley reflected on what motivated him:

> Well, I don't think we've reached nirvana or anything yet, but it seems to be working one heck of a lot better. I have always had this idea, Daley's Law: the more you give teachers to do, the less they give students to do. If you've got 150 students, you're obviously not going to give them an essay to write every other day because you don't have the time to grade all those papers and, as a result, school is reduced to a ritual—the worksheet, the textbook, the short-answer test; learning is reduced to a formula or a regimen. Both teachers and students suffer from this kind of circumstance, and we all know that it might be easier, but it certainly is more boring. I like being able to reverse Daley's Law.

Another motivator for all of them came in the form of frequent requests to make presentations to other teachers. Elizabeth and Betty had driven quite a distance to make a 40-minute presentation entitled "Teacher as Generalist: Out on a Limb." Although Elizabeth thought the session had been a disaster—a "three-aspirin" session—she and Betty had caught the irony. They had tried to present a very complex topic in 40 minutes. It was just like their old teaching conditions, which had caused similar problems. As a result, they had learned again about the importance of adequate instructional time. Despite their harsh personal evaluation of the session, the presentation had provided them with the opportunity to connect to another interdisciplinary team that had been newly formed. These new teachers, from a different part of their state, had asked as many questions as they could squeeze into the breaks and on the walks to and from lunch during the course of the day. The new team kept referring to the two veterans, Elizabeth and Betty, as their "mentors" and were hopeful that they might make reciprocal visits soon.

The benefits of these speaking engagements were substantial. The team members were forced to examine their own practices and to evaluate the pros and cons. They were forced to organize their own materials so that others might be able to use them. They gained valuable insights from the comments and suggestions of participants, and they learned new strategies and solutions from the efforts of others.

Challenges

Although a number of people and conditions existed that had made change possible for them, there were simultaneous forces at work that Elizabeth believed had impeded her team's work. She noted that there was a great deal of paradox in change: oftentimes those circumstances that enabled change also constrained it. She also believed that some of the challenges, such as their personal fears, had diminished over time, while others—including lack of support and resentment from the larger faculty—remained a constant source of difficulty.

Personal Fears

Just as their own personalities had enabled them to undertake this work, their own fears had played a part in restricting them. Elizabeth had felt fearful of a number of circumstances. "I was very concerned about working with my colleagues. I felt that there might be a time when I would have to let down my guard and let them know that I didn't know everything I was supposed to know. I felt very vulnerable."

"Becoming a generalist also caused anxiety for me." Elizabeth was referring to Number 8 of the Common Principles, which states that teachers and principals should perceive themselves as generalists more than as specialists. Such a stance allows teachers to interconnect various disciplines for students and to take greater responsibility for the whole student.

Defending Change

Elizabeth had been uncertain about her ability to defend the changes she believed she needed to make. Although she had looked forward to closer relationships with her students, she had felt unprepared for the responses of principals and parents, largely because she was just beginning.

> During that first year, the first sources of contention were the parents of some of my students and the interim principal. Because all of this was new, I was somewhat insecure in what I was doing. I did not have the same sense of security and confidence I have now. I was not sure if I could answer some of those criticisms. ("Why is your classroom so noisy? You know, a good classroom is a quiet classroom." or "I want my kids to get into college. I don't want them doing anything different.") I didn't have enough in my heart to say to myself, "This is good for your students; you know what you're doing." One day the principal said to me, "I've been a teacher for many years and my students learned all they needed to learn while they were at their desks. Why do they have to leave your classroom or wander around the room?" I wondered whether I was doing the right thing. It was frightening to me because my professional credibility was being challenged. It literally made me physically ill. I just didn't know how to respond.

Administrative Turnover

A third major challenge to the team's work at Newline was the whole issue of administrative turnover. A number of transitions had taken place over the previous 3 years which confounded the team's work. Most notably, they had had three principals in less than 2 years. Although the first principal had been their champion, he had left hastily in the middle of their first year. The interim principal had not been not familiar with the Coalition, nor had he been a supporter. Elizabeth described the impact the interim principal had on their time. "We spent an enormous amount of time convincing him, explaining, pleading." Although his successor, Mr. Smith, worked to expand the number of teams, Elizabeth and her colleagues still worked hard to gain his support.

In a local newspaper interview when the School-within-a-School Program was identified as a model program, Mr. Smith was quoted:

Traditional education is not going away. There's just a thousand different ways to teach. This is just one step to improve education. I'd like to get away from the School Within a School title, because this is just one program in our school. We are all a part of Newline High School as a whole. I don't think education has deteriorated. I think it is the parents' and the students' interest in education that has deteriorated.

Lack of Administrative Support

In the midst of the team's work, the basic structure of the program had undergone significant transition as well. During the third year, the school board had voted to expand the program, utilizing existing school monies. (The original 3-year, nonrenewable grant had been used up, but the governor had become an ever stronger supporter, which had added political pressure for the district to maintain the program.) The administration had decided to do this by creating a second team of teachers. Elizabeth and her colleagues had submitted a report outlining their recommendations for the expansion of the program, most of which were ignored; their input was not solicited. Course titles and, consequently, course content had been changed back to basic discipline configurations—math, science, English, and history. Students no longer volunteered for the program; they were enrolled randomly.

Because the principal had hoped that the program would be institutionalized throughout the school, the teachers had been asked not to hold meetings for parents or to describe their purposes to their students. He had felt that this would stress differences too much and raise potential controversy. He had suggested that if the program were not billed as an option or as something different, and if the courses had the same names as in the larger program, participants would accept it more readily, with less of a fuss. When parents and students complained, feeling that the kids had been segregated in some way, the teachers had felt unable to convene a meeting of the new parents with the parents of the students who'd been through the program for 3 years. In addition, the expanded program had been established for only 1 year. As a result, Elizabeth and the other team members felt very insecure. Furthermore, the principal selected the teachers who would serve on the expanded team. He chose two beginning teachers and another teacher in whom parents traditionally had little confidence, even though some of the best teachers in the school had applied.

In dealing with the larger state educational context, none of the school-based educators perceived that the state laws governing public education would bend easily to support their work despite the fact that the state was a member of Re:Learning. (Re:Learning is a partnership between the state, the Coalition of Essential Schools, and the Education Commission of the States to create a policy environment that would support schools in making significant changes.) None of their conversations with the state department of education indicated that changes in graduation requirements, Carnegie units, or in discipline-centered requirements would be easy to change. In addition, requirements, which governed teachers' work lives, made it difficult for them to change the curriculum. "Because I must document my students' mastery of a whole host of basic skills, I am sometimes in conflict with what I know I 'should' teach and the goal of 'Less is more.'"

Student Resistance to Change

Another challenge was the transition students went through on entering the program. Elizabeth noted that her team's 4th year was almost a repeat of the 1st year. Students weren't used to having the same four teachers for all of their core subjects for 3 years. In addition, because the team had chosen to reorganize periods so that teachers had 2-hour blocks with their students, the students' schedules were different from those of many of their friends. One student felt that it would hurt her chances for college. Another student said he just plain didn't like being asked to think up questions.

> Kids do not want to be different. They have to work hard, and they are unused to it. They meet in 2-hour blocks and nobody else does. We don't use textbooks like everybody else does. One girl noted that the other classes have read 10 short stories already and we have only read 5. We've been at this for 9 weeks, and I feel from my students the same hesitations, the same apprehensions, even the same animosities that I felt 3 years ago. I am just now beginning to see a glimmer of light in some of their eyes— an indication that they are coming to the realization that maybe they do have partial responsibility for their learning and an interest in making more decisions about what they are doing.

Although she was beginning to see progress, Elizabeth noted that each new group of students that entered the program encountered difficulties as both the students and their parents weathered the transition.

Faculty Resistance

A fifth impediment proved to be more quietly troublesome. The rest of the faculty in this large comprehensive high school knew very little about their program other than that these teachers were given fewer students and an extra planning period. Asked by their administrators to be quiet about their program, all of Elizabeth's team members indicated that their relationship with their colleagues in the school at large was tenuous. Peter Daley explained.

> There is some tension with the teachers who are not in the program. We never know what they're thinking. Obviously the tension comes from the fact that we have 73 students and they have a 150, we've got two planning periods and they've got one. It's always under the surface, but I feel it and I'm sure it's there.

Elizabeth and her colleagues despaired that no forum existed for them to share their experiences with their colleagues. A number of times they had suggested informal sharing sessions but had been refused by the administration. Even if they were given the opportunity to share information about their program, they were unsure whether they could dispel the tension because any discussion of change tended to make many people defensive. Although they had gained enormously from their teaming, they felt increasingly isolated from the larger faculty.

Elizabeth summarized the challenges they faced in an image that surfaced again and again. When they started the program, the dream had been that the whole school would eventually become involved.

> The whole environment, you know, is generally not conducive to change. The image I have is that we—my team and my students—are all standing on the starting line of a new kind of event, and we're waiting for someone to fire the gun; my fear is that we're going to go on like this for years—at the starting line waiting for someone to tell us to really take off. We know a lot and we've been practicing hard, but no one ever gives the signal. The event never really starts.

Essential Lessons

Elizabeth's case reveals several lessons that echo findings in the previous cases and contributes a couple that are unique.

Parents and Kids and Resistance

Elizabeth and her colleagues found that parents and kids both were resistant to change. Generally, like many teachers and administrators, they felt uncomfortable with unfamiliar practices. In their first 3 years, the teachers held a number of meetings for parents to help them understand what it was they wanted to create for their children. They also spent considerable time explaining to students why they were doing what they were doing. In addition, they were firm; they persisted and they had the backing of a local prestigious foundation and the governor. Over time, both the students and their parents became their strongest advocates. Later, when they were not allowed to provide adequate information for parents, their discomfort grew. They remind us that students and parents require the same kind of educational opportunities and open discussion that fosters positive change for teachers and administrators.

Benefits Over Time

Both Kathryn and Elizabeth carried their students for more than 1 year, and both thought it to be an important contributing factor to their ability to better support student growth. Elizabeth and her colleagues noted that most parents and students were initially reticent to agree to this because kids frequently found themselves in conflict with some teachers. Three years would be too long! The teachers had come to believe that they had shifted their own attitudes about troublesome kids. They learned that there was always someone in the group who advocated for a student someone else found difficult. They learned from each other to see the strengths of each student and taught each other how to build on students' interests and competence. This team was also convinced that their students and their parents had grown to believe that this change was in the best interest of their kids.

The Disappointment of Temporary Funding

Elizabeth and company learned an old lesson about change. While they had outside funding, they had been able to do what they wanted and had felt that the support of the foundation strengthened their position. Once the funding dried up, however, support did too, until the program was all but eliminated. Many of the federally funded programs of the 1960's and early 1970's came to this end (Berman & McLaughlin, 1978). It is difficult to figure out how to change without some extra funds to help people retool, think, and practice. The trick is to figure out how to use the extra funds only for those extras people feel are expendable. In Elizabeth's case, the principal had told the larger faculty that it was the grant that paid for the extra planning time and the reduced student load. Because faculty had resented these perks and the principal had been unwilling to consider how these conditions might be made available for all teachers, these important conditions disappeared once the funding dried up, an all too common occurrence.

New Roles Bump Up Against Old Systems

Newline High School was a rural, county high school in a conservative part of the country. Hierarchical decision making was the norm: administrators made most of the decisions; and most administrators were men. When Elizabeth and her colleagues were given the autonomy to make decisions about their program, they had assumed that they would then share in the decision making about what happened to the program. Once the administrators shifted, this was clearly not the case. Seldom was the teachers' input solicited. When respectfully given, solicited or not, it was seldom considered. Simple requests like having a faculty meeting to talk frankly with the larger staff about what they were doing or inviting parents to an evening meeting were denied. These teachers believed that several norms worked against them: half of their team members were women, and all of them were teachers in a system in which teachers were allowed to make few programatic decisions.

What proved most frustrating for them was that as they learned to share leadership and responsibility among themselves, as their roles changed, and as they became more convinced that what they were doing worked better for students, they were less able to share with others, restricted by practices that they no longer used in their own classrooms or amongst themselves. The lesson here seems to be that changing roles for teachers is insufficient without synergistic changes throughout the system. Common practices, like decision making, need to shift system-wide if teachers are truly to be able to transform classroom practices and students' experiences.

Definitions of Teaming and Interdisciplinary Curriculum

This team took yet another cut at what teaming meant and how it might be done to support students. They believed that the primary purpose of teaming was to know students better and, therefore, agreed at the outset that they would carry them for 3 years. In order to engage students more rigorously, they had built what they called interdisciplinary curriculum by engaging in parallel processing of their various disciplines: when the history teacher did the Greeks, the math teacher did Pythagorean theorem and the English teacher did myths. They had used their daily team planning time—the last period of the day, the same period that Judd and his colleagues found so tough to use—to work on curricular connections, to talk about providing better support for students, to help each other understand what was happening in their classrooms, and to deal with various administrative requests and with requests for visitors and presentations. They had ensured that the time would be well spent by rotating responsibility among themselves by assigning a COW, the coordinator of the week. The COW kept the agenda, kept them on task, and took care of any details that needed attending to during that week. The fact that they had built a system like the COW ensured that they used their time better; the fact that they had continued to work within their own disciplines suggested that they were not necessarily ready to give up their discipline-centered affiliation.

What was perhaps most compelling for Elizabeth and her colleagues was their sense of the possibilities. They all felt that they were really just beginning in this work, but the vision they shared of what could be if they all just kept going and kept pushing was very motivating. Sally Watkins started to describe their vision:

> In the best of all possible worlds, every child would belong to some unit or family group in school. Throughout the whole system teachers would all be teamed, in threes at least, so that they could enjoy and grow from those relationships. Parents would be thrilled at the progress their children were making and the kids would decide that they didn't need to have jobs to pay for cars because they would be doing work which they believed was important—

Peter interrupted her to say that the class load might be even smaller, which would allow teachers to find more real-world connections for kids in their school work. Tom Whitman added the hope that the curriculum would be built as a real continuum.

> We would continue what we started on the first day and connect it up throughout the whole year, and then on to the next. The mini-Exhibitions and experiments would build one on another so that there was a progression. Although teachers are led to believe that this is the way, the textbooks are terribly repetitive and don't provide kids with the kind of depth that can hold their interest. They repeat a lot of stuff, year after year after year. We wouldn't do that.

Elaine Martinson chimed in to say that student teachers would be able to work with a team during their student teaching, which would really expand their exposure to more teachers and teaching styles.

"Let me sum up all this dreaming," said Elizabeth, eyes flashing, her face reflecting both teasing and conviction.

> We will not be a comprehensive high school. We'll be a total Essential school. And the quality of our students' capabilities and the work they do in their final Exhibitions will convince others to join us. We'll be off the

starting blocks—way down the track. The only uneasiness I'll be feeling then will be from worrying about what to wear on Katie's national news show. She's going to have her own weekly show, I have no doubt, and she'll do a special. It'll be on the improvement of American schools. I just hope I don't gain any more weight between now and then!

A loud hurrah went up from all.

SINCE THEN . . .

During the year I studied Elizabeth, she did a television interview with the governor of her state on the kinds of changes schools need to make; their work with students was widely recognized as exemplary. She and her colleagues published an article about their experiment in a leading educational journal. The next year, she took a leave of absence to get her master's degree. She left because she felt exhausted from struggling with the current district administration, which did not envision the program in the same way she and her colleagues did. At the same time, another of the original team members left to do his doctoral work—also fed up with the lack of decision making ability the teams had. On her return to school in the fall of 1991, Elizabeth found the original conception—a team of teachers carrying a common group of students through their high school years—dismantled because the larger faculty was angry about the original program, and because the principal had been charged by the superintendent to get more people involved. He did that by making teaming available, but he eliminated the complication of carrying students over time. He promised to schedule any teachers who were interested with their partners and to give them a common planning period. Elizabeth teamed with a geography teacher; together, they continued to work on developing more valuable practices. Elizabeth was very disappointed that the experience that had been so powerful for her and for her students was no longer possible. At the same time, she was encouraged that more people on staff were involved. The division between her team and the larger faculty had been painful.

When she returned for the 1992–93 school year, nine teachers on the faculty were teamed. There was still no arena in which the whole faculty might discuss change or work towards communicating about teaming. The administration had turned to a new focus—Tech Prep—the preparation of non-college bound students for vocational programs. At the beginning of the 1993–94 school year, only one team remained. Elizabeth chose not to participate until she understood what kind of support they might be given. The principal retired, and the new administrator might well have been a carbon copy of Mr. Smith in his reluctant support. To make matters worse,

he had no personal history with the students or parents who had benefited from their original program.

Looking back at her school, Elizabeth felt as if they had begun a journey that would have resulted in much more powerful schooling for their students. "I feel like we just chase every old rabbit—one right after another. We
can't seem to stick with one thing. Don't have the courage to go the distance. I'm not sure anymore that one teacher or a group of teachers can
make a difference. We can make a difference for our students, but not for
the whole school."

> If I look back at what we were doing in 1989–90, everything was focused
> on personalization—making sure that we knew the kids well enough to
> get them involved. Now I'm adding to that the development of their
> habits of mind. We had eight students—the geography teacher and I—
> who weren't doing very well. We pulled them out of the class to build
> their intellectual habits. We made progress with them, but they hated
> being pulled out. Next I'm going to try doing that without pulling them
> out of the classroom.
>
> I love working with my students and with the other teachers in the
> school. I do feel like I imagine adopted children feel—you know, they love
> their adopted family, enjoy being with them, but always wonder about
> their true parents, always hope that they'll run into them on the street or
> find them after 30 years. I feel that what we did with that group of kids we
> had for 3 years was my real school, and that what we're doing now is my
> adopted school. I haven't given up hope. I'll keep working on finding a
> real school.

7

Common Places

A lthough any number of cross-case comparisons are possible when looking back at the journeys of these teachers, several common places emerge as most compelling, most deserving of reflection and examination. These are places where each of the teachers and their colleagues stopped along the way. They were not mandated to pause where they did, nor were these stops recommended by the Coalition as appropriate. They were chosen by the teachers themselves; thus, they give us greater insight into what teachers choose to do when charged with the redesign of their practices. There they grappled with teaming, the interconnectedness of curriculum, pedagogy and assessment, changing conceptions of teaching and learning, shifting leadership, and the nine Common Principles. Each pause is fraught with its own dangers—misinterpretations, faulty assumptions, possible overconfidence—and each illuminates the promise of changing practices.

TEAMING

Little and McLaughlin (1993) make the point that high schools are places where multiple professional communities exist, and that it is quite possible that two teachers, teaching side by side for years, experience the school quite differently, and despite their proximity, these same teachers may not know each other at all. Their research reveals that the primary community within high schools is the subject area department—the English department, the social studies department, and so forth. They point out that departments represent the power bases within schools: they compete for resources, influence the schedule, generate their own grading and tracking policies, assign classes to individual teachers, and so on. Departments are described as sturdy, micro-political organizations within most schools.

Teachers in this study elected to challenge the department structure by forming cross-disciplinary teams. Although the Coalition makes no recommendations about teaming, it is perhaps the single most common strategy adopted by CES schools nationwide. The fact that all of these teachers selected teaming as a strategy suggests that they were dissatisfied with their traditional professional communities to at least some degree, that the focus on disciplines narrowed students' learning opportunities too significantly, and that the teachers felt the need to experiment with other forms of collaboration. These cross-disciplinary teams challenged most of the micropolitical norms of their schools.

Purposes

In each these cases, the teachers suggested that they undertook teaming for a variety of reasons. All of the schools had multiple purposes in mind; some had more than others. The purposes of teaming were not formally delineated, but emerged as teachers talked about why they were doing what they were doing. Some were clearer than others about what they hoped to achieve from teaming, and their teams reflected the clarity or lack thereof that they themselves were able to articulate. Most of them mentioned that teaming had been a strategy in the sixties, but that it had faded. They suggested that there was little information about why teaming was undertaken then, what went wrong, and why, but believed that it was an important strategy to pursue. They also noted that there was little information written about teaming that might have helped them as they built their own teams. The reasons for teaming included the following:

- To reduce teacher isolation
- To make curricular connections for students
- To know students better
- To increase parent involvement
- To gain greater flexibility in time, for both learning activities and for teacher and student work
- To blur curricular distinctions in favor of thematic or problem-centered learning
- To build continuous professional growth opportunities for teachers

These purposes are different from those that undergird discipline centered schools, and as a result, it is not surprising that they provoke challenges to the existing system. Although Huberman (1993) suggests that individual work may be more creatively compelling, these teachers made choices that suggest that collaborative work provides more benefits for both students and teachers. They indicate that working collaboratively enables teachers to strengthen support for children while fostering their own professional growth.

Challenges

Moving to teams provoked several major challenges for these teachers. It required that they replace the autonomy in which they had worked for years with a willingness to collaborate. It was no longer possible for them to close the classroom door completely or to make decisions independent of others. Relegating one's individual authority to the authority of the group proved extremely uncomfortable for teachers steeped in years of independent work.

Also, they required more time to meet and plan together; less of their planning could be done at night at home after their own kids were in bed because they had to do it in the company of their colleagues. Thus the work day seemed extended because they had lost the ability to schedule their own planning time around their family routines.

The major challenge Judd, Jennifer, and Elizabeth encountered was resistance from the larger faculty. Their schools were larger than Mary's and Katherine's, and engaging the entire faculty in support of changes like teaming simply did not happen.

Almost every aspect of teaming constituted some challenge to their colleagues who were not on teams. Traditional budgeting procedures provided a good example. Each year, in all of these larger schools, departments submitted budgets to the principal and competed for limited resources. When the teams, which crossed disciplinary boundaries, worked together, they needed resources—extra planning time, release for conferences, support for visitors, new materials. They constituted a new bargaining unit, one which affected, and often reduced, the competitive power of the individual departments. Because the teams asked for and got highly valued resources, many of the faculty were resentful.

Teaming caused other disruptions to the normal order of business. Counselors needed to schedule kids differently. Pullout programs required new thinking. Lunch schedules had to be refigured. Most of the teams involved teachers from core subjects—math, English, science, and history. When teams asked for scheduling considerations like longer blocks of time, other staff who weren't in core subjects worried that their jobs would eventually be jeopardized if the whole school went to teaming—they worried that there simply would not be enough time in the day for teaming and electives. Still other faculty felt that they had been left out of the decision making about the formation of the teams, and as a result, suspected that it would soon be a mandate for everyone; without the ability to discuss and to decide, teaming seemed to them a questionable goal.

Another set of dynamics contributed to the resistance of the larger faculty. . . . Jennifer, Judd, and Elizabeth *were* hopeful that the whole school would eventually be on teams. Their colleagues did not miss for a minute that those on teams held those goals, regardless of everyone else's lack of enthusiasm. To further confound things, whether they intended to or not, the teams' stance suggested to their colleagues that those on teams were working harder and doing more for kids than those who were not yet teamed. This was communicated when the teams made presentations to the faculty in which they pointed out that they were trying to address student motivation, to eliminate passive learning, and so forth—implying that the rest of the faculty were not. Many of them felt that their responsibility was to "sell" the larger faculty on teaming so they spoke only of the advantages, of how well things were going for them, how much their students were benefitting. Their non-teamed colleagues were not naive enough to miss the pitch and often felt manipulated by it. At other times, the kids or their parents suggested that the teams were really trying to address some of the major educational problems. Regardless of who delivered the message, it made those not teaming resentful of the implications.

For all of these reasons and more, insider/outsider dynamics developed. Teams, the insiders, received the attention and additional resources—extra planning periods, reduced student loads—while the rest of the faculty felt themselves to be uninformed, excluded, and undervalued. Both groups—the teamed and the unteamed—saw their counterparts as unwilling to cooperate.

Although the resistance teaming generated in the three larger schools may in large part be directly connected to the larger faculty's lack of participation in the decisions to team, it seems clear that until the source of this resistance is addressed, teams will be challenged to justify their existence and to maintain their roles.

Benefits

From these teachers' perspectives, there were important benefits to teaming that, in their minds, counterbalanced the challenges. In Mary's and Kathryn's schools where the entire school moved to teams, teams became the new professional communities and were described as richer, more meaningful. They learned from each other information that would never have penetrated their individual worlds. Teachers felt compelled to think beyond their own disciplines, which was refreshing, interesting, and growth producing. Several of them mentioned that they felt renewed enthusiasm for learning itself, freshly conscious that there was so much to learn outside their own disciplines. They gained respect for their colleagues, what they knew about their disciplines, about teaching, about individual students. They gained validation for their own work as others adopted some of their suggestions. They shared strategies, techniques, and materials and talked over problems. After years of isolation, such conversation was very restorative.

All of the teachers gained respect for their students. Because they could talk to several other adults about their students, they gained insights that they had not been able to gain on their own. Each teacher had additional observations and knowledge about individual kids, which proved helpful to all of them. Knowing a kid was an expert in science made the English teacher more appreciative and also gave her a clue as to how she might hook that particular student in English. Teaming diminished the them-against-me experience that many teachers talk about. Those teachers who carried students for several years described their relationships with students as deeper because they were able to expand their understanding of each other through continued shared experiences. They noted that watching students grow and mature from one year to the next was perhaps the greatest reward of teaming.

Having teammates made individual teachers more confident about when to contact parents, how to contact them, what kind of involvement to suggest. Again, the collective brainstorming that the teachers did made them more comfortable about including parents in the support network for children.

In addition, as the teachers became more comfortable with teaming, they began to see greater benefits in teaming for the kids, too. Kids learned from each other, helped each other, and talked their way to new understandings. Teaming helped teachers so that they could use time more flexibly; if students needed more time to work on a particular activity, they could negotiate those arrangements. Similarly, if teachers needed time to organize materials or field trips, that time, too, could be arranged. Mary, Kathryn's colleague at Westgate, said that she actually felt like a criminal when she went to a bookstore during school hours for the first time. She behaved furtively, looking around to make sure that no parents saw her!

New Skills; New Roles

Teaming required a whole new set of skills not commonly practiced in traditional schools. Several years ago, Saxl, Miles, and Lieberman (1989) developed training materials that emerged from a study of teacher leaders. Teachers leaders, working with their colleagues, suggested that they needed assistance to build skill in six skill clusters, which enabled them to:

- Build trust and rapport
- Engage in organizational diagnosis
- Build process skills
- Deal with resource utilization
- Manage new work
- Build skill and confidence in others to continue

All of these skills were valued by these teachers as well, despite the differences in their responsibilities. They needed good communication skills—active listening, checking for understanding, honesty, directness; and good negotiating skills—the ability to deal with conflict, to understand multiple perspectives, to negotiate mutually acceptable compromises. Running meetings, establishing agendas, building in reflection, critiquing, and accepting the critique of others all required new roles and skills which focused on building common work. These teachers, accustomed to thinking of professional development in terms of new curricular trends or new instructional methods, found it difficult, and at times embarrassing, to request help to gain the skills they needed to assume these new roles; however, their assuming new roles and gaining the requisite skills had a great deal to do with the effectiveness of their teams.

Teacher Leadership

The close collaboration and new responsibilities in teaming generated new needs for teacher leadership. Going to meetings and gathering and creating curriculum materials all required that someone of the group keep things moving and organized. And, as the cases demonstrate, the teams were more or less successful depending on the quality of internal leadership that the team constructed and/or acknowledged. These teams offer glimpses of several teacher leadership arrangements: Mary had no special release time, but was supported in the development of leadership skills in a weekly meeting with the other team leaders and Adrienne. Kathryn's team had a teacher on half time release to keep the team organized and focused on instruction. Similar to department heads in her school, Jennifer was given an extra planning period for each team she coordinated. Elizabeth and her colleagues developed the COW, coordinator of the week. They chose to rotate leadership responsibilities. Judd's team, to their own detriment, had not set up any kind of internal leadership structure.

Analyzing their leadership roles makes one conscious of the power of leadership in a given setting. The teacher leaders in Kathryn and Mary's settings operated similarly to the principals in their schools—encouraging open and honest discussion, bringing out conflict, fostering the resolution of conflict, holding the team to its vision. In Jennifer's case, she operated much like her first principal. Elizabeth's team consciously worked to establish a new norm of leadership.

Again, the quality of the leadership in large part determined the success of the team. Given the predominant egalitarian norms in teaching—that everyone has equal status, differentiated only by the number of years' experience—this aspect of teaming also assaulted traditional norms. On the other hand, these teachers suggested that they benefitted from increased

responsibility and appreciated the opportunity to spread leadership responsibilities through their own ranks.

Teaming, selected by all of these teachers, constituted a major strategy
in each of these schools. Not counting the rest of the staff in Mary's school,
or the other teachers in Kathryn's school, the teams represented in these
cases include 36 teachers. When asked in general what made the changes
they'd made most potent, all of these teachers claimed that fresh opportunities to work with colleagues was a significant benefit and motivator. In
addition, they confirmed McLaughlin's (1993) findings about highly collegial
places. They had a renewed commitment to teaching, great enthusiasm,
heightened interest in their own professional growth, a willingness to inno-
vate, and a belief in shared responsibility. Kathryn and Mary offered a summary the rest of these teachers agreed with when they suggested that they
no longer considered it a privilege to work collaboratively because cooperating is difficult for even the best of friends. They did, however, agree that
teaming was a professional responsibility because they gained a great deal
personally—clarification of focus, new strategies, more immediate feedback,
a closer community, a sense of shared responsibility, and better articulated
beliefs—and believed that they were able to serve their students better.
None of them would go back to working alone; however, they recognized
that simply building a team was not enough. Teachers needed to clearly
understand the purposes of new roles and the new skills needed before
teaming made a difference for them and for their students. In addition, many
of them felt that they had miles to go before they felt assured that their non-
teamed colleagues were willing to go along with them.

THE INTERRELATIONSHIP OF
CURRICULUM, PEDAGOGY, AND ASSESSMENT

Along the way, most of these teachers had come to a central insight about
the interrelationship of curriculum, pedagogy, and assessment that fueled
and provided support for much of what they were doing. In their previous
school experiences, curriculum had reigned supreme. They had worked in
discipline-based departments; they had worried about standardized tests
within their disciplines; and they had been expected by the state and/or district to teach and to cover a specified curriculum. As a result, they had
thought most about curriculum—the discipline-centered work they had to
cover. Coverage, making it through all the prescribed topics, always too

many, had been their central teaching responsibility. Curriculum had been what they planned in advance of the term.

Closer to the actual day the curriculum would be delivered, these teachers had thought about pedagogy. Most of the teachers suggested that this had been a less demanding task because they had drawn from a relatively limited repertoire of teaching techniques: lectures, demonstrations, worksheets, conferencing with individual students on their projects or assignments, reviewing homework. Conferences had consisted mostly of telling students what teachers thought might be changed to make a piece stronger. Reviewing homework had meant that teachers demonstrated at the board. Less attention had been paid to engagement; more to finding instructional methods that ensured that teachers were able to cover everything they wanted to.

Closer to the end of the unit, these teachers had begun to think about assessment. Tests had been necessary to ensure that students could demonstrate knowledge of the material covered. Again, these teachers had suggested a limited repertoire of assessment practices: text-tests or their own multiple-choice tests, short-answer essays, research papers, reports, essays, and an occasional project. The emphasis had been on students' recall of the curriculum. Projects, student-initiated investigations, critical thinking, and practical application had been fewer, because they took too much time and interfered with curriculum coverage.

As these teachers began to concentrate on engaging students more thoroughly, on thinking about performance assessment, on curriculum connections, they found themselves unable to separate curriculum, pedagogy, and assessment into the neat, rather linear schedule they had previously followed. When they did follow the old format, something slipped: If the curriculum was planned first without thought to pedagogy, teachers didn't have adequate time to get the information into a form that kids could use themselves; if they left the assessment to the end of the unit, kids frequently had not organized the information in a form that would allow them to demonstrate convincingly what they'd learned. As these teachers continued to bump up against these kinds of complications, they began doing a kind of simultaneous planning. The conversation would begin with what they wanted to cover (old habits die hard!); someone would ask how they were going to get the kids to interact with the material in a more substantial way; then someone would ask how they were going to know whether the kids had actually learned what teachers wanted to ensure they understood.

Eventually, it seemed that together these three strands comprised the fabric of teaching. Eliminate one, and the strength of the whole fabric fell apart. By the time I followed Kathryn, she had had considerable experience in blending the three. Each assignment Kathryn gave—while the students were doing their literary comparisons of justice, or the role play to understand how and why bail is set—was leading up to the culminating mock trial. In order to do well at the trial, students had to practice organizing an argument and presenting a point of view before the big event. They had to have a number of opportunities to practice during the course of the unit. Had she not had the final assessment in mind from the outset, students may not have had adequate opportunities to build the skill and confidence they needed to do well. Had she lectured rather than providing them with less important presentation activities, they would again have been hampered.

Recognition of the interconnection of these three aspects of teaching suggested major changes within each domain as well. Understanding of the interconnection is strengthened by a seemingly contradictory exploration of each individually.

Curriculum

Discipline specific curriculum has long dominated in most secondary schools in this country. As these teachers worked to build better practices, they found themselves questioning and undoing some of the most commonly held truths of curriculum. They came to believe that connections between the disciplines were more potent than a single minded focus on their own discipline, that texts were less valuable as the centerpiece of a course than material of their and their students' devising, that depth of student understanding is preferred to coverage of material. Each had resounding effects on their daily work.

Curriculum Connections: Interdisciplinary or Integrated?

Every one of the teams chose to connect various disciplines in some way. However, it was initially confusing because most of them used the terms *interdisciplinary* and *integrated curriculum* synonymously. Closer observation suggested that their practices varied from school to school and that they could be better understood by the distinctions Heidi Hayes Jacobs (1989) suggests in her work on integrated curriculum. She notes that the various approaches these teachers used fall along a kind of continuum from parallel processing (teaching Greek myths in English while teaching about the Republic in history) to integrated curriculum (the Project Challenge strategy, as described in chapter 5).

Interdisciplinary curriculum meant that teachers taught within their own disciplines but made connections through a chronological or thematic alignment. (In Elizabeth's school, they were discussing what each would teach when they covered the Greeks, for instance.) The rationale here was that individual teachers maintained their discipline-centered expertise while attempting to help kids make the connections between disciplines. When

integrating curriculum, teachers took responsibility for more than one discipline and did not draw attention to the distinctions between disciplines.
The rationale for integrated work, according to these teachers was to present learning closer to its natural state. Integrated curriculum also allowed
kids the latitude to explore the given topic or question from some vantage
point that interested them. It also lent itself to more practical application of
the issues under investigation and was less dictated by a chronological, or
linear approach. Kathryn's study of "What is Justice?" is an example. Students
were exploring justice in works of literature, in their own writing, in the
daily newspaper. In following a contemporary rape case, they went back
in time to explore the building of precedents.

The further these teachers moved on the Jacobs continuum, the more
they attempted to build a curriculum that incorporated more choice for students and began with some connection to students' daily lives. To integrate
meant further changes in teachers' roles, in the schedule, and in curriculum than did interdisciplinary work. The further they moved toward integrated curriculum, the more they balanced the emphasis on curriculum with
the emphasis on students' learning.

Regardless of which tack they took, these teachers all noted that by con-
necting the curriculum, they believed they provided students with better
understanding about the nature of knowledge and more realistic learning
experiences. The teachers acknowledged themselves that it may not be
more efficient to concentrate on a single discipline at a time and that students need to have the capacity to understand the interconnected nature
of knowledge, to unravel various aspects, and to combine pieces into complex wholes.

Coverage Versus Depth

Prompted by books like *Horace's Compromise* (Sizer, 1985) and *A Place
Called School* (Goodlad, 1984) and their own discontent, these teachers all
realized that many of their students were disengaged in school partially
because of the race to cover. Moving through material so fast that many
couldn't fully absorb its meaning and its utility left them feeling insecure and
disinterested. Jennifer noted that every year students got stuck in the same
places in math, but she had no time to stop and help them because she had
too much material to cover.

Rapid coverage of curriculum has implications that have been clearly
documented in McNeil's powerful work, *The Contradictions of Control*
(McNeil, 1988). Complex material is oversimplified; discussion of controversial issues is avoided—too emotional, too volatile. Kids miss contemporary examples and experimentation with practical applications. Coverage
is supported by the bell curve, which justifies that only 25% of students will

learn any given topic well, while the rest do moderately well to nothing at all. Pushing fast, leaving many with sketchy knowledge is justified as mer- itocratic—survival of the fittest—and undergirded by the belief that not all students are capable of learning.

These teachers claim that by opting for depth, they narrow the range of topics to be covered in any given year, but take the time to allow students to explore more deeply in any given topic—to build practical applications or extended projects, to move backward and forward in time. For instance, in US studies, students may still investigate the Civil War, but might do that by contrasting it with the circumstances in Bosnia/Herzogovina. This requires that teachers determine the critical skills and concepts students must not miss, coordinate with colleagues who taught the kids previously in order to understand what they know, and inform those teachers who will have them next so that they can build a coherent curriculum. Then, teach- ers must build a variety of activities that will allow *all* students to gain deep understanding. This shift is undergirded by the belief that all students can learn and must be given the opportunity.

Moving from coverage to depth does not suggest that students relin- quish responsibility for the memorization and drill that are part of skill build- ing. It does suggest that the need to master a skill emerges for students from the larger problem or project context, so that students can see the utility of the skills they need. At the same time, these teachers have been convinced by the futurists and their own inability to keep up as thoroughly as they'd like in their own disciplines that knowing all the important information— times, dates, places, people, or vocabulary—is no longer as possible as it once was; that there is simply too much to know. They have come to agree that it is more important for kids to know where to get that factual infor- mation and how to use it once they find it, than to spend time storing it in their short-term memories.

Moving from coverage to depth suggests its own set of challenges for these teachers. It implies that curriculum in a given system should be built to provide students with a coherent experience that in most traditional systems is very casually monitored, if at all. This, in turn, requires still greater cooper- ation among teachers who teach different age groups. The move from cov- erage to depth caused these teachers some healthy anxiety about whether their students would do as well on standardized tests as other students because these measures are critical for college entrance. Although the most recent sta- tistics continue to suggest that students can still manage the tests, and although more colleges and universities are willing to consider performance assess- ments, the evidence is not broad enough yet to be thoroughly reassuring.

In addition, teachers raised in a system designed to encourage special- ization have to grapple with their own beliefs about the need for greater expertise, especially in math and science. Will students who've covered less than kids in other, more traditional schools be able to compete when they get to the college courses designed to eliminate the less competitive? Again, limited anecdotal information suggests that they will be, and that they are competitive, but again the evidence is not compelling enough to be a surety.

Pedagogy

Hoping for heightened engagement from students and looking for techniques to move them out of passive roles in school, most of these teachers found themselves thinking more seriously about pedagogy than they had previously. As they searched for new techniques, they analyzed their own role in the classroom. All described teacher-centered roles in their previous jobs and noted that they relied most heavily on whole group instruction. The norms pressing for quiet and control overshadowed their interest in the quality of student comprehension. In retrospect, they all agreed that there had been little focus on instruction either in their college preparatory courses or in their continuing education. Now, however, all of them were using group work, building collaborative tasks for students, taking themselves out of the center but circling closely around each group to understand better what students were doing, what they were having difficulty with. They were attempting to locate a more appropriate metaphor like coaching or directing or construction-site supervising. They were aware, some for the first time, that students need to struggle with material themselves to gain the same kind of understanding and appreciation that teachers themselves have.

Tired Teachers or Tired Students?

At first, the old joke about teachers being so tired at the end of the day because they'd done all the work seemed appropriate to these teachers. Soon, however, as their understandings about the changes they were making deepened, they found the joke inept. They were more tired than ever at the end of the day even if they did have fewer students! And they weren't up in front all the time either. Fewer students and classroom practices that moved the students into active roles did not translate into time off for teachers. Fewer students whom they knew better required more attention. The teachers found it necessary to build a range of activities for each class, some which attended to the process of learning, others which attended to content. Two examples illustrate: Jennifer asked the students to log in, to recount their progress, to work in their groups on a new task, to report on both their progress and their group process, and to design the activities they'd need to go through to plan a vacation, paying particular attention to the necessary math skills. Kathryn had students work on writing independently while she conferenced with individual students—not correcting their papers for them as she used to do, but asking questions to prompt them to see their own errors and to clarify their thinking so that she could get to know better how they worked. Then she orchestrated a discussion, followed by a role play. Each class period was varied and moved from individual to group activity, from generative to reflective practices.

The planning required for such diverse activities included thinking about many possible directions students might take and various decision points teachers might encounter. Working with more varied instructional techniques, and spending more time watching and listening, these teachers noticed that kids brought varied approaches and skills to class. Variation in activities clearly became important access points for kids, all of whom were different and responded to different stimuli. These teachers, through their own experiences with kids, came to agree with Gardner's (1983) theory that students come to school with multiple intelligences. Growing understandings like these brought these teachers to a new respect for the professional responsibilities of coaches, supervisors, and conductors.

Diagnostic Skill

Most of these teachers described a new skill that they believed to be key to supporting their students better. Although Saxl, Miles, & Lieberman (1989) noted that teachers needed to be better organizational diagnosticians, these teachers needed to be better diagnosticians of individual student's learning. Although the medical analogy might be inept because these teachers did not see their patients as diseased, the term was helpful in a number of ways. As they moved away from whole group instruction, the teachers had more time to watch kids work. Gradually, they began to pick up clues about how individual students were processing information, organizing their time, and interacting with others. They found themselves working harder to understand each learner individually so that they could prod each along to greater capacity. To do that, they gathered data by watching and listening closely, by asking questions and making suggestions, by watching again and making further modifications. Such close observation had not been possible when they were teaching to the whole group. This new skill required closer attending, observing, synthesizing, and reformulating, but there still seemed to be too many kids in the classroom to do this thoroughly for each.

Seeing the critical need for better diagnostic skill helped these teachers to move from the traditional focus on curriculum to a shared focus on the subject and students. As a result of this and their collaborative discussions about students with their teammates, they perceived students in a different light—puzzles, individual challenges, which they, as teachers, were responsible for piecing together while guiding students through new material. This shift, again, was quite profound, because all of the teachers described that previously they had spent much of their time blaming students for inadequate performance without consideration either of teacher performance or student abilities, learning preferences or prior experience.

An Ever-Expanding Repertoire

During the course of the study, all of the teachers struggled with the differences between their teaching now and the pedagogical techniques they'd used previously. They tended to be dismissive of their previous teaching roles, yet irritated when someone pointed out that they were using some of the same pedagogical techniques visible in any school. Several of them worried about visitors because there were days when they used every old technique they'd every learned—pop quizzes, lectures, note taking, reading out of a text. They did not see this as a matter of reverting to old behaviors. Instead, they had come to see that they were constantly building their repertoire of instructional techniques. And they needed as many techniques as they could possibly gather. They stopped seeing any one technique as the villain, but did agree that overuse of any one technique was villainous on their parts! Although it was temporarily discouraging to some to understand that they would always be engaged in the process of building a stronger repertoire, they understood that their discomfort was a result of their previous conceptions of teaching as something that could be mastered with right techniques. Acknowledging that teaching was a craft to be honed over a lifetime was encouraging because it suggested continuous growth, heightened interest, and cumulative skill and wisdom.

Assessment

Challenged to determine whether students really know what had been taught, most of these teachers were attempting to move from recall tests to performances. Still daunted by state competency tests and standardized tests, many of the teachers were attempting to build end-of-unit assessments, which they called exhibitions or mini-exhibitions. In some cases, they were also working to develop broader assessments—portfolios—which would move with the kids, or with final graduation exhibitions. In both Mary's and Kathryn's schools, this took place by whole school committees.

New Skills

New assessment measures predictably suggested that teachers needed new skills and a comparative understanding of various forms of assessment. In Elizabeth and Kathryn's case, the mini-exhibitions they were doing were much like final unit writing assignments in traditional English classes. The differences were that students were encouraged to shape their own approaches, that multiple forms were acceptable—videos, reports, creative writing—and that students were expected to share their findings with others. Initially teachers reported great frustration at students' lack of skill or effort. On further examination and conversation with students, the teachers learned that students did not necessarily have the skills needed for more complex approaches, nor did they have enough experience with these new forms to judge quality. Adequate practice and reflective evaluation of examples done by others had to be combined in the unit in order to ensure that kids had the personal experience to produce a good final product.

Assessments for the Assessments

A number of the teachers talked about their ill preparedness to score performance-based assessments. Straight A–F grading seemed inadequate; they recognized the need to give kids more feedback on their performances and on their presentation skills in addition to their written material. Many were engaged in building scoring guides or rubrics for performance assessments. In addition, students' work was more varied so they had to find ways to grade it that calibrated effort, experience, innovation, and quality. As student tasks grew more complicated, the grading task became more complicated, so that, again, they had to go in search of new practices.

These teachers and their teammates uncovered two insights that changed their teaching lives profoundly. First, they discovered that it was no longer feasible for them to address curriculum, pedagogy, and assessment as if they were three separate aspects of teaching. Secondly, they determined that the interconnection of the three propelled serious changes in each aspect. Coming to understand that these three aspects of teaching were inextricably intertwined led teachers to an acceptance of planning that is more recursive—moving backwards and forwards between the pieces of a unit. They came to accept, not without frustration, that teaching itself is more unpredictable and messier, but still requires careful and thorough planning. "Winging it as an acceptable strategy is not part of what I learned!" said Judd at the end of our work. In addition, seeing teaching as multidimensional enabled them again to acknowledge the power of collaborative work; different people worried about different aspects of teaching. Finally, although their work seemed more complex, most of these teachers agreed that they'd come miles closer to understanding the true nature of their profession.

THE NINE COMMON PRINCIPLES

Having a set of ideas to interpret is an unfamiliar practice in schools used to the models and mandates of the 1970's and 1980's. The strategy is based on voluminous research suggesting that commonly held beliefs propel school faculty towards more coherent and educationally sound practices. (Fullan, 1989, 1990; Sarason, 1971) As a reform strategy, the ideas require that teachers, students, administrators, and parents call on their own intellectual resources to determine what each principle means in their specific context. The principles were designed so that once that kind of effort was invested, schools might be clearer about their purposes and direction, that they might be less inclined to abandon their efforts whenever the next approach appears on the reform horizon. Teachers in these cases had different experiences with the principles as an interpretive tool to guide their work.

Judd noted that, because the principles seemed so simple and straightforward to begin with, his staff found it hard to return to them, to work with them over time. Judd himself found them unnerving; the longer he and his teammates worked together, the more he realized how complicated the ideas they were working with actually were. He felt discouraged, too, because the ideas were too easily turned into slogans. Ironically, with slogans, concrete meaning seems to diminish in direct relation to their broad acceptance.

Kathryn felt that though she and her colleagues seldom talked about the principles directly, aspects of them peppered their mutual planning. She noted that the principles were like onions, ring and layer after ring and layer of understanding, each revealed as she worked to go deeper. She noted that they were only as useful to her as the effort she expended to use them.

Elizabeth and her colleagues talked about them regularly and acknowledged that they were implementing all of them at once as they built their original program. When her administrators intervened to change what they had created, she recognized that they did not have the same understanding of the ideas or the same commitment to them.

It seems from looking across the cases that ideas are only as useful to a school as the effort the faculty expends to understand them and to use them as a guiding tool. If schools work towards common understanding of the principles, it is more likely that they will be able to design practices that match their agreements. Traditional faculty meetings have worked against the kind of sustained, substantive discussion that fosters shared understanding. These teachers described faculty meetings as the time when staff got together to listen to announcements about the daily running of the school, up and coming events, and so forth. Because of hierarchical patterns of leadership, the structural emphasis on expertise by disciplines, and time constraints, these teachers suggest that these meetings do little towards facilitating discussion about what the faculty believes about its practices and its responsibilities to students. Unfortunately, several of these teachers noted that they had engaged in activities to generate "mission statements" for the school. They participated in tightly controlled processes over a short period of time, and the expectation that they would attempt to analyze whether their practices matched their mission seemed nonexistent. Generating a mission seemed often to be an end in itself; one never had actually to do it.

Without that common set of beliefs, it is too easy for each individual to proceed on individual definitions, which are often quite different from those of others. The autonomy in which most teachers have worked persists, and teachers are robbed of the ability to learn from their colleagues through discussion and argument. Prestine (1993) confirms that a school that spent time understanding the principles was able to sustain its efforts to change during and beyond a very difficult year of innovation because it had a common understanding about its goals and direction.

Coming to an agreement about what they mean is only the first step. As Elizabeth suggested, she and her colleagues were constantly asking whether they were actually translating the ideas into their daily activities. This is another recurrent and recursive process, one which requires time to work on together.

Obviously, ideas have long been compelling in the history of humankind. Teachers in these cases suggest that ideas such as the nine Common Principles can provide a beneficial support for educational reform when used to build common understanding and to assess whether actions taken match goals established.

CONCEPTIONS OF TEACHING AND LEARNING

In the midst of rethinking curriculum, pedagogy, and assessment, forming and working with teams, and working towards the implementation of the nine Common Principles, most of these teachers ascertained that their basic beliefs about teaching were shifting. Piaget (1987), Sarason (1971), Fullan and Miles (1992), and Gardner (1991) have for years pointed out that just such a shift is necessary. Constructivists are gaining influence and writing extensively about the necessity of this shift (Prawat, 1989, and Brooks & Brooks, 1993). Teachers' beliefs about how learning takes place must shift from understanding teachers as the deliverers of knowledge to the facilitators of students' own learning. Fischetti, Dittmer and Kyle (1993), in an article that traces the roots of the constructivist theory, suggest aptly that teachers must determine how to provide minimum assistance, whereas their previous training suggested to them that they had to provide it all. What is quite hopeful and confirming is that these teachers came to the same conclusions as a result of their own experimentation.

The work of several notable educators helps us to gain a deeper under-standing of the nature of this change in beliefs. As teachers begin to see their roles differently, they search for new descriptions of their philosophy and their responsibility. Gardner (1993) and Perkins & Blythe (1994) suggest that they are really teaching for understanding. When teachers teach for under-standing, they are not satisfied with the simple recall of factual information. Instead, they want students to apply concepts, formulas, and events to new, fresh circumstances. By analyzing students' applications, teachers are able to assess whether or not they have a deep enough understanding to be able to use knowledge gained. The important distinction here is utilitarian in the best sense of that word—knowledge must be useful, must add to a student's own repertoire of learning techniques.

Newmann and Wehlage's (1993) work on authentic instruction delin-eates a series of characteristics describing the kinds of techniques that pro-vide evidence of the necessary shift in conceptions of teaching and learn-ing. These criteria include evidence of higher order thinking skills, depth of knowledge, connectedness to the world beyond the classroom, substantive conversation, and social support for student achievement. These criteria pro-vide a good analytic tool for review of the teaching in these cases and help teachers to understand whether their actual daily work with students match-es the rhetoric of their beliefs.

The shift from believing that teachers are the repository of knowledge to believing that students must construct their own knowledge requires a much more difficult transition than any description of it can convey. Teach-ers must grapple with their own childhood school experiences where many of their attitudes about what constitutes good teaching were formed. They must confront their training, hours of listening to lectures. They must ana-lyze their own teaching experiences. Once the shift becomes apparent, there is still more work! It is far more confusing to find, to build, and to practice new techniques than the definitions of the set of criteria convey.

CHANGING LEADERSHIP

Although some aspects of teacher leadership have already been considered as they relate to teaming, the issue of leadership in general is important enough to merit a broader discussion. Although there is almost unanimous agreement in the reform literature that leadership roles and practices must change if schools are to be better places, what this actually means in terms of their daily interactions is, unfortunately, not nearly so clear to principals and teachers. Several years ago I was at a friend's for dinner and a woman said to me, "My principal thinks she's into school-based management and shared leadership, but we think she really wants to be queen." I love this description because it captures the confusion that exists for nearly everyone about shared leadership and shared decision making. Most principals experience a great deal of confusion over what it means to share power while still providing what every one notes as essential—leadership. The administrators in these cases provided multiple examples of leaders trying to unravel the meaning of shared leadership; some didn't believe in it at all; others struggled; and a couple seemed to be forging new paths.

Adrienne from Cityscape and Rebecca from Westgate High cannot be dismissed as important examples of new leadership simply because they created new schools. Their bold actions helped others to articulate new practices and to see new forms of leadership in action. Both of these women put new decision-making structures in place and gave up the formal teacher evaluator role. These two changes alone allowed them to support change better. In decision making, although no one was unaware of their very real informal power, they were able to participate as nearly equal voting members, allowing them to be as honest as they hoped others would be. It also prevented them from putting programs or projects in place with which the staff did not agree and would most likely ignore. They were also able to function as provocateurs, to nudge people along, while holding in place the goals and the vision they and others shared about what the school might become. They kept one eye on current practices and the other on discrepancies, next steps, and future possibilities. Furthermore, they represented the school at the central office and the state department to ensure that the kinds of changes teachers were making met with support rather than dismissal. Their roles were complicated, far reaching, and intensely interconnected with teachers and students. To a large extent, they embodied the cultural norms they wanted for the school and gained power, not from their positions, but from their commitment to teachers and students.

It is also important to note that both of these leaders chose to build small schools. Size obviously has a direct bearing on leaders' abilities to know staff, students, and parents well, and thus to better assess the values and the tolerance of their communities for change. The importance of school size becomes apparent when we understand that the difficulties of change were exponentially magnified for the three larger schools in the study.

The three other schools are from two-and-a-half to four times bigger than Eastgate and Cityscape. They each have long, and in some cases illustrious histories of traditional, hierarchical practices. All of them have customs and norms that predate this study by decades: Faculty meetings in two are planned and run by the principals and focus on information dissemination rather than on substantive discussion about teaching and learning. In all, departments compete for limited resources; the schedule supports the old conception of learning and the departmental organization of high schools.

Still, within these larger structures, the principals took different stances. One of the principals was quite content with business as usual. The other two believed that they were working hard to change these old customs and norms and their own roles, but were perhaps trapped, as teachers frequently are, by their own most familiar practices. In both Judd's and Jennifer's schools, when the principals began to build the change efforts, they appointed people or anointed volunteers (in itself a hierarchical act) rather than institute a whole-faculty decision-making structure that would have involved everyone. As a result, the larger faculty were excluded from the formative discussions, which would have allowed them to participate in the generation of strategies, purposes, and the vision. Such participation might have reduced the staff's fears that they were being attacked yet again or mandated to change. With no part to play, most of the larger faculty in both schools opted to be resistant.

There are other examples that suggest that these principals thought they were engaged in changing practice, but in reality, they were being quite traditional. In Andy's case, he delegated responsibility to the team but did not share it with them. He withheld his voice, thinking that he was obligated to do so when "sharing." Jennifer's principal, similarly, did not meet with the teams, but with Jennifer, his designee. Delegation, an old bureaucratic practice, continued in the midst of intentions to share, sending contradictory messages to those involved.

Shared leadership is understandably complicated. One of the primary tasks is to understand the difference between hierarchical decision making and shared decision making. In hierarchies the emphasis is on specialization, on delegation, and on efficiency, whereas in shared decision making the emphasis is on shared responsibilities and mutual goals and aims. This shift, too, suggests enormous competence from leaders—they must be able to envision the as-yet-unrealized school, validate that vision through group participation, ask questions, and prompt people to move in that direction. Quite naturally, there is constant tension between establishing direction and manipulating; between guiding and sharing; between sharing responsibility and abdicating responsibility. Again, the re-creation of the common conceptions of leadership requires that everyone shift their expectations, their personal responsibilities, and examine their past practices to better understand the consequences of their actions.

In many ways the shift expected from principals is much the same as the shift expected from teachers. Principals, too, need better diagnostic skills to listen and watch teachers work and to guide them in reflective, analytic behaviors. They need to engage teachers in the co-construction of their beliefs and daily practices and in greater collaborative effort; and they need to see whether teachers' practical applications suggest deep understanding of their new, shared beliefs.

Kathryn, Mary, Jennifer, Elizabeth, and Judd, with their teammates and administrators, were all trying to make sense of the whole combination of these changes. When considered all together, the combination of changes constitutes a very different kind of professional work and responsibility. Isolation, once a predominant characteristic of the world of teachers and administrators, gives way to collaboration. Single subject matter organization gives way to interdisciplinary or integrated curriculum. The dominance of curriculum gives way to a new understanding of the interconnectedness of curriculum, pedagogy, and assessment. Teachers search for methods that take them out of whole group instruction and that engage kids in significant ways; they search for assessment measures that allow students to demonstrate what they know and how well equipped they are to use it. Planning changes, resources change, and teaching materials change. Hierarchical structures give way to new shared responsibilities. Strong leadership from both teachers and administrators is essential if all of the effort expended is to have any real benefits for students.

Several aspects of the examination of the cases surprised me. When I was doing the cases, they seemed radically different. The context was quite different in each of these schools: from urban poor to a less debilitated urban population, from suburban to rural, from resource rich schools to schools that were impoverished. And yet, the strategies these teachers elected were generally quite similar. It is possible that membership in the larger Coalition network facilitated the general trends, although these teachers did not all have access to regular communication with other Coalition teachers and administrators. It is also possible that given the freedom to determine what is best for students, the teachers' instincts led them to the same conclusions as educational philosophers like John Dewey, and contemporary researchers cited herein.

At the same time, there were some very interesting and productive variations influenced, most assuredly, by local leadership and norms. These welcomed creativity and encouraged local and regional diversity, freedom from the crushing sameness—a McDonald's on every corner and a TV in every home—that pervades this country.

In the end, considering the changes that they made, most of these teachers felt as though they'd grown enormously and that they'd achieved better success for their students. The fact that they were willing to dig in at all, and that they were willing to examine their common practices in the company of colleagues and to make changes and reexamine those again without the external pressure of a mandate from the state legislature or from the department of education or the central office is important. It suggests that intellectual activity, and the great promise thereof, is alive and well in the midst of our schools.

8

Epilogue

A s this journey to collect images of teaching done differently draws to a close, a pause is needed to determine the distance traveled, the distance left to go, to think about what we, the teachers and I, have learned in the process. A series of questions surfaces from an imaginary audience: You wanted to collect images of teaching done differently. What did you end up with? Was the journey worth it—from the teachers' perspective? From the researcher's perspective? What was learned that might enable others as they proceed on their own journey? What questions remain to be asked of others who choose this same path? The answers to these questions help to estimate the distance come, and to mark the far horizon.

IMAGES OF TEACHERS IN THE MIDST OF CHANGE

As I got to know these teachers, their contexts, their particular interests and dreams, it became apparent to me that my original intention was misguided. Teaching is not easily transformed, nor is the transformation process something that one completes; my insight as a researcher was similar to theirs as teachers: teaching is complex enough, compelling enough to provide teachers with a career of growth, change, and ever deeper understandings about how students are best supported. Teachers do not arrive. They do not ever learn everything there is to know about teaching. Although for some this is humbling, and for others discouraging, it also promises a career rich enough in complexity and potential inquiry to hold a professional's interest for more years than a typical working lifespan allows. Such knowledge helps to combat the old disparager that haunts teachers: "Those that can't, teach." Teaching is, in reality, only for those who can—learn, hone, reflect, and then investigate again.

DO STUDENTS BENEFIT IN PRODUCTIVE WAYS?

This is a question that this study does not adequately answer. Because the focus was on teacher change, the data gathered was insufficient to make determinations about student performance. Even though one would expect teachers to confirm that their work has been worthwhile, their comments are still of interest to those who want to know if these changes are productive for students.

For the most part, these teachers believed that their work had produced the kinds of results they were aiming for. Although they were not yet satisfied that students were making all the gains possible, they did believe that their students were making uncommon progress as a result of their—teachers and students—efforts. Kathryn noted that watching her kids in their mock trials and in the law firm convinced her that the kids were learning concepts, communication skills, and leadership skills more thoroughly than the students she had worked with previously. Despite Judd's dissatisfaction with his team's progress, their students, as a result of consistent attention from their teachers, were staying in school. Elizabeth looked at the examples of student work—the student's re-creation of the concluding chapter of *Of Mice and Men*, among others—and concluded that kids were taking more risks, thinking more deeply, and working longer and harder on their mini-exhibitions. Jennifer had far fewer complaints about math from students and their parents. She also had the advantage of comparing conventional classes with her project based classes. "Everybody knows that math is hard for kids, that a lot of kids don't get it. I'm having fewer complaints since the kids are engaged in project work, and I'm hopeful that we'll see that what they learn sticks with them better." She also believed that the kids in her project classes got better attention from her; she was able to watch them, to understand their thinking processes as they solved problems, and thus, to provide them with better diagnostic support. Mary and her colleagues believed that their students were learning to cooperate, to dig deeper, to finish difficult projects. Students' real accomplishments, such as completed video tapes and reports on waste management, enhanced their self esteem, which the team believed key. Unfortunately, they noted that self esteem is largely ignored in general formulations of student achievement.

Collectively, all of these teachers believed they could demonstrate that their students were meeting some of their original objectives. Most of them were convinced that their students were doing better work, and that they could prove it if they had access to comparative samples drawn from students who'd worked with them previously. Measuring their students' growth against other kids in other more conventional classes seemed problematic to them, unless daily observations of both sites could be included. In three of the five schools, teachers were working on establishing portfolios and public exhibitions of student work so that their students' progress could be assessed by others in the community. Believing that their students were gaining increased competence and confidence, none of these teachers suggested that they were anything but encouraged.

WAS THE JOURNEY WORTH IT?

From all of the teachers' perspectives, regardless of the difficulties, undertaking change was and is a worthwhile process. Different from previous efforts to change with which they had been involved, this time each of them had come to the same conclusion: that change was necessary for both students and adults. In addition, they worked collaboratively to think about what should be done. Some made enormous progress; others were stalemated by the surrounding context or by their own lack of familiarity with reflective practice, but all of them learned enormously. All of them talked about a recommitment to teaching as a profession, a heightened investment and interest in their work, a greater sense of their own professional responsibilities and capacities, and a renewed belief in students' substantial potential. Their professional communities expanded so that they felt more connected to others in their work place and to other educators beyond their own school. In short, their own professional self-esteem rose.

From a researcher's perspective, the journey was very fruitful. A number of researchers like Michael Fullan, John Goodlad, Ann Lieberman, Judith Warren Little, Milbrey McLaughlin, Seymour Sarason, and Ted Sizer among others have suggested that the changes these teachers are making are necessary. I was able to watch teachers unwittingly concur as they, oftentimes unfamiliar with much of the research, generated their own ideas about what needed to be done to improve student performance. In watching them play out these reforms, I was able to gain a more thorough understanding of the contextual complexity that either confounds or supports teachers' best efforts. What appears as a recommendation in the research takes on a whole new meaning when translated into practice!

In addition, I, like the teachers, gained renewed respect for teachers who had the courage to undertake this extra effort to change. Clearly, in order to move forward, they became more intellectually active in problem-solving daily practices, student capabilities, organizational structures, and so on. They expended enormous energy to move from previous practices to new, and from autonomous work to collaborative work. These teachers, even when they weren't as successful as they would have liked, were eager for feedback to learn about their own progress so that they could push further forward. They were willing to undergo public scrutiny and were courageous enough to hold problems up to the light so they, and others, could grow from them. Moreover, the incentives that encouraged them were simply heightened professional efficacy. More often than not, they received no more money, had less flexibility in their use of time, and encountered all kinds of circumstances that they hadn't encountered previously. I gained a greater sense of hopefulness for reform in American schools, a renewed sense of the potential that rests in our teaching force.

WHAT LEARNED?

From watching these teachers in action, several fresh understandings emerged. These are issues that helped me to clarify what's involved in school change and I hope they will help others to strengthen their own efforts. Although these issues are numbered, they are by no means listed in any order of importance.

1. Emerging Characteristics of Collaborating Teachers

Looking across these teachers, I am led to the conclusion that they share some distinct characteristics that are different from the set of characteristics that describe most practitioners working in conventional schools. These teachers:

- Move students to the center of the learning activity
- Understand that activities, problem solving, and/or projects provide students with worthwhile intellectual work and compelling experiences
- Are diagnosticians of individual student's intellectual development and skill
- Select from a wide range of instructional techniques and are constantly expanding their instructional repertoire
- Accept uncertainty as central to the learning process, both for themselves and for their students
- Understand that school has to connect the interests of students, teachers, and the local community, and that they are primarily responsible for providing the connections
- Discover that curriculum, pedagogy, and assessment are planned and reshaped simultaneously
- Move from a focus on coverage of curriculum to a focus on depth of students' understanding

- Use student performance as a guide to their own efficacy
- Are unwilling to work alone because of the personal limitations it places on them
- Are able to be a critical friend to others and to benefit from the feedback of others
- Have significant responsibility for making decisions that affect the school and accept that responsibility
- Have a philosophy and a set of ideas, which they share in common with their colleagues, that guide their work. They know why they are doing what they are doing.
- Accept new responsibilities (new, closer relations with parents) and forfeit old freedoms (the ability to close one's classroom door)
- Examine school practices and structures vis-a-vis their goals for students and change those that aren't in sync
- Share responsibility and leadership with their administrators and their teaching colleagues
- See change as productive and essential to learning rather than as criticism, and seek it out
- Understand that change for themselves means change for others and work to facilitate that
- Know their students and their families very well: what they like, what they do in their spare time, what they hope for
- Learn that teaching is an activity in which the teacher as well as the students must always be learning

As more teachers begin to change their practices, there is a growing need to redefine what it means to teach. I do not suggest a narrow, limiting definition but an expansive one, one that suggests growth and productivity. This list may prove helpful because it can fuel good debate and discussion that leads to greater clarification and agreement.

2. The Need for Stability in the Midst of Change

Several of these cases demonstrate that teachers' efforts to strengthen students' education is only as good as the stability of the system that surrounds them. When superintendents or principals or team members leave, much of what teachers have undertaken is frequently undone. Established as an interdependent hierarchy, the conventional system suggests that people at the top have the overriding authority to make decisions about the focus of effort for a given school or district. Belief that children need more various experiences in schools suggests that these decisions must be shared by teachers, principals, central office folks, and policy makers, and that those newly hired or elected need to be informed of and committed to sustaining the work underway. Although it would be overly naive to suggest that those involved in school change stay put, it is not impossible that measures can be taken to protect those who remain. System wide, those who begin efforts to change need to secure policies and practices that make it likely that people's best efforts will be sustained and valued over time. Governors and legislators need to commit their resources to state efforts for periods that extend beyond their potential tenure. Qualifications to fill new positions need to include recognition of work underway that requires the support of potential candidates. At the school and district level, teachers need to be involved in hiring principals. Principals and teachers both need to be able to influence central office hiring. It is possible that school boards might establish much lengthier terms of commitment to individual efforts at the outset. In the face of personnel turnover, unless provisions are made to protect efforts begun, schools will continue to change direction with each new hire. The more horrifying effect of this is that teachers and principals, once interested and committed to change, will continue to develop into the difficult, resistant cynics we sometimes see in the educational ranks today.

3. "Everybody Changes; Nobody Stays the Same"

These cases make it abundantly clear that unless traditional procedures, policies, and roles change throughout the system, teachers will be severely restricted in their efforts to improve student performance. Sizer (1991) wrote about the fact that everybody needs to change their role, that no school personnel will be untouched because once change is underway, it begins to affect everything and everyone. He wrote this to assuage the fears of teachers in elective fields who could not originally see how they might be included and worried that their positions might be eliminated. His point was that teaching kids to use their minds well does not take fewer people; it requires that people think about working in different ways in order to achieve different, more powerful ends for students. These cases demonstrate that everyone involved in the educational system needs to be involved in order for deep and lasting change to take place. We can see from the cases that within the school, teachers', counselors', and administrators' roles change. It is equally important outside the school: in the district office, in schools of education, in state departments.

One insight is particularly striking. There appears to be marked similarity between the changes we hope for in the various roles different players hold. We hope that students will demonstrate intellectually lively interest in their school work. We hope that teachers will be more compellingly involved in ascertaining students' growth, needs, and strengths. We hope that principals will be more thoughtfully engaged in the construction of school programs that promote student engagement, and so on. Everyone is interested in engaging their primary constituents more actively in the learning process, which requires that everyone needs to be using their minds well. Secondly, in order to accomplish this, everyone is interested in sharing decision making, power, and responsibility. Kids are more engaged when teachers involve them in determining the direction their final exhibition will take. Teachers are more involved when principals ask them to determine what professional development they need as a group. And on it goes. Shared responsibility and heightened involvement seem to be key for everyone involved, no matter where they are in the system.

Without a doubt, this effort will also only be as good as its ability to extend into schools of education. To suggest that teachers are trained conventionally and then transformed once they get into the schools is both costly and foolish. Schools of education need to help new teachers, principals, teacher leaders, and superintendents develop the kinds of skills the teachers in these cases have found necessary. Professors, like teachers and administrators, need to examine their pedagogical processes and techniques to ensure that they are modeling what they hope their students will learn and emulate.

The fact that there is a kind of synergy in the retooling that everyone needs is important; it suggests that it will take us all to redesign schools so that students are better prepared for the world in which we live. It also indicates that we will all learn together what it means to engage others, to share leadership, and to rethink our basic beliefs about what teaching and learning are. Suggesting that everybody changes, nobody stays the same confirms a point Sarason has made repeatedly over the years. Schools will not change for students unless they also change for adults.

4. Change as a Continuous Process

These teachers demonstrate that change is not a single "Ah-ha," or two or three gestalt-like events; it is, instead, a continuous process that includes recognizing a problem, learning about it, experimenting with potential solutions, integrating those that work, reflecting on what's lacking or missing, and beginning again. There are several implications of this understanding. Fostering change, cannot be shaped into a tightly organized, linear program that is completed in 2 months or at the end of a course. Change takes more time, more time than any of us, even those who long ago recommended ongoing support, imagined. Although there are those who would cry that we don't have the time, that teachers should be mandated to change, their cries are misguided. We know from experience that trying to short circuit the time it takes for people to change their practices and their beliefs also reduces the likelihood that meaningful, sustained change will take place.

Teachers need time and continuous opportunity to work with new ideas and practices. In some cases they need to revisit a particular point or issue a number of times before it strikes them as significant. Then they need to try beginning to interpret it in their own context, in the midst of the history of their own experiences. The implications of this insight are terrific for those who would foster teacher change. It suggests that teachers, like children, need to work on building skills and activities that are currently of interest and relevant to them. At the same time, staff need to be exposed through seminars, reading groups, and discussion groups to new ideas and techniques to ensure continuous growth, but the decisions about what they will work on should be left to the individual or the team. They need multiple opportunities to consider a particular issue or problem, as they, like students, are ready at different times.

The third implication is that those who would foster teacher growth also need to support teacher development of analytic, diagnostic, and reflective capacities. It is not enough, as we saw in Judd's case, for teachers to build new practices without the skills to take stock. They must be able to gather data on whether their new plans and activities are as productive as they had hoped. Although Donald Schön (1983) has taught us a good deal about the need for and the means by which to build reflective capacity, these need to be included not in separate courses, but incorporated into teachers' own professional development plans.

—

Naturally, in a study of this nature, one concludes with more questions than one gains in new understandings. I am left wondering how we'll know and convince others that students are better prepared by teachers like these, in schools like these. Here we see through fairly thick description what change means in the daily life of these teachers. I wonder what it is like for those who are not in such sharp focus. What are kids doing? What does their work look like? Is it better? What are principals doing? How are they rearranging their past practices? What about the union, state department people, governors and their aides, central office people, university professors? I wonder, too, whether we can build a collective sense of what it means for all of us to create schools where students learn to use their minds well. Can we, together, build a coherent vision of an educational system that serves all its students and leaves them on the doorstep of a nation that so desperately needs an intelligent, energetic, thoughtful populace? We haven't managed this in the past. Is it possible now? Peter Marin (1969) wrote that schools make us all smaller than we are. Can we, together, build schools that make us all greater than we dreamed?

As if responding, Mary, Kathryn, Judd, Elizabeth, Jennifer, and all of their colleagues dream a new image, a counterbalance to one that expressed their worst fears at the beginning of the book. Here, they move beyond their own current practices to create an image that conveys the essential nature of a life in teaching: growth and change. Does this describe their current circumstances since we left them? Is it a distant future? Beyond this, what other images are possible?

Two students, high school freshmen, walked down the hall of their high school with their parents to register for the first day of school. The feeling in the school was familiar. For the parents, the school seemed much the same as it had when they attended— new paint; old smells. But there were new signs everywhere: Central American School, with an arrow; Health and Society, with its own arrow; The New European Community, (written in French, Spanish, and German) and an arrow; Ancient Civilizations and Modern Perspectives, with a pyramid pointing upstairs; The American School, the arrow pointing north.

The students were excited; the school seemed bigger than their previous school, more adult, sophisticated, but they knew they'd be working in a smaller school within the larger building. In the spring, students from the high school had come to their middle school and explained the philosophy of the school, which really housed five schools of 200 students each. Students voted to ascertain the focus in each of the houses each year.

The two students checked at the office to confirm that they were enrolled in the Central American School. Then, knowing that it was still summer and likely to be vacant, the students and their parents headed off to locate their classroom.

They found the room, but it was three classrooms turned into one and it was definitely not empty! As they walked in, they saw an absolute hum of activity. The teachers, eight of them, the CD player playing Spanish canciones, were working in different groups. One teacher was up at a large map of Central America, gesticulating wildly. Clearly he wanted to get his point across. Several teachers were lounging behind desks, with pads of paper or computers in front of them, watching him, nodding or shaking their heads. Two teachers were arranging several potted palms into a kind of tropical landscape in one corner of the room. It was beginning to look like some kind of a Spanish patio or maybe a plaza. Two other teachers were sitting on a couch with books, magazines, and all kinds of other material around them. They looked up when the new students and their parents came in. Ms. Emery beamed and welcomed them.

She was the Central American School team leader. Her age was inestimable—older but not old. She hugged both parents, who knew her. She had taught them when they were in high school! "Oh , oh," thought the kids. Immediately, her gaze dropped to the two freshmen and she held out her hand, which each of them shook in turn. "Jito, I am so delighted to meet you. I have been looking forward to working with you this year; And you must be Hannah. It's going to be such an exciting year. Habla espanol?"

"Si," Hannah said shyly.

"Nope," said the Jito.

"Bueno!" she responded to Hannah, and turned to Jito, "Neither do I, very well, but we'll learn together. Mr. Guittierrez, over there at the map, is our expert and he's been absolutely relentless with us teachers all summer." Mr. Guittierrez turned to them

while phrases in Spanish rolled like ripe berries, sweet and round, out and around them. The kids giggled, turned red and shook their heads. They'd understood nothing but the beauty of the sounds. "Eventually," he said to them in English, "and it won't be long!"

"Ms. Emery, what's happened here? This is nothing like when we went to school. What do you think of it? Will our kids get a better education here than we did?" asked Jito's mother.

"Better? It seems better to me, but it's hard to tell. Times have changed; the world has changed; kids have changed; so we've had to change too. I think it's better because kids are doing more and are really involved. On the other hand, I thought it was good when you were here as students!"

Jito's mother said softly, "Your humanities class was my favorite in high school. Do these kids get to read classics, connect the past to the present, and think hard about real issues like we did?"

"Definitely! They certainly read classics—though they may be Latin-American classics instead of European classics. Many days, I think the kids have to think harder and longer about things now, but then, I've learned a lot more about how kids learn and what makes them think. Let me tell you a little bit about what we'll be doing."

She pointed to a long wall, slowly being covered with questions. "This is our inquiry center. You can see we've been finding some of the really big questions that face the Central American countries; some of them are historical, like 'How do countries with such diverse peoples blend their interests?' Your first job," she looked at Hannah and Jito, "this year will be to develop your own essential question on which you will work during the year with a team of colleagues and an advising teacher. At the end of the year, parents and community members will be invited back when you exhibit the fruits of your labor and defend it. Last year we had students who organized a telecommunications conference with students in Russia. Their task in a one hour program was to help students to define the benefits of political change."

"Wow," said Hannah, eyes huge.

"Wow, is right! It's on video tape. You'll see it. There is our world currency market." She pointed to a corner that had clocks registering the different time zones of Central and North America, and computers lining the counter. "The computers enable us to connect to the individual national market reports that come out daily so that we can keep track of how the individual economies are doing, how their currency is holding up, and so forth. Some of their economic reports are quite different from ours, which is interesting for students to work with. Ms. Jefferson is familiarizing herself with them now, and she and the students will set up daily tracking procedures and analysis procedures too. Then over here we have our own very limited but constantly rotating Library of Central American works. We've subscribed to a newspaper from each of the countries and we are borrowing books from all over the country via inter-library loan. So part of the time we will be reading original works in Spanish. At first we'll have translations, don't you worry; but before you know it, Mr. Guittierrez will have us reading Spanish as if we were born in Guatamala!"

While asking questions of the students, probing for their interests, Ms. Emery described that there would be a community service component to the students' work and that, embedded in the focus on Central America, they would build their skills and understandings in language, science, math, history, computer literacy, and English.

One of the parents made a plea, "Can I help? I'd love to help. I get several hours a week from my company to do community service work. I work at the phone company and maybe I could arrange for someone to explain how the telecommunications cables work. . . ."

They conspired, met the other teachers, and Jito and Hannah helped to lay a few tiles before saying goodbye so that the teachers could carry on with their planning. As Ms. Emery waved them down the hall she heard Jito ask, "Mom, I never did any of this stuff before; it's going to be hard, huh?" And Hannah, talking to her father, "Dad, could you understand what he said? He talked so fast. I thought I knew Spanish pretty well . . ."

"Another year! Where did the summer go? We're not ready yet!" Ms. Emery had a moment's panic. Then she turned back to Ms. Naiquist who drove her a little nuts, but who had promised to help her understand the differences in the governmental structures before school begins. "Let me do them on the chalkboard," Ms. E. said. "Then I can erase them when I mess up." As she moved to the board and picked up the chalk, little clouds of chalkdust puffed off the chalk tray, off the chalk. Suspended in the air for just a moment—miniature clouds—then gone, stirred to new horizons. . . .

Appendix A

SUPPORTS, CHALLENGES, AND ESSENTIAL LEARNINGS

Teachers	Support	Challenges	Essential Learning
Kathryn	Structure Collaboration Teacher leadership Starting slow Building configuration Principal The kids	Bigger responsibility Collaboration Group decision making New relationships with students No rest	Structure counts Systemic support Role changes Changes in beliefs
Judd	Funding Re:Learning Willing team	Time to plan Collaborative skills Experience of team Changing leadership Lack of professional develop- ment for teachers Interpretation of the 9CPs	Insider/outsider Dynamics Early fame Personal agency
Jennifer	The kids Leadership The 9CPs	Personal fears Listening, not talking Collaboration No models Teaching as continuous growth	Insider/outsider Dynamics Teaming for personalization Need for stable support Mathematics and change

(cont'd.)

213

Supports, Challenges, and Essential Learnings (CONT'D.)

Teachers	Support	Challenges	Essential Learning
Team	Decision making structures Culture of honesty and directness Shared leadership expectation for experimentation	Rhetorical agreement and follow through Finding time Dealing with uncertainty and ambiguity Question of rigor and quality	Whole school culture Tension between expectations and student experience Team works
Elizabeth	A champion for change The CES network Teammates Time, money and autonomy The kids	Personal fears Defending change Administrative turnover Lack of administrative support Student/parent resistance Insider/outsider dynamics	Parents, kids resistance Benefits of carrying kids for three years The problem of temporary funding New roles/old systems

End Notes

―

CHAPTER TWO

[1]Kathryn and I struggled to find terms that would describe her past teaching practice. She preferred the term *conventional* to *traditional* because she felt it less pejorative. *Conventional* refers to a particular kind of teaching that has received considerable attention throughout the history of schooling. The predominate image of a conventional teacher suggests that the teacher delivers instruction to students. Students are vessels waiting to be filled with knowledge. It is important to note that there are both brilliant and dismal conventional teachers. Good conventional teachers employ a number of teaching strategies from Socratic dialogues to lectures to activities in which students must demonstrate their comprehension. Good conventional teachers are typified by Mr. Chips, Miss Brooks, Mrs. Zajac in *Among School Children* and Robin Williams' role in *Dead Poets Society*. Examples of dismal conventional teachers can be found in the works of Charles Dickens and Mark Twain and in the movies *Teachers* and *Ferris Bueller's Day Off*.

[2]"Student-as-worker" implies that knowledge is constructed by the learner, not handed over by the teacher. Further, it implies that the goal of classroom activity is to teach students to be self-regulating and enterprising learners; that is, the work they do must help them to develop the skills to learn — the skills of question formulation, investigation, synthesis, and analysis, among others. The work students are involved in must be educative with a clear performance objective in mind, so that the larger purpose of any given activity is to help the student make independent choices. For a fuller discussion, see Wiggins (1988).

[3]Each house comprised five or six advisory groups—one teacher and approximately 15 students per group. The house system guaranteed that each student had a smaller, more personal community in which to work. The house planned several whole-group activities each year, and the house teachers met once a week in order to plan events and to communicate on students' progress.

[4]The term generalist refers to principle number 8. It suggests that in schools which put student learning first, teachers must take on multiple responsibilities rather than perceive themselves simply as subject-area specialists. As generalists, teachers develop curricula that make connections among disciplines and between the learning world in school and the world at large. As generalists, they also function as coaches, counselors, and managers, taking greater responsibility for the whole school.

[5]Essential questions are an important part of rethinking the curriculum in Essential schools. Essential questions become the centerpiece around which the curriculum is built, rather than the curriculum being organized around right answers. Essential questions go to the heart of the discipline; they do not have obvious, single right answers; they require that students engage in higher-order thinking skills; and they allow for personalized interest. For a more complete discussion, see Wiggins (1987).

[6]"Mini-Exhibitions" are an adaptation of principle number 6, which encourages schools to find alternative ways in which students might meet the requirements for a diploma. A graduation Exhibition is a culminating public demonstration of the student's mastery of a limited number of skills and areas of knowledge chosen by the faculty as essential to the school's program. Kathryn and her colleagues developed mini-Exhibitions, exercises which allowed students to demonstrate mastery at the end of a unit of study. The end-of-the-year mini-Exhibitions in humanities would require that students demonstrate their understanding of the essential question, What is justice?

[7]Bloom's *Taxonomy* has been interpreted as a linear scale of learning activities that moves from the least difficult (knowledge acquisition) to the most difficult (synthesis of material). See Benjamin Bloom, *Taxonomy of Educational Objectives*, vol. II (New York: D. McKay, 1956).

[8]Kathryn noted that although I did not observe any of these conventional methods, she certainly used them on occasion; for instance, she quizzed students on their reading. However, she used the quizzes to stimulate discussion rather than for grading purposes.

[9]The full texts of these studies report the dismal results of costly staff development programs in recent years. The conditions in which teachers work seem particularly resistant to significant change. See Fullan (1989); Lambert (1988); Little (1988).

CHAPTER FOUR

[1]Jennifer had obtained this exercise from the Connecticut Multi-state Performance Assessment Collaborative Team (Compact), a project sponsored by the Connecticut State Department of Education and the National Science Foundation to develop rigorous state-level math and science assessment instruments. For a copy of the complete dog pen problem or for more information on the Connecticut project, contact COMPACT, Box 2219, Connecticut Department of Education, Hartford, CT 06145.

[2]This activity was taken from Malcolm Swan, *The language and function of graphs*. Nottingham, England: Shell Centre for Mathematical Education, Dale Seymour Publications, 1984.

CHAPTER FIVE

[1]The Ropes Course is an actual patented course taught in many schools and camps. It consists of a series of physical and mental challenges that teach trust, build collaborative skill, and encourage people to stretch beyond their current capabilities.

[2]Project Challenge is a pseudonym for Project Adventure. For more informtion about Project Adventure, write to: P.O. Box 100, Hamilton, MA. 01936 or call: 508-468-7981.

[3]The Foxfire Teacher Outreach Network offers courses on developing student centered curriculum much like Eliot Wigginton, Foxfire's founder, describes in *Sometimes a shining moment: The Foxfire experience.* New York: Anchor Books, 1986.

CHAPTER SIX

[1]In *Shopping Mall High School* (1985), the authors describe the kinds of treaties which exist between teachers and students—"Don't ask me to work too hard and I won't cut up in class." "Don't give me any grief and I won't push on you to extend yourself." Elizabeth's new group of students was used to treaties of this nature and, as a result, initially often felt uncomfortable in her classroom.

[2]Elizabeth worked with four groups of students each day. I chose to include her most difficult group for two reasons. First, almost every teacher I know has one class that is more challenging than the rest, and they are the most likely group to cause teachers to revert to old teaching behaviors. In addition, this group best demonstrates the difficulties students experience when asked to become "workers." They were unfamiliar with the kinds of tasks asked of them, they were unfamiliar with group work, and they were unaccustomed to dealing with choices in the classroom.

[3]"Learning to use their minds well" refers to principle number 1. I have learned from hours of observation in conventional secondary schools around the country that too many students are not required to use their minds well, if at all. They engage in rudimentary tasks: They copy facts, dates, and definitions off the board; they describe information contained in texts by answering questions at the end of the chapter; they fill in blanks on worksheets, using information given to them in lectures or textbooks. None of these tasks requires that students engage in any of the higher-order thinking skills of analysis, synthesis, or interpretation. Nor do they require that students learn the process of determining and then investigating a problem. To learn to use their minds well, students must be actively engaged in problem-solving, in making connections between the subject of study in schools and the outside world, in the analysis, synthesis, and imaginative re-creation of knowledge and experience.

"Less is more" refers to Principle Number 2, which suggests that students actually learn more when they cover less. The pressure to "cover content," to get through the text, encourages teachers to skim the surface of complex material so that students acquire a broad but disjointed, disconnected understanding, rather than that they achieve mastery of a more limited number of skills and areas of information. By covering less, teachers enable students to engage in more thorough learning.

References

Berman, D., & McLaughlin, M. (1978). *Federal programs supporting educational change, Vol. VIII: Implementing and sustaining innovations.* Santa Monica, CA: Rand Corporation.

Bloom, B. (1956). *Taxonomy of educational objectives* (Vol. 2). New York: D. McKay.

Brooks, J., & Brooks, M. (1993). *The case for constructivist classrooms.* Alexandria, VA: Association for Supervision and Curriculum Development.

Cohn, M. H., & Kottcamp, R. B. (1993). *Teachers: The missing voice in education.* Albany: State University of New York Press.

Darling-Hammond, L. (1990). Teachers and teaching: Signs of a changing profession. In W. R. Houston (Ed.), *Handbook of research on teacher education* (pp. 267–290). New York: Macmillan.

Darling-Hammond, L., & Ancess, J. (Forthcoming). Authentic assessment and school development. In J. B. Baron & D. P. Wolf (Eds.), *Performance-based student assessment: Toward access, capacity, and coherence: Yearbook of the National Society for the Study of Education.* Chicago: University of Chicago Press.

Dewey, J. (1938). *Experience and education.* New York: Collier

Fischetti, J., Dittmer, A., & Kyle, D. (1993). *Shifting paradigms: Emerging issues for educational policy and practice.* Manuscript submitted for publication.

Fullan, M. (1989). *The meaning of educational change.* New York: Teachers College Press.

Fullan, M. (1990). *The new meaning of educational change.* New York: Teachers College Press.

Fullan, M., & Miles, M. B. (1992, June). Getting reform right: What works and what doesn't. *Phi Delta Kappan, 73*(10), 745–752.

Gardner, H. (1983). *Frames of mind: The theory of multiple intelligences.* New York: Basic Books.

Gardner, H. (1991). *The unschooled mind: How children think & how schools should teach.* New York: Basic Books.

Gardner, H. (1993). *Multiple intelligences: The theory in practice.* New York: Basic Books.

Glickman, C. D. (1990, September). Pushing school reform to a new edge: The seven ironies of school empowerment. *Phi Delta Kappan, 72*(1), 68–75.

Goodlad, J. I. (1984). *A place called school.* New York: McGraw Hill.

Goodlad, J. I. (1990). *Places where teachers are taught.* San Francisco: Jossey-Bass.

Hampel, R. L. (1986). *The last little citadel.* Boston: Houghton Mifflin.

Huberman, M. (1993). The model of the independent artisan in teachers' professional relations. In J. W. Little & M. W. McLaughlin (Eds.), *Teachers' Work* (pp. 11–50). New York, Teachers College Press.

Jacobs, H. (Ed.). (1989). *Interdisciplinary curriculum: Design and implementation.* Alexandria, VA: Edwards Brothers.

Kerchner, C. T., & Koppich, J. E. (1993). *A union of professionals: Labor relations and educational reform.* New York: Teachers College Press.

Lambert, L. (1988, May). Staff development redesigned. *Phi Delta Kappan, 69,* 665–668.

Lieberman, A., & Miller, L. (1984). *Teachers, their world and their work: Implications for school improvement.* Alexandria, VA: Association for Supervision and Curriculm Development.

Lieberman, A., & Miller, L. (Eds.). (1991). *Staff development for education in the '90s* (rev. ed.). New York: Teachers College Press.

Lieberman, A., & Rosenholtz, S. (1987). The road to school improvement: Barriers & bridges. In John I. Goodlad (Ed.), *The ecology of school renewal, Eighty-sixth yearbook of the National Society for the Study of Education, Part I* (pp.79–98). Chicago: University of Chicago Press.

Little, J. W. (1988). Assessing the prospects for teacher leadership. In A. Lieberman (Ed.), *Building a professional culture in schools* (pp. 78–106). New York: Teachers College Press.

Little, J. W., & McLaughlin, M. (Eds.), (1993). *Teachers' work.* New York: Teachers College Press.

Lortie, D. (1975). *Schoolteacher: A sociological study.* Chicago: University of Chicago Press.

Marin, P. (1969, January). The open truth and fiery vehemence of youth. *The Center Magazine, 2*(1), 61–74.

McLaughlin, M. (1993). What matters most in teachers' workplace context? In J. W. Little & M. W. McLaughlin (Eds.), *Teachers' work* (pp. 79–103). New York: Teachers College Press.

McLaughlin, M. & Talbert, J. (1993, March). *Contexts that matter for teaching and learning: Strategic opportunities for meeting the nation's educational goals.* Stanford: Stanford University, Center for Research on the Context of Secondary School Teaching.

McNeil, L. (1988). *Contradictions of control: School structure & school knowledge.* New York: Routledge.

Newmann, F., & Wehlage, G. (1993, Spring). Standards of authentic instruction. In *Issues in restructuring schools* (Issue Report No. 4, pp. 3–6.). Madison: University of Wisconsin, Center on Organization and Restructuring Schools, School of Education, Wisconsin Center for Education Research.

Perkins, D., and Blythe, T. (1994, February). Putting understanding up front. *Educational Leadership, 51* (5), 4–7.

Piaget, J. (1987). *Possibility and necessity: The role of necessity in cognitive development.* Minneapolis: University of Minnesota Press.

Powell, A. G., Farrar, E., & Cohen, D. K. (1985). *The shopping mall high school.* Boston: Houghton Mifflin.

Prawat, R. S., 1989. Teaching for understanding: Three key attributes. *Teaching & Teacher Education 5*(4), 315–328.

Prestine, Nona. (1993). Feeling the ripples, riding the waves: Making an essential school. In P. Hallinger & J. Murphy (Eds.), *Restructuring schooling* (pp. 32–62). Newbury Park, California: Corwin Press.

Sarason, S. (1971). *The culture of school and the problem of change.* Boston: Allyn and Bacon.

Sarason, S. (1991). *The predictable failure of educational reform: Can we change course before it's too late?* (rev. ed.). San Francisco: Jossey-Bass.

Sarason, S., Davidson, K., & Blatt, B. (1988). *The preparation of teachers: An unstudied problem in education.* Cambridge, MA: Brookline Books.

Saxl, E., Miles, M., & Lieberman, A. (1989). *Trainer's manual.* Alexandria, VA: Association for Supervision and Curriculum Development, Assisting Change in Education.

Schön, D. (1983). *The reflective practitioner: How professionals think in action.* New York: Basic Books.

Sizer, T. (1985). *Horace's compromise: The dilemma of the American high school.* Boston: Houghton Mifflin.

Sizer, T. (1991, May). No pain, no gain. *Educational Leadership, 48*(8), 32–34.

Swan, M. (1984). *The language and function of graphs.* Nottingham, England: Shell Centre for Mathematical Education, Dale Seymour Publications.

Wasley, P. (1991a). *Teachers who lead.* New York: Teachers College Press.

Wigginton, E. (1986). *Sometimes a shining moment: The Foxfire experience.* New York: Anchor.

Wiggins, G. (1987, Winter). Creating a thought-provoking curriculum. *American Educator, 11*(4), 10–17.

Wiggins, G. (1988). *The metaphor of student-as-worker.* (Available from Coalition of Essential Schools, Brown University, Box 1969, Providence, RI 02912.)

Wise, A. E. (1988). Legislated learning revisited. *Phi Delta Kappan, 69* (5), 328–332.

Bibliography

Alberty, H. & Alberty, E. (1962). *Reorganizing the high school curriculum* (3rd ed.). New York: Macmillan.

Center for the Study of Testing, Evaluation, and Educational Policy, Boston College. (1992). *The influence of testing on teaching math and science in grades 4–12*. National Science Foundation grant no. SPA8954759. Boston: Author.

Cohen, D. (1988). Teaching practice: Plus que ca change . . . In P. Jackson (Ed.), *Contributing to educational change: Perspectives on research and practice* (pp. 27–84). Berkeley: McClutchan.

Cohen, D., McLaughlin, M., & Talbert, J. (1991, Fall). Revolution in one classroom (or, then again, was it?). *American Educator, 15*(2), 16–23, 44–48.

Cohen, D., et al (Eds.). (1993). *Teaching for understanding: Challenges for policy and practice*. San Fransisco: Jossey-Bass.

Cuban, L. (1990). Reforming again, again, and again. *Educational Researcher, 19*(1), 3–13.

Diamond, M. (1988). *Enriching heredity: The impact of the environment on the anatomy of the brain*. New York: Free Press.

Dworkin, M. (Ed.). (1959). *Dewey on education, selections*. New York: Teachers College Press.

Evans, R. (1989, May). The faculty in midcareer: Implications for school improvement. *Educational Leadership, 46*(8), 10–15.

Evans, R. (1992). *The human face of reform: Meeting the challenge of change through authentic leadership*. Unpublished manuscript, The Human Relations Service, Inc. Wellesley, MA.

Hargreaves, A. (1990). *Contrived collegiality: A sociological analysis*. Paper presented at the XIIth meeting of the International Sociological Association, Madrid, July 9–13, 1990.

Hargreaves, A., & Dawe, R. (1990). Paths of professional development: Contrived collegiality, collaborative culture, and the case of peer coaching. *Teaching and Teacher Education, 6,* 227–241.

Lieberman, A., & Miller, L. (Eds.). (1991). *Staff development for education in the '90s* (rev. ed.). New York: Teachers College Press.

Little, J. W. (1986). Seductive images and organizational realities in professional development. In A. Lieberman (Ed.), *Rethinking School Improvement* (pp. 26–44). New York: Teachers College Press.

Little, J. W. (1987). Teachers as colleagues. In V. Richardson-Koehler (Ed.), *Educators' handbook: A research perspective* (pp.491–518). New York: Longman.

Little, J. W. (1989, Summer). District policy choices and teachers' professional development opportunities. *Educational Evalutation and Policy Analysis, 11*(2), 165–179.

Little, J. W. (1992). Teacher Development and educational policy. In M. Fullan & A. Hargreaves (Eds.), *Teacher development and educational change* (pp. 170–193). London: Falmer.

Louis, K. S., & Miles, M. B. (1990). *Improving the urban high school: What works and why.* New York: Teachers College Press.

McDonald, J. (1991). *Dilemmas of planning backwards; Rescuing a good idea* (Studies on Exhibitions No. 3). (Available from Coalition of Essential Schools, Brown University, Box 1969, Providence, Rhode Island, 02912.)

McDonald, J. (1992a). *Steps in planning backwards: Early lessons* (Studies on Exibitions No. 5). (Available from Coalition of Essential Schools, Brown University, Box 1969, Providence, Rhode Island, 02912.)

McDonald, J. (1992b). *The process of planning backwards: Stories from three schools* (Studies on Exhibitions No. 7). (Available from Coalition of Essential Schools, Brown University, Box 1969, Providence, Rhode Island, 02912.)

McDonald, J. (1992c). *Teaching: Making sense of an uncertain craft.* New York: Teachers College Press.

McDonald, J. (1993, February). Three Pictures of an exhibition: Warm, cool, and hard. *Phi Delta Kappan, 74*(6), 480–485.

McDonald, J., Smith, S., Turner, D., Finney, M., & Barton, E. (1993). *Graduation by exhibition: Assessing genuine achievement.* Alexandria, VA: Association for Supervision and Curriculum Development.

McQuillan, P., & Muncey, D. (in preparation). *Contested power and negotiating school change: An educational reform movement in multiple contexts.*

Meier, D. (1992, Summer). Reinventing teaching. *Teachers College Record, 93*(4), 594–609.

Muncey, D., & McQuillan, P. (1993, February). Preliminary findings from a five-year study of the Coalition of Essential Schools. *Phi Delta Kappan, 74*(6), 486–489.

Muncey, D. & McQuillan, P. (1992). The dangers of assuming consensus for change: Some examples from the Coalition of Essential Schools. In G. A. Hess, Jr. (Ed.), *Empowering Teachers and parents; School restructuring through the eyes of anthropologists* (pp. 47–69). Westport, CT: Greenwood.

Oxley, D. (1993). *Organizing schools into smaller units: A planning guide.* Philadelphia: Temple University, Center for Research in Human Development and Education.

Rosenholtz, S. (1989). *Teachers' workplace: The social organization of schools.* New York: Longman.

Senge, P. (1990). *The fifth discipline: The art and practice of the learning organization.* New York: Doubleday/Currency.

Sirotnik, K. (1987). Evaluation in the ecology of schooling: The process of school renewal. In J. I. Goodlad (Ed.), *The ecology of school renewal: Eighty-sixth yearbook of the National Society for the Study of Education* (pp. 41–62). Chicago: University of Chicago Press.

Sizer, T. (1992). *Horace's school: Redesigning the American high school.* Boston: Houghton Mifflin.

Tripp, D. (in press). *Critical incidents in teaching: Developing professional judgement.* London: Routledge.

Wasley, P. (1991b, Fall). Stirring the chalkdust: Changing practices in essential schools. *Teachers College Record, 93*(1), 28–58.

Index

About the Author

PAT WASLEY is the Senior Researcher for Change at the Coalition of Essential Schools at Brown University. In this position, she spends time in Coalition schools documenting and writing about how students, teachers, principals, and others in the system go about improving educational practices on behalf of student learning. She represents the Coalition in a variety of national symposia on school restructuring throughout the United States. She completed her Ed. D. at the University of Washington. Pat taught in elementary and high schools, and she held several administrative positions before she turned to research. She is the author of *Teachers Who Lead* (1991) and a number of articles on restructuring. Currently she is finishing a 3 year study following 150 students in four states through their high school years in changing schools, and she is working on a book about the depth of reforms in Coalition Schools.